ALONG the
RIVER ROAD

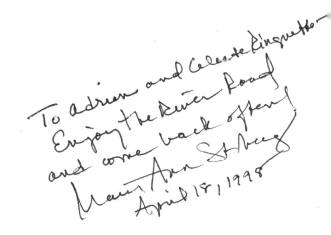

To adrian and Celeste Linguette
Enjoy the River Road
and come back often!
Mary Ann Stberg
April 18, 1998

ALONG the RIVER ROAD

Past and Present on Louisiana's Historic Byway

MARY ANN STERNBERG

Louisiana State University Press
Baton Rouge and London

Copyright © 1996 by Louisiana State University Press
All rights reserved
Manufactured in the United States of America
First printing
05 04 03 02 01 00 99 98 97 96   5 4 3 2 1

Designer: Michele Myatt
Typeface: Sabon
Typesetter: Impressions Book and Journal Services, Inc.
Printer and binder: Thomson-Shore, Inc.

Library of Congress Cataloging-in-Publication Data

Sternberg, Mary Ann.
    Along the river road : past and present on Louisiana's historic
byway / Mary Ann Sternberg.
       p.   cm.
    Includes bibliographical references and index.
    ISBN 0-8071-2055-3 (cl : alk. paper)
    1. River Road (La.)—History. 2. River Road (La.)—Guidebooks.
3. Historic sites—Louisiana—River Road—Guidebooks. I. Title.
F377.R58S84   1996
976.3—dc20   96-12542
                                                                        CIP

The paper in this book meets the guidelines for permanence and durability of the
Committee on Production Guidelines for Book Longevity of the Council on
Library Resources. ∞

Endpapers: Detail from Marie Adrien Persac's map "Plantations on the
Mississippi from Natchez to New Orleans, 1858." Courtesy Louisiana and
Lower Mississippi Valley Collections, Hill Memorial Library, LSU.

CONTENTS

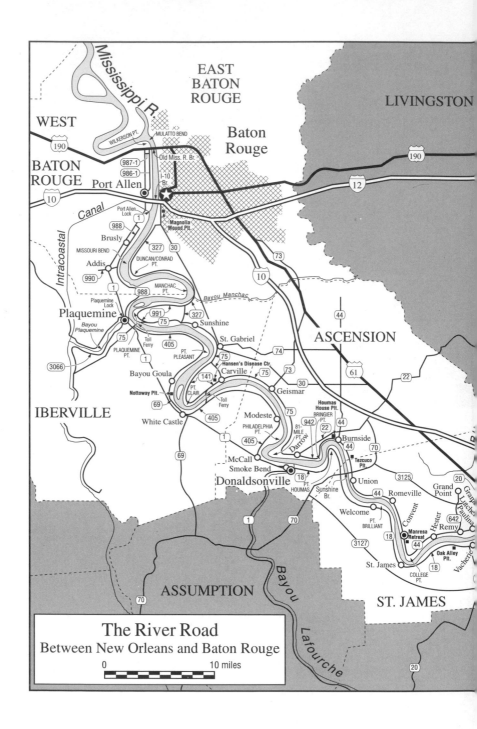

The River Road

Between New Orleans and Baton Rouge

0　　　　　　　　　　　10 miles

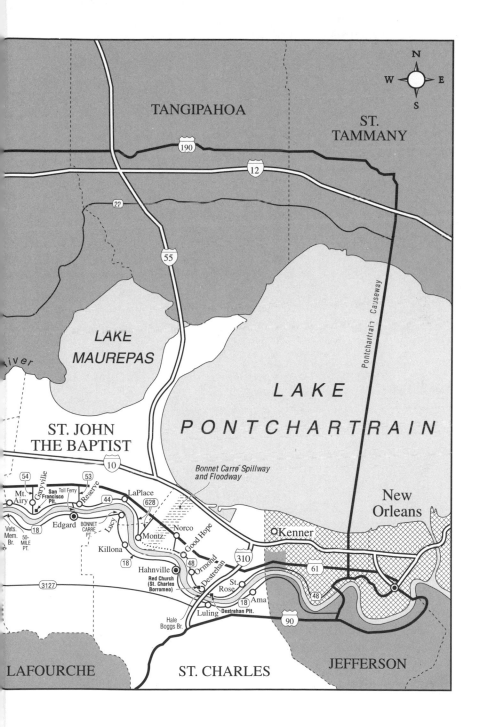

ACKNOWLEDGMENTS

To Joan Oppenheim and Norman Marmillion, my two disparate River Road travelers, whose divergent perspectives on the River Road unwittingly created this project. And to Joanna, Katie, and Jay for their interest, love, and encouragement, which kept me mostly on track.

My deepest thanks to the following for providing information and insights as this project developed: the late Mark T. Carleton; Louisiana Preservation Alliance; Glenn Timmons, Cinclare Plantation; Louisiana Division of Archaeology; Louisiana Office of Historic Preservation; U.S. Army Corps of Engineers; H. Parrott Bacot, LSU Art Museum; the Foundation for Historical Louisiana; Robert Heck; Jay Edwards; Rebecca Saunders; Louisiana Division of the Louisiana State Library; Faye Phillips and her staff at Hill Memorial Library, LSU; Dr. and Mrs. Robert Judice; Irene Tastet; Jo Ann Amort; Debra Purifoy; Helêne Crozat; Faye Russell; Stacy Ryan; Frances Peltier; O. J. Dupuy; the St. James Historical Society; Rose Marie Perrilloux; Emily Guidry; Ronald and Hazel Scioneaux; Andrew Capone; Cindy and John Hill; Horace Wilkinson IV; Lucy and Walter Landry; Gwen Edwards; Kevin Harris; Oscar Richard, and Lynda Waguespack. And enduring gratitude to Martha Yancey, Don Stanford, Marc Goldstein, Patricia Cooper, Fred Benton, and Ron Boudreaux, who rode the road, and to Margaret Dalrymple and Gerry Anders, successive editors at the LSU Press, who helped shape a likely idea into a worthwhile project.

INTRODUCTION

What is the River Road?

Polite confusion sometimes arises in trying to distinguish between the River Road and the Great River Road. The latter, a federally designated land route first conceived by the Mississippi River Parkway Commission in 1938, roughly traces the Mississippi River along much of the meandering 2,350 miles from its Minnesota source to the last point of solid land south of New Orleans. The route was intended to supply travelers with a broad focus on the history and culture of the Mississippi River Valley. Between New Orleans and Baton Rouge, however, the Great River Road follows Louisiana Routes 1 and 18 and U.S. Route 90, all on the west side of the river and incorporating only a small section of what is locally known as the River Road.

"Our" River Road, on the other hand, is an aggregate concept—shorthand for the pair of undistinguished rural routes that closely parallel the Mississippi between Baton Rouge and New Orleans, one along the east bank, one along the west, winding through the parishes of St. Charles, St. John the Baptist, St. James, Ascension, Iberville, and parts of East and West Baton Rouge. Each roadway, although narrow, pocked with potholes, devoid of lane-striping, seldom straight, and whimsically numbered, is really an asphalt tracing that defines a landscape of history and culture, of real people and legend.

This book is the direct result of a pair of unrelated encounters in which I heard two highly divergent opinions of "our" River Road. The first, from a longtime New Orleanian, was provoked after she had taken visitors for a day's sightseeing. "There's nothing there anymore," she lamented. Beyond the few plantation houses open to the public, the travelers had spent their day in an unexplicated world of cane fields and pastures, a sprinkling of majestic oaks, various industrial complexes, and many ravaged structures—their stories unknown—sporting rusting tin roofs, flapping walls, and weathered boards at a tilt. She and her friends could well understand why the National Trust for Historic Preservation had declared the area one of the country's most endangered historic places.

Just a few weeks later, however, I happened upon a man with a passionate and delightfully myopic sense of the River Road. He delivered a breathless litany of structures, sites, characters, and stories that twined through a fascinating monologue about the River Road's history, culture, and meaning. To him, the River Road was a constant source of delight, a place of past, present, and—he hoped—future fascination.

It seemed impossible to have heard two such opposite opinions of the same place. The discrepancy clearly suggested that a link was missing between my two River Road travelers—between the former, an interested visitor who was not able to identify much of what she saw, and the latter, an aficionado to whom the River Road is a familiar neighborhood and a passion.

To a writer, a missing link usually means a book, so I set out to find one that might serve this purpose and made two significant discoveries: first, the book I sought did not exist, or rather, existed in pieces, in hundreds of books; second, information about the River Road is truly encyclopedic.

The River Road has been the backdrop on which the traditions of diverse peoples—Indians, French, Germans, black slaves from Africa and the West Indies, free people of color, Acadians, Spaniards, Anglo-Americans, Italians, and others—have been deposited like geological strata and compressed together, forming a distinct and unusual culture. And the centerpiece of this culture was the Mississippi River, creating an endless and daily struggle between man and nature. The river linked people and separated them, attracted and repelled them, functioning both as a source of transportation, food, fuel, and irrigation and as an agency of destruction and ruin.

What was needed to explicate this remarkable area was a comprehensive volume that did not focus solely on plantation houses or colonial economies or the history of a single parish or steamboats but gave an overview, an insight into the area as a whole. A comprehensive work, I determined, would analyze each mile of the River Road along both banks, with detailed timelines and large-scale maps showing individual properties. It would give the history of each place, including information not only about changes of ownership and boundaries, but about the people who lived there— their domestic lives, business pursuits, whatever could be learned. The definitive River Road book would cover three centuries of land use, life-styles, cultures, and architectural styles; river movements and their effects on settlements, settlers, and land; the intertwined genealogies of river families and the politics that enmeshed them; and the rich anthology of legends, stories, and tales that animates the region. Such a volume would take a decade to prepare and be too heavy to lift.

For better or for worse, I did not write that book.

Instead, I have tried to create a portable reference and companion to link my two disparate River Road travelers. It includes a brief historical outline to furnish context, a bit of explanation about often-used local terms, some background about the dynamic of the river system and man's interaction with it, a glimpse of the most familiar architectural forms, and a brief overview of the most significant aspects of agriculture and industry, all flavored with bits of natural and social history and a colorful tale or two. These chapters are background to two linear routes plotted for the casual visitor, one upriver along the east bank, the other downriver along the west bank, with *some* of the interesting places, past and present, noted to make a meander along the River Road more enjoyable and meaningful.

A few explanations and caveats about using this book are in order. First, although New Orleans was (and in many ways still is) the cultural, social, and commercial hub for the River Road, I have specifically omitted it because many fine and detailed books devoted to the greater New Orleans area already exist. Second, in attempting to present a broad view that ranges from prehistoric to contemporary times, I have inevitably treated many things superficially. Third, locations are sometimes approximate due to the vagaries of the river and altered land usage; however, I have been as accurate as possible and have noted such discrepancies where known. And last, many sites unfortunately are omitted altogether for lack of sufficient information. Perhaps in a later edition . . .

One of the quirks of a trip along the River Road is the inconsistent numbering of each roadway. Covering a distance of about a hundred miles, the continuous, levee-hugging east bank route successively follows Louisiana Routes 48, 628, 44, 942, 75, 141, and 327; on the west bank, the highways are La. 18, 20, 405, and 988. To me, this inconsistency effectively illustrates why the River Road has an identity problem and has not been properly appreciated *en tout*.

Driving this multinumbered byway is occasionally precarious. The River Road is a local road, shared equally by behemoth trucks that careen around curves presuming themselves to be the road's sole occupants and by residents drifting from one community to the next, to the store or a neighbor's, under the pleasant assumption that directional signals and highway protocols need not apply among friends.

Sightseeing along the River Road is predominantly just that—an occasion to see and view, but with few opportunities for visiting because most of the properties are privately owned and closed to the public (I have designated as "open to the public" any that are accessible). And sadly, many areas are derelict, dirty, or otherwise lacking in visual interest. But the River Road is no exhibit under glass or theme park, and even its scars and warts must be seen as part of a dynamic place that is continuously changing—not always for the better. Given a dash of historical context and a measure of pride, however, perhaps even these will improve. Most unpleasant of all to me as an author is the fact that some places or buildings noted along the linear routes will no longer exist by the time this book is published. For these I offer apologies but take no blame.

Access to the river itself is a challenge. Much of the levee is private and posted, making the Mississippi all but invisible and unattainable. But it remains a natural wonder and essential to comprehend in order to gain an appreciation of the River Road. So where public access is available, I urge you to take a drive or hike up the levee and view the river and whatever vista is at hand. In the few areas where ferries still run, take a ride to gain an insider's perspective on the awesome Father of Waters.

In the end, I hope that you will relish all that is worthwhile and remarkable Along the River Road as it wanders through the cultures of yesterday, today, and tomorrow. I also hope you will be inspired to visit again and again, with new eyes and greater enjoyment.

ALONG the RIVER ROAD

RIVER ROAD TIMELINE

Prehistory

The earliest evidence of human settlement in the River Road area is thought by archaeologists to date from about 3000 B.C., when various indigenous peoples lived in the area that is now St. James Parish. (*Indian* was, of course, the designation given to these native North American inhabitants by European explorers, following Christopher Columbus' misidentification in 1492 when he landed in the Western Hemisphere believing he had reached the East Indies.)

Archaeologists have identified several important Indian cultures whose range included parts of south Louisiana during the centuries before Europeans arrived:

1500–500 B.C.: *Poverty Point culture.* Living on high ground by streams, these people engaged in intensive hunting, gathering, and fishing as well as rudimentary agriculture. They built large ceremonial mounds and other earthworks, most notably near what is now Epps, in northeast Louisiana. That was the culture's principal site, but more than a hundred lesser ones have been discovered all across the Gulf South.

200 B.C.–A.D. 400: *Tchefuncte culture.* Mainly coastal dwellers but sometimes living along streams, these people fished, gathered, practiced agriculture, and made the earliest known pottery in the region. Large middens of discarded mollusk shells characterize their sites.

A.D. 100–550: *Marksville culture.* Named for the south Louisiana town at which their principal site was discovered, this group pursued agriculture, hunted, fished, and gathered and created the first conical burial mounds found in the region.

A.D. 500–1300: *Troyville–Coles Creek culture.* The Troyville built temple mounds and ceremonial centers and specialized in hunting and fishing. The Coles Creek culture extended that of the Troyville.

A.D. 1200–1700: *Plaquemine–Mississippian culture.* These were the peoples first encountered by European explorers. Tribal groups who lived in what is now southeastern Louisiana included, among others, the Houma, Bayougoula, Acolapissa, Quinapisa (Mugulasha), Tangipahoa, and Okelousa. Descended from the Troyville–Coles Creek culture, some of these groups built large ceremonial centers with two or more flat-topped pyramidal mounds flanking a central plaza. They created a distinctive style of decorative pottery and were quasi-settled rather than nomadic, relying relatively heavily on agriculture and fishing for sustenance. Crops included corn, beans, squash, tobacco, sunflowers, gourds, and pumpkins. Settlements were located along the natural high ground of streams and riverbanks. Houses, constructed of poles with mud-plaster fill and roofed with palmetto leaves, were easily erected—an important feature, since groups changed settlement sites every few years. Offshoots of the Mississippian culture included the language groups of the Tunicas, Chitimachas, and Muskogeans; descendants of the Plaquemine culture are thought to have been the Taensa (Tensas) and the Natchez language groups.

European settlers became much indebted to these native inhabitants, who shared with them valuable knowledge about indigenous plants and animals, medicine, boatbuilding, navigation of local waterways, and hunting, fishing, and agricultural techniques.

Early Explorations to Present

The following are historical highlights that had an impact on life along the River Road. (The list is, of course, far from comprehensive.)

1541–1542: Spanish explorer Hernando de Soto discovers the Mississippi River. De Soto's expedition created considerable disruption among the native populations, especially by introducing diseases to which they lacked natural resistance. After de Soto's death in 1542, his lieutenant Luis de Moscoso led the remainder of the expedition as far as what is now east Texas before returning to the river. There the Spaniards built boats and floated downriver—probably camping along what would become the River Road—to the Gulf and thence to Spain's outposts in Mexico. Of the more than six hundred men who had begun the exploration with de Soto in Florida in 1539, only about three hundred survived to reach Mexico.

1673: French explorers Jacques Marquette and Louis Jolliet traverse the Mississippi River from the north to the mouth of the Arkansas River. Their journey confirms that the Mississippi must flow to the Gulf of Mexico, not the Pacific Ocean.

1682: Robert Cavelier, sieur de La Salle, is the first to descend the entire length of the Mississippi, and claims for France all territory between the Great Lakes and the Gulf Coast. He names this vast territory Louisiana in honor of his reigning monarch, King Louis XIV. La Salle's expedition was attacked by members of a Quinapisa village near the present location of Hahnville, in west-bank St. Charles Parish.

1699: The Iberville/Bienville expedition founds France's Louisiana colony by landing some two hundred soldiers and settlers near present-day Biloxi, Mississippi. Iberville locates the mouth of the Mississippi River and becomes the first explorer to enter the river from the Gulf of Mexico. His party ascends the Mississippi to the confluence of the Red River. His journals document an encounter with Bayougoula Indians (who joined his party as guides), the discovery of a stream (now believed to be Bayou Manchac), and observation on the Mississippi riverbank of a *baton rouge*—a red pole, which the local Indians called *istrouma* and which seemingly indicated an intertribal territorial boundary. On the return journey, Iberville uses a shortcut back to Biloxi Bay via Bayou Manchac, Lake Maurepas, and Lake Pontchartrain as suggested by the Indian guides.

1712: In an attempt to cut costs, the French government allots to wealthy private citizen Antoine Crozat exclusive rights as proprietor of the struggling colony for fifteen years.

1714: France establishes Fort St. Jean-Baptiste, its first permanent settlement in present-day Louisiana, on the Red River at what is now Natchitoches.

1717: The Company of the West, a French enterprise under the leadership of Scots-born financial wizard John Law, takes over an

P⁷ ᴸᴱ MOYNE
E5 53 D YBER VILLE

Pierre Le Moyne, sieur d'Iberville, founder of France's Louisiana colony.
Courtesy State Library of Louisiana

exclusive twenty-five-year charter for the development and super-
vision of Louisiana from Crozat. The total French population in
the colony is approximately 400. Law's charter mandates that he
enlist 6,000 colonists and 3,000 slaves before the decade's end. In
return, he receives a trade monopoly, the right to lease and sell land,

Jean Baptiste Le Moyne, sieur de Bienville, Louisiana's principal leader for
most of its first four decades.
  Courtesy State Library of Louisiana

and control of forts, the military, and the appointment of public officials. Between 1717 and 1722 the colony will expand rapidly as the Company of the West—soon renamed the Company of the Indies—grants large "concessions" of land to wealthy French citizens, begins importation of African slaves, and recruits thousands of German small farmers, wishing to escape unrest in their homeland, to immigrate to Louisiana. For a time, the company also sends to the colony large numbers of involuntarily deported French criminals, male and female.

Meanwhile, French speculators avidly buy stock in Law's company, creating the price run-up and eventual collapse known as the "Mississippi Bubble" (at the time, the colony was still widely referred to as "Mississippi"). Much of the income from what amounts to a pyramid scheme goes into private pockets rather than into financing the colony.

1718: At the direction of the Company of the Indies, Bienville begins the groundwork for a permanent settlement on the Mississippi River (a step to which Iberville had once objected on the grounds that the river was too difficult for big ships to enter from the Gulf). He chooses a site on relatively high ground along a crescent-shaped bend of the river and near a portage to Lake Pontchartrain long used by the Indians. The settlement will become New Orleans. Bienville is named commandant of the colony.

1719: The first large consignment of black slaves—451 men and women in two ships—reaches Louisiana. Like most of the African slaves who will be imported to the colony under French rule, they come from the Senegal-Gambia (Senegambia) area of West Africa.

1720: German farm families, lured by advertisements promising an agrarian paradise, begin arriving in substantial numbers, many under indenture contracts. Eventually, they settle mainly on the west bank near the present-day St. Charles/St. John Parish boundary; the area becomes known as *la Côte des Allemands*—the German Coast. At least two of the several small villages (really clusters of huts) are on land first cleared by Indians.

In France, the Mississippi Bubble bursts when mismanagement, skimming of investment income, and other difficulties cause the Company of the Indies to miss dividend payments to stockholders. The stock plummets to worthlessness almost overnight, giving Louisiana its first recognition for major scandal. The company administration is forced to reorganize.

1721: German settlers continue to arrive. Unlike those of 1720, most of these newcomers are unidentured and the recipients of small land grants. One large group is led by Karl Friedrich of Arensbourg, Germany, who became known by the French as d'Arensbourg and who served as commandant of the German Coast for forty years. D'Arensbourg's compound, built at the river's edge, is called Karlstein, as is the settlement downriver from his property. On the upriver side, the new settlement is called Hoffen; it extends along the "Coast" from present-day Glendale downriver to approximately Killona. After flooding caused by a hurricane in 1722, many residents relocate to the river's natural terrace, the highest ground in the vicinity. Despite natural disasters and Indian attacks, the German settlement survives and becomes known as the breadbasket for New Orleans as the industrious farmers haul their surplus produce downriver by pirogue on weekends to sell to the "city dwellers." In 1724 the first church in French Louisiana, St. Jean des Allemands (St. John of the Germans), is established at Karlstein. By 1746, the German Coast is the second largest settlement in the colony, after New Orleans.

1722: New Orleans becomes the colonial capital, succeeding Mobile.

1724: The colony's population of blacks slaves having grown significantly, Bienville issues the *Code Noir,* or Black Code, a set of rules based on those of the Saint-Domingue (Haiti) slave trade. Although aimed largely at controlling slave behavior and preventing revolts, the code also gave slaves certain rudimentary rights. For example, forced marriages between slaves were prohibited, as was the sale of young slave children apart from their mothers; also, care and support of slaves by the master was made compulsory, and slaves were allowed to appeal to the attorney general against injustice or cruelty. Other provisions of the code restricted the activities of the colony's free blacks, established Catholicism as the official religion, and banned Jews from the colony.

1729: A surprise attack by Natchez Indians at Fort Rosalie (present-day Natchez) kills some 250 settlers—roughly a tenth of the col-

"Savages of Several Nations," drawn in Louisiana in 1735 by Alexandre de Batz, engineer, architect, and artist. Among representatives of various American Indian tribes, de Batz included an African boy (second from right).
Courtesy State Library of Louisiana

ony's free population—and undermines the colonists' already-shaky security.

1731: After years of poverty, famine, epidemics, Indian attacks, and other trials, the colony is stagnating. The Company of the Indies, having spent vast sums with little return, retrocedes Louisiana to the French Crown. Nevertheless, Law and his company are credited with firmly establishing the colony.

1732: Bienville, who had returned to France, is appointed governor of the colony and assumes an even larger role in its history. He is credited with introducing the first cattle, hogs, and chickens, growing and exporting the first cotton and tobacco, and conducting experiments with indigo and silk. He remains until 1743.

1751: In New Orleans, the Jesuits introduce Louisiana's first successfully grown variety of sugarcane.

1762: In a move best characterized as "cutting his losses" (although some theories suggest that it was to compensate the Spanish for their loss of Florida to the British and to acknowledge their support in the Seven Years' War), Louis XV secretly cedes to Spain France's money-draining colonies west of the Mississippi River as well as the Isle of Orleans; however, the Spanish do not exert formal authority until 1766. The colony's population is approximately 8,000, including roughly 4,600 blacks and 3,800 whites.

1763: In the Peace of Paris, France cedes to England all of its Louisiana territory east of the Mississippi River, including that part of the modern state that lies north of Bayou Manchac and Lakes Maurepas and Pontchartrain.

1764–1765: Some of the first Acadians arrive in Louisiana and settle along the river in the St. James Parish area, called the First Acadian Coast.

1766: The first Spanish governor, Antonio de Ulloa, lands at New Orleans.

1768: Unhappy at living under a Spanish regime, French Creoles, Acadians, and residents of the German Coast mount an insurrection against Governor Ulloa. Ulloa and Spanish officials flee.

1769: Irish-born Spanish general Alejandro O'Reilly arrives from Havana with a large military force and regains control of the colony, dividing it into administrative districts called "posts" and twenty-two ecclesiastical parishes.

1779: War having been declared between Spain and England, Spanish territorial governor Bernardo de Gálvez marches from New Orleans and captures the British forts at Manchac and at New Richmond (present-day Baton Rouge), returning the West Florida territory to Spain.

1785: The Spanish government attracts to Louisiana approximately 1,600 Acadian refugees who had been living in France. Acadian immigration to the colony between 1765 and 1788 totals roughly 3,000.

1792: Governor Francisco Luis Carondelet appoints the equivalent to a justice of the peace in each district, drawing his appointees from the planters in the area, who were responsible to the syndics—

essentially, divisions like wards. Syndics had increasing powers, including responsibility for levees, roads, and drainage.

1795: Etienne Boré successfully granulates sugar on a commercial scale.
    Pinckney's Treaty grants Americans permanent trade privileges in New Orleans.

1796: The first certainly identified epidemic of yellow fever in Louisiana breaks out in New Orleans.

1800: By the Treaty of San Ildefonso, Spain secretly returns the Louisiana territory west of the Mississippi to France, although France does not take control until 1802.

1803: Americans fear that France, now under Napoleon, will close their access to New Orleans. President Thomas Jefferson sends James Monroe and Robert Livingston to Paris to discuss the purchase of the Isle of Orleans. To their surprise, Napoleon, needing money for a looming war with England, offers not only the Isle of Orleans but the entire Louisiana territory west of the Mississippi. In the transaction known as the Louisiana Purchase, the United States pays $15 million for this vast tract—about 4 cents per acre for 900,000 square miles of territory from the Mississippi River to the Rocky Mountains. The treaty is vaguely worded, and the United States claims to have acquired all the territory included in French Louisiana; however, Spain continues to assert title to West Florida.

1804–1805: Congress divides the newly acquired lands into two districts: the "Territory of Orleans" includes most of what is now Louisiana; the "Territory of Louisiana" includes all the rest of the Louisiana Purchase lands. The Territory of Orleans is divided into twelve counties to function in the realms of judicial and administrative oversight. William C. C. Claiborne is appointed governor of the Orleans territory.

1807: The Territory of Orleans is divided into nineteen districts called "parishes."

1808: A federal law goes into effect prohibiting importation of slaves into United States territory; it does not, however, outlaw the growing interstate commerce in slaves.

1810: Residents of West Florida declare independence from Spain and defeat Spanish troops in a brief battle. The West Florida Republic is established with its capital in Baton Rouge. President James Madison orders Governor Claiborne to occupy the Republic, which soon thereafter becomes United States territory.

1811: A slave insurrection in St. Charles and St. John the Baptist Parishes is forcibly quelled. Historians have described the uprising as numerically the largest in North American history. Led by Charles Deslondes, a slave at Woodland Plantation in east-bank St. John Parish, as many as five hundred rebels armed with cane knives, axes, and other tools marched down River Road toward New Orleans. Woodland's owner, Manuel Andry, was wounded; one of Andry's sons and planter Jean François Trepagnier, who refused to abandon his home, were killed. Few other whites suffered physical harm, having been forewarned to flee. At the Jacques Fortier plantation (now Ormond Plantation), the slaves encountered a force of west-bank white residents who had crossed the river. Soon troops also arrived—federal soldiers from Baton Rouge and a militia company from New Orleans led by General Wade Hampton, who owned plantations along the River Road. Vastly outnumbered and outgunned, the rebels were quickly overcome. A tribunal met at Destrehan Plantation to determine sentencing. Sixteen of the rebellion's leaders were executed and their heads piked along the river as a warning to others inclined to follow their example. Although subsequent slave insurrections were plotted in Louisiana, the 1811 revolt was the last to take place.

1812: Louisiana is admitted to the Union as the eighteenth state, with William C. C. Claiborne elected as its first governor.

> *Historian Alcée Fortier noted that Louisiana retained the French language even after the Purchase and statehood. The legislature employed an interpreter for each house at a salary of $2,000 to translate the speeches of members. It was, Fortier wrote, amusing to see a Creole lawmaker abusing an American colleague who remained perfectly unconcerned until the interpreter translated the hostility.*

The first steamboat to navigate the Mississippi River arrives at New Orleans, introducing the steamboating era to the lower Mississippi Valley.

The steamer *Empire Parish* at anchor at Baton Rouge, 1863. The boat was a floating headquarters for Union general Nathaniel Banks.
Courtesy State Library of Louisiana

1832: A massive outbreak of cholera, combined with a yellow fever epidemic, kills thousands of Louisianians—as many as five thousand in New Orleans alone.

1846: The seat of state government is moved to Baton Rouge, where it will remain until 1862.

1849: The new, neo-Gothic state capitol building is completed in Baton Rouge.

1853: Louisiana's worst epidemic of yellow fever claims some 5,000 victims.

1856: A hurricane destroys the resort of Ile Dernière off Louisiana's coast, killing more than 200 people, including many vacationing River Road residents.

1861: Louisiana secedes from the Union and is an independent nation for two months before joining the Confederacy. Over the next four years, the Civil War devastates the River Road. Action is especially fierce during 1862 and 1863.

1862: New Orleans and then Baton Rouge fall to Union forces. Admiral David Farragut's fleet commands the river. Opelousas becomes the temporary Confederate state capital, to be succeeded by Shreveport.

1864: Henry W. Allen becomes Confederate governor of Louisiana; Michael Hahn becomes Federal governor of the state.

1865: The Civil War ends with the Confederacy's defeat.

1868: Louisiana adopts a "Radical" Reconstruction constitution and is readmitted to the Union.

1870: The steamboats *Natchez* and *Robert E. Lee* stage their famous race from New Orleans to St. Louis; the *Lee* is victorious.

The Louisiana Seminary of Learning moves from Pineville to Baton Rouge, where in 1877 it will become Louisiana State University and Agricultural and Mechanical College.

1873: Lieutenant Governor P. B. S. Pinchback is appointed governor, the first black to hold that office in the state.

1877: Reconstruction ends when President Rutherford B. Hayes recalls the army after the longest occupation of any state.

1879: Baton Rouge is designated the permanent state capital; the government returns to the city and, soon thereafter, to the renovated Old State Capitol building.

1884–1885: The World's Industrial and Cotton Centennial Exposition is held in New Orleans.

1901: Louisiana's first successful oil well comes in near Jennings.

1909: Standard Oil establishes a giant oil refinery in Baton Rouge.

1914: Southern University moves to Baton Rouge from New Orleans, where it was founded in 1880.

1915: A hurricane kills 275 people, mainly in south Louisiana, and causes heavy damage in the River Road area.

1925: Louisiana State University moves to a new campus on the old Gartness plantation.

The Old State Capitol in Baton Rouge. Gutted by fire during the Civil War, the building was freshly renovated when this photograph was taken in the early 1880s. The steel turrets atop the original towers were added in the renovation but were later judged unsightly, removed, and scrapped.
    Courtesy Louisiana and Lower Mississippi Valley Collections, Hill Memorial Library, LSU

1927: The worst flood in United States history occurs along the Mississippi River, inundating nearly one-third of Louisiana.

1928–1935: Huey P. Long is elected governor and later United States senator, becoming a virtual dictator of the state before his assassination. Among his many building projects is the skyscraper-style new State Capitol Building in Baton Rouge.

1940: The Huey P. Long–O. K. Allen Bridge opens at Baton Rouge, the first bridge to cross the Mississippi River between New Orleans and Vicksburg.

1963: The Mississippi River–Gulf Outlet shortens the marine distance between New Orleans and the Gulf of Mexico by seventy-six miles, boosting river commerce.

1964: The Sunshine Bridge, the first span between New Orleans

Huey P. Long orating.
Courtesy State Library of Louisiana

and Baton Rouge, connects the Mississippi's east and west banks at river mile 167.5.

1965: Hurricane Betsy, one of the most devastating storms to hit the New Orleans and River Road areas, causes enormous property damage.

1973: During the highest water of the century, all 350 gates of the Bonnet Carré Spillway are opened, averting the threat of a catastrophic flood.

1983: The Corps of Engineers again opens all gates of the Bonnet Carré Spillway to prevent flooding.

TERMS, PEOPLE, AND PLACES

Note: The most commonly used phrase in this book, *the River Road,* refers not only to the separate east- and west-bank roadways that follow the Mississippi River, but also to the settlements and culture that evolved along them.

Acadian: The Acadians, today colloquially called "Cajuns," were people of French descent who had lived in Nova Scotia—*Acadie*— until they were expelled in 1755 by the British, who had taken over their territory in 1713. The exiles were widely dispersed along the Eastern Seaboard and elsewhere. Some began arriving in south Louisiana in 1764 and 1765, drawn because the colony was French, despite its recent cession to Spain. Of several thousand Acadians who had made their way to France, about 1,600 were induced to immigrate to Louisiana in 1785, and others even later. The Acadians were Catholics, most of them small farmers, artisans, or traders. They settled along the river in St. James, Ascension, and Iberville Parishes, as well as in other parts of south Louisiana.

Acadian Coast: The term encompasses both the east and west banks of St. James and Ascension Parishes, heavily settled by Acadians. In St. James, the Acadian Coast was later infiltrated by Americans and a large contingent of Italian immigrants. Descendants of John Law's original German settlers moved to St. James and were absorbed into the French culture.

allée: French for "alley." Two parallel rows of trees planted to form a lane leading from the river or road to a plantation house.

arpent: A French measure of land, either linear or areal. A linear arpent, sometimes known as an *arpent de face,* was approximately

192 feet. (Fractions of an arpent were often broken down into *toises*, a toise equaling about 6.4 feet.) Land grants were made along the river based on their arpent frontage with a standard depth of forty arpents or a double depth of eighty. In square measure, an arpent equals roughly five-sixths of an acre.

batture: Thought to have been derived from the French *battre*, "to beat." On the lower Mississippi, the term denotes the land, deposited by siltation, that lies between the levee and the river at low or moderate water levels. At such times, the batture is used for recreational or commercial purposes. At high water, however, it is flooded.

bayou: From the Choctaw *bayuk*, for "creek" or "river." In south Louisiana, the term applies to a sluggish stream that can change direction according to amounts of rainfall. Bayous intersecting the lower Mississippi River, however, always flow away from the river.

belvedere: From the Italian *bel*, "beautiful," and *vedere*, "to see." A railed rooftop platform on a plantation house, originally used as a vantage point from which to see steamboats on the river or to view the fields. Sometimes a belvedere is enclosed with a cupola.

bend and point: Where the river curves, the curve itself is called a "bend," as is the land that follows the outside of the curve. The thrust of land on the inside of the curve is called a "point." Deepest water is usually on the outside of a bend where the river tends to cut away the bank.

borrow pit: The excavation that results when dirt from the water side of a levee is "borrowed" for the purpose of constructing the levee. Borrow pits were dug more or less haphazardly until the United States Army Corps of Engineers specified that they be relatively shallow and separated by a wide berm from the levee. When the river is high, the pits fill with water, which they may continue to hold after the river recedes.

Bonnet Carré: French; literally, "square bonnet." Several landmarks located at approximately river miles 133–134, in St. John the Baptist Parish, are named Bonnet Carré, including the sharp turn of the river, a point on the west bank, and the bend on the east bank. The formation was so named because it resembled the back of the square bonnets worn by rural Louisiana women into the 1920s.

bousillage: Pronounced "boo-see-ahj." A French term for a mixture of mud and Spanish moss, or of river sand, horsehair, and moss, applied over a web of sticks and used as infill between timbers framing a house. The French adopted this technique from the Indians.

Bringier family: A prominent River Road family—the name is pronounced "brahn-jzay"—whose holdings over time included the St. James Parish plantations of White Hall, Bagatelle, and Union, and four plantations in Ascension Parish—Bocage, the Hermitage, Tezcuco, and Ashland (owned by later generations).

briqueté entre poteaux: "bricked between timbers"; French term for construction using brick infill between the wood framing of a house.

concession: During the French colonial period in Louisiana, concessions were large properties granted to wealthy Frenchmen who agreed to develop them for agricultural enterprise. Notable concessions along this portion of the River Road included the Duverney concession at the village of the Bayougoula Indians, that of Diron D'Artaguiette at Baton Rouge, and that of the marquis d'Ancenis at the village of the Houmas Indians. In a quasi-feudal system, concessions utilized large numbers of laborers, either Indian or black slaves or white indentured workers, supervised by a manager. Owners visited but did not live on their properties. Records indicate that concessions were laid out much like plantations, with a main house and various outbuildings. Directors, supervisors, accountants, workers, and slaves formed the hierarchy. In theory, each concession was also to have had a chaplain, but in practice, that did not materialize.

côte: French for "coast." In Louisiana the word often denoted a string of settlements or some otherwise identifiable area along a bank ("coast") of the river. Also, *côte* or *anse* denoted a concave bank of the river as seen from a boat. A convex bank was an *ile* or *pointe.*

Creole: From the Spanish *criollo* or the Portuguese *crioulo.* Originally, a slave of African descent born in the New World. In south

Louisiana today, no single definition of the word can be maintained; in fact, several conflicting definitions are acceptable. In one usage that apparently arose after the Civil War, Creoles were the colonial French and Spanish settlers' white descendants born in the New World—either in the West Indies or Louisiana. Another definition encompasses Louisianians descended from the European colonists, but especially the French, and includes those of mixed African and European heritage. A third, commonly seen in records from the eighteenth and antebellum nineteenth centuries, harked back to the original usage by denoting slaves born in the New World, as opposed to those born in Africa; however, it also applied to free people of color, including those of mixed African and French or African and Spanish background.

Creole has also evolved as the name for the language and folk culture that developed in south Louisiana from the cultural mélange of French, Spanish, and African inhabitants. Creole French, a dialect that developed among African-Americans in Louisiana, was spoken by many blacks and some whites in the southern part of the state until after World War II. Creole cooking is the culinary expression that arose in south Louisiana, and especially New Orleans, incorporating French, Spanish, and African influences. Creole architecture is the style that evolved in colonial Louisiana combining introduced elements of construction, native materials, and adaptive applications.

crevasse: From the French for "break" or "separation"; a fissure. When a specific area of levee is weakened—whether by natural forces or human incursion—the innate power of the river causes the weakness to enlarge until the levee breaks under great pressure. Through the break—a crevasse—rushes a torrent of such force that it gouges the landscape, often to a depth of several yards. The resulting water-filled depressions may remain as permanent pondlike or swampy areas, called "sloughs," after the flood recedes. Crevasses almost always meant severe flooding and loss of property.

According to documentation made between 1849 and 1927, the average crevasse along the lower Mississippi River created a breach in the levee between 500 and 1,000 feet long, and the force of the river through the break scoured the earth behind the break to an average depth of 12 feet.

delta: That part of the lower Mississippi River Valley in which distributaries of the river are located. The delta is a wide, flat plain

"Crevasse on Chinn's Plantation, West Baton Rouge, Louisiana," as depicted in *Harper's Weekly* in 1866.
Courtesy Fred Benton Collection

averaging approximately fifty miles in width and includes the five former Gulf outlet channels from which the river moved to its present course.

distributary: A river or stream that flows away from the main channel (opposite of a tributary, which feeds into the main channel). Distributaries are part of the natural river system, furnishing outlets for excess flow during high-water periods. Because of the height of the natural levees, at low water the junction of a distributary and the river was dry, although the distributary stream bed itself retained some water. Along this portion of the River Road, Bayous Lafourche, Plaquemine, and Manchac were primary distributaries of the Mississippi.

Dorr, J. W.: A journalist who traveled upriver from New Orleans by buggy in 1860, sending back descriptive reports for publication in the New Orleans *Crescent.* Dorr's firsthand observations of the appearance and culture of the River Road reflect a somewhat romantic sensibility mixed with practical information:

The further I journey up the [German] coast, the more anxious do I feel to vindicate this beautiful country from the aspersions cast upon it by tourists who dash down the Mississippi in steamboats and . . . dismiss the . . . banks of the lower Mississippi [as] low and monotonous and the scenery tame and uninteresting. So the picture doubtless looks to them, framed, as it is . . . with the muddy and rubbish-covered banks of the river outside the levee mound. But let them travel inside the levee . . . [and see] splendid villa-like or castle-like mansions of the planters, the cheerful and comfortable villages of Negro houses, the magnificent old trees with their wavy glory of moss, the beautiful gardens filled with the rarest shrubs and plants, the affluent vegetation of the broad fields, the bundant greenery with which lavish nature coats every inch of this prolific soil . . . the broad tide of the Father of Waters swelling through the long reaches of its winding channel and dotted with steamers and other craft.

Florida parishes: The eight parishes north of Lake Pontchartrain and east of the Mississippi River that prior to 1810 constituted West Florida. This area was transferred from France to England in 1763, when the rest of the River Road had been ceded to Spain. The area was invaded and occupied by Spain in 1779 and was not included in the original Louisiana Purchase in 1803. The Florida parishes—which include East Baton Rouge Parish—became United States territory in 1810 in the aftermath of the West Florida Rebellion and were attached to Louisiana with statehood in 1812.

freedmen: Former slaves emancipated as a result of the Civil War. Before the general emancipation, Louisiana blacks who were born free or had been granted their freedom were known as "free people of color."

gallery: A porch or balcony.

garçonnière: From French *garçon,* "boy." Bachelor quarters; often a separate building from the main house or a part of the house separated from the principal living quarters.

German Coast: The area of the east and west banks of St. Charles and St. John the Baptist Parishes where the Germans recruited by John Law settled. The designation is actually linguistic; the new arrivals came from numerous small kingdoms and other geopolitical entities in the region that would not actually become Germany until 1871. The original settlers were small farmers whose industriousness in this fertile area earned their settlement the flattering appellation "Golden Coast."

hogshead: A large wooden barrel or cask. Hogsheads typically had a capacity of 100 to 140 liquid gallons. Along the River Road in the eighteenth and nineteenth centuries, they were the standard container for storing and shipping sugar, of which they could hold approximately 1,000 pounds.

Iberville and Bienville: Pierre Le Moyne, sieur d'Iberville, and his brother Jean Baptiste Le Moyne, sieur de Bienville, were French-Canadian explorers commissioned by the French Crown to establish a settlement on the Gulf of Mexico. They sailed from France in October, 1698, and arrived early in 1699 at what is now called Ship Island, just off Biloxi, Mississippi, in the Gulf of Mexico. Iberville, commander of the expedition, is regarded as the founder of the Louisiana colony. Bienville became commandant of the colony in 1701 and remained a dominant political force for almost half a century. The Le Moynes' reputation for self-interest, especially profiteering, is well documented, but their skill, energy, and persistence were vital to the early colony's survival.

Ile Dernière: Last Island; literally the last island off the Louisiana coastline before the open Gulf. Ile Dernière was a popular resort destination for wealthy antebellum Louisianians, including River Road planters. Many built summer homes on the island; others sojourned at the island's rambling frame beach hotel. In August 1856, at the height of vacation season, a hurricane swept across the low-lying island, demolishing buildings and killing an estimated two hundred vacationers. Tombstones in cemeteries along the River Road allude to death at Last Island. The 1856 hurricane and later storms cut the island into a chain of separate islets known as the Isles Dernieres.

Isle of Orleans: The colonial territory centered around the settlement of New Orleans which is defined by the water boundaries of Lakes Borgne, Pontchartrain, and Maurepas, the Mississippi River, and Bayou Manchac.

levee: From *levée*, French for "raised" or "elevated." An artificial embankment built along a stream or river to prevent flooding. Levees have been used for flood control for all of recorded history, including levees along the Nile River 4,000 years ago. A *natural levee* is relatively high ground built up by silt deposition along the course of a river during repeated flooding over the centuries.

This view of San Francisco Plantation sometime before 1920 shows extensive front grounds that have since been lost to levee setbacks. The photograph is from the collection of Augustin Lasseigne, one of the last owners of the property before its sale to corporate interests.
Courtesy Doris L. Carville and St. John the Baptist Parish Library

levee setback: When the river changes course, or to prevent this from happening, levees have been relocated, or set back. A levee setback produces a sharp curve or angle in the lay of the levee, rather than following the wide natural curves of the river; correspondingly, the River Road, which follows the levee, takes the new sharp curve or angle. Such dramatic, manmade turns can be clearly recognized. Often they affect the angle at which houses face the road. When the road is redirected, a house may simply be moved back on its tract but left facing in the original direction. If so, the changed position of river, levee, and road make the house appear sideways or angled on its tract.

Mississippi Bubble: The graphic term for the misadventure of those who invested—or speculated—with John Law in the Company of the Indies in the fabulous New World land of Louisiana. Great fortunes were made and lost; it was the losses that gave rise to the image of a bubble burst.

Paret, Father: Father Joseph Paret made watercolor drawings of early-eighteenth-century St. Charles Parish plantations and build-

Father Joseph Paret's watercolor of Bouligny Plantation shows a sugar refinery, quarters, and other buildings, but the plantation's big house apparently had been lost to flooding.
Courtesy Marcel Boyer from the watercolors of Father Joseph M. Paret

ings. These artworks, published in 1859, are not only delightful, but also provide extraordinary primary-source material on the properties, big houses, outbuildings, landholdings, and other aspects of local culture.

parish: The unique Louisiana designation that is the equivalent of county in other states. The term originated with the administrative subdivisions of the Catholic church during the Spanish colonial period.

peripteral: An architectural term meaning "with columns on all sides." Along the River Road, some large plantation houses are square and surrounded by columns, which are surmounted by a horizontal entablature.

Persac: Marie Adrien Persac was one of Louisiana's most important nineteenth-century artists, best known for his gouache paintings of plantations—although it is said that the human figures in these artworks were snipped from magazines and collaged onto the paintings. Persac was married in Baton Rouge in 1851 and died at Man-

chac in 1873. A cartographer, surveyor, and architect in addition
to being an artist, he is widely recognized by historians and historic
preservationists for a diagrammatic map, "Plantations on the Mississippi River from Natchez to New Orleans, 1858," considered
one of the most important land-use documents from the period.
This extraordinary diagram, also called "Norman's Chart of the
Mississippi River," crystallizes a point in time—the year 1858—
and presents in unbroken sequence the chain of individual Mississippi River landholdings. Inscribed on it are the names of planters
and plantations, crops, roads, landings, and outstanding geograph-
ical features. References to Persac in this book apply to this map.

quarters: The row or rows of identical, multifamily cabins that
housed the slaves on a plantation. A single unit is a quarters cabin.
After the Civil War, quarters residences were used by freedmen and
tenants.

ratoon cane: The several additional annual growths that come from
a sugarcane plant after the initial crop and before the land has to
be made fallow and replanted.

river miles: The distance, calculated by following the channel of the
river, between a given location and Head of Passes, where the river
splays into several channels to the Gulf of Mexico. For example,
the Port of Greater Baton Rouge is 229 AHP (229 miles upriver
Above Head of Passes). The Corps of Engineers measured river
miles from Cairo, Illinois, downriver until the 1930s, when they
switched directions and measured from the Gulf of Mexico upriver.
The portion of the River Road included in this book begins at river
mile 115, at the Jefferson/St. Charles Parish line, and extends to
river mile 234.5, in East and West Baton Rouge Parishes.

surnames: The River Road's diverse cultural background, and especially its French heritage, is reflected by the surnames of the people living there. Examples: French Creoles who arrived from the
West Indies after the slave uprisings in 1791—Colomb, Tureaud,
Gentil, and Malarcher; French who migrated south from the Illinois
country—Armant, Balot, Beauvais, Blouin, Chauvin, Dufresne, Durand, Lambert, Louvier, Manuel, Maurien, Mercier, Peltier, Per-
tuis, Tessier; French-Canadian refugees from Nova Scotia who settled along the Acadian Coast—Arcenaux, Babin, Bernard, Breaux,

Bergeron, Blanchard, Boudreaux, Bourg, Bourgeois, Clouatre, Comeaux, Cormier, Dugas, Duhon, Gaudet, Gautreaux, Gravois, Guidry, Guilbeau, Hebert, Landry, Leblanc, Martin, Melancon, Mire, Mouton, Pierre, Poirier, Prejean, Richard, Robichaux, Roy, Saunier, Theriot, Thibodaux, and Trahan; gallicized German names—Dubs to Toups, Edelmeyer to Lemaire, Foltz to Folse, Heidel to Haydel, Huber to Oubre, Lesch to Leche or Laiche, Manz to Montz, Reinhard to Reynard, Scheckschneider to Schexnayder, Trischl to Triche, Traeger to Tregre, Wichner to Vicknair; late-nineteenth-century Italian farmers—Bosco, Migliore, Perino, Vitrano.

towhead: A low alluvial island or shoal located in midriver. Towheads result from formation of a wider channel on one side, which produces a slackened current and allows deposits to settle and build up.

upriver and downriver: Because of the river's twists and turns, directions given in terms of north, south, east, and west can be confusing. It is often clearer to designate positions relative to the source of the river (upriver) or the mouth (downriver). For example, the site of Golden Grove Plantation is upriver from that of Sport Plantation—Golden Grove is farther than Sport from the river's mouth. The terms *upriver* and *downriver* are used in navigation on the river as well as for points along its banks.

PARISHES: WHAT AND WHY

The political subdivisions of the state of Louisiana, including the seven in this region along the River Road, are called "parishes," unlike those in the rest of the continental United States, where they are known as counties. This peculiarity derives from the initial congruence of the secular territorial divisions of the colony with the ecclesiastical jurisdictions of the Roman Catholic Church.

During the colonial period, the Catholic church and the colonial governments were partners—at least unofficially—in developing the territory. The 1717 charter of John Law's Company of the West, for example, stated that the company "shall be obliged to build at its expense churches at the places where it forms settlements . . . also to maintain there the necessary number of approved ecclesiastics . . . all under the authority of the Bishop of Quebec."

Catholic missionaries arrived with groups of settlers or independently to establish church parishes, convert non-Catholics (including native populations), and serve as nonsecular diplomats for the reigning monarch. Both the French and the Spanish governments paid the clergy's salaries, collected tithes, and selected bishops. The French government permitted only the Roman Catholic religion to be practiced in the colony; French Huguenots (Protestants) were not allowed to immigrate. Although some German settlers were already Catholics, others were converted. During the Spanish colonial period, the authorities initially welcomed non-Spaniards who would convert to Catholicism and swear their fidelity to Spain. After 1785, when a considerable influx of new settlers had been systematically attracted to the colony, the Spanish government allowed immigrants to be members of other religions; however, only Catholicism could be practiced openly.

The church played an instrumental role in stabilizing settlement along the River Road, and individual churches were established as colonists dotted the coasts. Although Father Paul du Ru constructed a hut of some description for the purpose of conducting religious ceremonies in 1700, the first church built along the River Road was St. Jean des Allemands (St. John of the Germans) at the west-bank settlement of Karlstein *circa* 1724. It soon fell to ruin, but the void was filled when St. Charles Borromeo Church was built near Destrehan, on the east bank, in 1740. Thirty years later, French Capuchin friars visited the new Acadian settlements on the First Acadian Coast at Cabahanoce (St. James) and established St. James Church. In 1772 the Church of the Ascension of Our Lord Jesus Christ was established at present-day Donaldsonville, on the Second Acadian Coast. The same year, an ecclesiastical presence returned to the west bank of the German Coast with construction of St. John the Baptist Church in present-day Edgard. A land grant to the Parish Church of Manchac was made in 1733, but a church building was not dedicated in the area until the founding of the Coast of Iberville Church of the Archangel St. Gabriel in 1773.

Each church supervised a church parish. The boundaries of these parishes did not jibe with the political divisions set up by the colonial government, but the primarily Catholic residents paid more attention to the ecclesiastical divisions than the political ones. The parishes of St. Jean des Allemands and St. Charles Borromeo churches were in the political district called the First German Coast. St. John the Baptist Church in Edgard was at the Second German Coast. The settlement at Cabahanoce/St. James was on the First Acadian Coast, the settlement at La Fourche des Chetimaches (Donaldsonville) on the Second Acadian Coast (the original Acadian Coast having been separated into two parts in 1770). Upriver jurisdictions included the Acadian settlement at St. Gabriel, the French/Acadian/English settlement at Baton Rouge, and the Acadian settlement at Brusly, in West Baton Rouge.

In 1805, after the Louisiana Purchase, the Territory of Orleans, roughly coinciding with what became the state of Louisiana, was divided into twelve counties. Along the River Road, these included the counties of German Coast (the two German Coasts again conjoined), Acadia (the two Acadian Coasts reunited), and Iberville. The boundaries approximately followed the church parish boundaries formed during the colonial period.

In 1807 the territorial legislature divided the Orleans Territory into nineteen parishes based primarily on the ecclesiastical boundaries of the Spanish colonial period. Among the parishes were St. Charles and St. John the Baptist (the two German Coasts separated again), St. James and Ascension (the two Acadian Coasts), and Iberville. However, the lawmakers did not abolish the original twelve counties at this time, so both terms—parish and county—continued to be applied. East Baton Rouge Parish was added after the Territory of West Florida was annexed and divided in 1810. When Louisiana entered the Union in 1812, *parish* began taking precedence as the preferred term of political subdivision, but not until 1845 did it become official.

A seeming oddity along the River Road is that several parishes (St. Charles, St. John the Baptist, St. James, Ascension, and Iberville) are split by the river rather than having it serve as a boundary. Why, for example, is all of St. Charles Parish not on one side of the river and all of St. John the Baptist on the other? A definitive answer is elusive, but it is most likely that the settlers found it is easier to paddle a boat across a river than to go some distance upstream along the same bank. The river was seen as an avenue connecting opposite banks rather than as a barrier between them. Thus, the early ecclesiastical parishes were drawn to accommodate settlements on *facing* banks rather than those extending along a single bank.

A notation from Spanish colonial documents regarding religious leadership needed along the River Road seems to support this supposition. The assessment was "for two parishes, Les Allemands, covering 10 leagues on each bank of the river; for two parishes at Kabahan-nosse and La Fourche des Chetimachas covering about 12 leagues on each bank of the river; for the parish of Iberville, making about 6 leagues in extent on each bank of the river."

A Thumbnail History of the River Road Parishes

The following brief sketch of how the parishes evolved is in alphabetical, not chronological, order.

Ascension: One of the original twelve counties and original nineteen parishes, Ascension was first settled in 1764 by a group of Acadians and was listed in 1805 as Acadia, part of the Second Acadian Coast. The name is derived from the church parish dedicated to the Ascension of Our Lord Jesus Christ by Charles III of Spain. The parish seat has always been Donaldsonville.

East Baton Rouge: The French words *baton rouge* translate as "red stick." The name was taken from a red-stained pole or stripped tree trunk that served as the boundary between two Indian tribes' hunting grounds, as noted by Iberville in 1699. The area was initially settled by the French, ceded to the English in 1763, and won by the Spanish in 1779. After the Louisiana Purchase, the area now known as East Baton Rouge Parish remained part of Spanish West Florida until the West Florida Rebellion of 1810, when it entered the Territory of Orleans as part of the County of Feliciana. Shortly thereafter, the county was subdivided. The parish seat is Baton Rouge.

Iberville: Named in honor of the Louisiana colony's founder, this was one of the original nineteen parishes and original twelve counties in the Territory of Orleans. In his early explorations, the sieur d'Iberville found a settlement of Bayougoulas on the west bank; in his wake, the Jesuit missionary Paul du Ru arrived to convert the natives and establish a church. Acadians settled the east bank at St. Gabriel in the 1760s. The first parish seat was Point Pleasant, on the west bank; the seat was moved upriver to Plaquemine in 1843.

St. Charles: Initially called *la Côte des Allemands* (the German Coast) and later part of the County of German Coast, St. Charles was named for the sainted sixteenth-century Italian bishop Carlo Borromeo. The area was originally settled by Germans enticed to the colony by John Law and was one of the nineteen original civil parishes of the Territory of Orleans. The first parish seat was called St. Charles Courthouse and was located on the west bank at present-day Flaggville/Hahnville. The parish seat today is Hahnville.

St. James: After the arrival of the Acadians in 1765, the area became known as the Acadian Coast (later Acadian settlement led to a distinction between the First and Second Acadian Coasts), and was part of Acadia County in 1805. St. James is thought to have been named for the patron saint of longtime commandant Jacques Cantrelle. The west bank of St. James Parish was first settled at the present site of St. James—an area then known as Cabahonnoce, an Indian word meaning "mallards' roost"—and at what is now Vacherie, a site the Indians called Tabiscana. Under the Spanish, the area was referred to as Cabahannoce, spelled with confusing diversity over the years: Cabanoce, Cabahanose, Cabahannose, Cabahhnoc, Cabahanoccer, Cabanosse, Cabanocey, Cabaanace, etc. The first parish seat was at St. James Courthouse, on the west bank near the Church of St. James; in 1869 the seat was moved to Convent, on the east bank.

> *Englishman Thomas Hutchins reported on the Acadians in 1770: "They are sober and industrious; they clothe themselves in almost every respect with the produce of their fields and the work of their hands."*

St. John the Baptist: First called the Second German Coast, the parish was named for the church established on the west bank, St. John the Baptist Catholic Church. St. John was one of the original nineteen parishes. The first parish seat was at Bonnet Carré Point (present-day Lucy), on the west bank, but was moved in 1848 to Edgard.

West Baton Rouge: Records of land holdings in the parish date from 1763. West Baton Rouge Parish was created in 1807 as part of the Orleans Territory. It is directly across the river from Baton Rouge and was included in the Louisiana Purchase territory when East Baton Rouge was not. San Michel was the first parish seat; Port Allen took over this function after San Michel was destroyed by the river.

Comparative parish populations:

	1860	1900	1990
Ascension	11,484	24,142	58,214
East Baton Rouge	16,046	31,153	380,105
Iberville	14,661	27,006	31,049
St. Charles	5,297	9,072	42,437
St. James	11,499	20,197	20,879
St. John the Baptist	7,930	12,330	39,996
West Baton Rouge	7,312	10,327	19,419

THE RIVER AND
SETTLEMENT ALONG IT

Almost half a league wide, deep, rapid and constantly rolling down trees and driftwood on its turbid waters. The current was strong. . . . If a man stood still on the opposite side of it, it could not be discerned whether he was a man or no. In places it was a league or more broad and of great depth, and the water always muddy.

—Hernando de Soto.

River Control

When European explorers came upon the Mississippi River, it was the centerpiece of an extensive natural system—what modern engineering jargon would call a "poised stream." The term means that the river and its dynamic existed as a set of balanced forces. Although the actions and reactions within this system might vary from year to year—cutting off bends, adding loops, and altering the channel—the river maintained an overall equilibrium and a generally stable length from source to mouth.

At low water, the river ran within a channel between natural levees created during flooding when heavy silt precipitated out of the overflow. The levees were higher by seven to ten feet than the flatland plain behind them, which sloped gradually another two or three feet lower to swamps. The swamps were the lowest areas and served as catch basins and mitigation pools by retaining floodwaters. Distributaries such as Bayous Manchac, Lafourche, and Plaquemine, as well as other, smaller waterways intersected with the river and served as natural outlets for the normally high springtime flow.

When the river overflowed its banks—usually as part of the annual cycle—floodwaters covered the lower, flatland plain and the swamps. During exceptional floods, the waters deposited silt over thousands of square miles of the Mississippi River floodplain, or alluvial valley, building a vast region of rich bottomlands that, in parts of the upper valley, extended to an average width of fifty miles.

The native peoples of the Mississippi River alluvial plain had adapted their lifestyle to the natural landscape and cycle of the river. The Europeans, seeking to "civilize" this new land, made more demands. When the French decided to move the capital of the Louisiana colony from Biloxi, on the Gulf Coast, to "the rich country bordering the Mississippi" (now New Orleans), they defined their intention to create along the river a permanent and stable community supported by a dependable economic base. This European model could only be accomplished by challenging the river's natural, and inhospitable, cycle.

Levee building, a historically proved technique documented since the ancient Egyptians' use of it along the Nile, was the French government's method of choice for controlling the Mississippi. Therefore, with each land grant along the river came a statutory requirement for the owner to build and maintain a levee along his water frontage. Although these documents mandated specifications for the levees, such rudimentary structures often failed to contain the river. Nevertheless, by 1731, a continuous—although hardly uniform—levee extended along both banks of the Mississippi as far as the upriver boundary of the German Coast.

In 1732 the French colonial government, aware that control of the river was inadequate, demanded that levees be six feet wide at the crest, with a foot-and-bridle path on the land side and a twelve-foot-tall boat-hitching post on the river side. But a flood in 1735 destroyed much of what had been erected. Recalcitrant landholders, frustrated at their constant battle with the forceful river, balked at replacing their levees, submitting only when threatened with expropriation of their property.

Little changed under the Spanish colonial government, which acknowledged the need to continue aggressive river control in order to maintain a permanent foothold in the valley. Governor Carondelet's Levee Ordinance of June, 1792, offered quite specific instructions:

The maintenance of the levees interests all the inhabitants where crevasses ruin in an instant the fruits of a year of labor. . . . Messrs. the syndics, will make forthwith a rigid examination of the levees of their district and will assign to each inhabitant the work that he will have to do there as soon as the crops will be finished. All the levees will be raised in proportion to the last rise . . . all ditches actually existing on the inside of the levee on the river side will be carefully filled and replaced by a spoil bank or embankment . . . which will be planted in short grass. . . . In the most dangerous places exposed to crevasses, the owner will have to have at all times a deposit of pickets, plants, Spanish moss and other articles necessary to stop the crevasses. . . . As soon as there will be a crevasse the syndic of the district will issue an order . . . to send to him the number of Negroes that he will judge necessary whose days' work will be paid to him by the owner of the land.

After the Louisiana Purchase, riverfront landholders continued to be responsible for levee maintenance, even as their protests grew stronger: it was unfair that, while land not fronting the river was gaining settlement, the owners of these backlands bore no responsibility for the levees. Simultaneously, although no means of enforcement existed, riparian landowners gradually came to agree that cooperation, rather than competition, among themselves in levee building might be worthwhile. By 1812, a continuous—but still far from uniform—levee ran along the east bank of the river from New Orleans to Baton Rouge.

The United States Army Corps of Engineers, formed in 1802 to oversee works of civil engineering for the federal government, soon became a presence in the Mississippi Valley. With the proliferation of steamboats on America's inland waterways in the 1820s, the Corps was dispatched to clear the Mississippi River of snags under the justification that the river's navigability was in the national interest. With this wedge, pressure increased to convince the political powers that the security of the levees was also a matter of national interest.

By 1856, state government had agreed that protection from the Mississippi affected all citizens, not just those whose property abutted the river; therefore, all should share in the burden of maintaining the levees. A system of levee districts, each run by a board of commissioners, was developed to maintain the levee by sections. Two years later, parish police juries (equivalent to county governing bodies) were designated as the parties responsible for maintaining levees, with the power to draft slave labor to combat crevasses. But success was short-lived: a major flood struck in 1858, followed by

Under the direction of a Union army officer, "contrabands" (former slaves) build a levee just downriver from Baton Rouge. The engraving is from an 1863 issue of *Frank Leslie's Illustrated Newspaper*.
Courtesy Fred Benton Collection

the outbreak of the Civil War, neglect of the levees, and more flooding in 1862, 1866, and 1867.

At the war's onset, levees were eight to ten feet high, eight feet across on the crest, and fifty to seventy-five feet wide at the base. They were still inadequate as protection from an angry spring river, but in wartime it was impossible to sell bonds to raise money for improvements. And after the war, neither impoverished state or parish governments nor hard-pressed local landowners had the resources—financial or human—for levee maintenance and repair. Throughout Reconstruction, the federal government was petitioned to become involved in reopening the river for commercial navigation; an unmentioned tangential benefit was that such an effort would help protect property owners along the river.

In 1879, after ongoing confusion and the lack of a unified authority over the river, Congress created the Mississippi River Commission—the first formal federal body dedicated to dealing with problems caused by the river. However, no money was allocated until after the flood of 1882, at which time the river south from

Constructing willow revetments, 1950. Within a few years this traditional material was abandoned in favor of reinforced concrete.
Courtesy State Library of Louisiana

Cairo, Illinois, was divided into four Corps of Engineers administrative districts. Their purview was the execution of the commission's policies, including the building and maintenance of levees.

Once the federal engineers became involved, levee construction became increasingly coherent and scientific. Levees were moved to stronger positions, often to the great displeasure of landowners who lost property. Standards for site preparation and construction were introduced, and steps such as clearing land for new levee bases, planting grass to combat erosion, and outlawing the cutting of levees or using the levee ridges as roadways were initiated. Willow-mat revetments—flats of stripped willow boughs woven tightly together—were introduced to provide additional protection against erosion on the riverside flank of the levee.

Engineers analyzed the system's hydrology on an annual basis and studied causes of levee failures. They defined three: overtopping (water rising higher than expected and flowing over the levee's crest), caving (caused by erosion from the river's current or wave wash), and seepage (resulting from structural weaknesses from any

Golden Grove Plantation house during the 1902 flood.
Courtesy St. James Historical Society

number of sources, including intrusions as seemingly insignificant as crawfish holes). The Corps and civilian engineers adopted increasingly sophisticated techniques to combat these problems.

Nature, however, proved smarter. The whole strategy of building levees, albeit politically expedient, ignored certain very important aspects of hydrology. By their very nature, protective levees cut off the river's overflow system. Without its distributaries and access to swamps and the alluvial plain, the Mississippi funneled down an unnaturally narrowed course with increased force, intensifying the pressure against the levees. Higher levees raised flood heights, subjecting the levees to still greater pressure—and demanding still higher levees. Moreover, predictions that the increased current would scour and deepen the river's channel, mitigating floods, turned out to be incorrect.

Flooding, no longer part of the annual cycle, became an occasional event with disastrous results. Serious flooding occurred in 1884, 1897, 1902, 1903, 1912, 1913, and 1922. Then, in April of 1927, came the Great Flood. Euphemistically referred to as "the climactic high water event on the Mississippi River in recorded history," the Great Flood dramatically and permanently altered man's relationship with the river.

The flood resulted from an already swollen river and weeks of torrential and incessant rains in the upper valley, where the Mississippi soon began to back up into its tributaries. Huge amounts of swiftly moving water poured into the lower river, where no release system existed—the natural distributaries had been cut off. Flooding affected the Mississippi Valley from Illinois downriver as the waters overflowed hundreds of miles in some places, drowning the devastated areas for up to two months. The River Road, for the most part, suffered less than many other areas of Louisiana, such as the Atchafalaya Basin. Nevertheless, as the great river roared rampant, Mark Twain's nineteenth-century warning rang presciently: "Man cannot tame that lawless stream. . . . One might as well bully the comets in their courses . . . as try to bully the Mississippi into right and reasonable conduct."

After the devastation of the Great Flood, Congress demanded that the Corps of Engineers tame the river once and for all—build a protection high enough, wide enough, and strong enough to withstand any possible future flood. But it had finally become apparent—and acceptable to admit—that a "levees only" control policy would not suffice; some outflow channels to mimic the river's natural dynamic must be reinstated.

The idea of building a series of floodways and spillways had first been expounded in 1851 but lacked political support until after the Great Flood. Now, sites were chosen and projects urgently pushed forward. The Morganza and West Atchafalaya Floodways and the Old River Control Structures above Baton Rouge were integral to this plan, as was the Bonnet Carré Spillway—today a significant presence in the area covered by this book—cut between the river and Lake Pontchartrain above New Orleans to protect the city.

Bonnet Carré, a historically dangerous bend where the river repeatedly overcame the levees at the elbow and frequent crevasses caused the loss of crops and property, lies very close to Lake Pontchartrain. The river naturally sought a shortcut over the low, flat land between it and the lake. The same factors that made the location a flood hazard recommended it as a site for a spillway; indeed, William Darby had noted as early as 1816 the river's predilection to follow this formation. After 1927, a controlled opening at Bonnet Carré was deemed acceptable.

As it happened, the spillway was actually built several miles downriver from Bonnet Carré Bend because, according to the engineers, that was the closest location where the soil base was stable

The Bonnet Carré Spillway with one floodgate open.
Courtesy State Library of Louisiana

enough to support heavy construction. The control structure and
fan-shaped spillway run were completed in 1932; highway and railroad crossings were in place by 1936, just a year before the gates
were opened for the first time. The spillway was judged an unquestionable success after a potentially ruinous flood became what
was subsequently referred to as simply "the high water of 1937."
(See the East Bank chapter for an explanation of the mechanics of
the spillway control system.)

    The Great Flood also impelled the development of new concepts
in levee engineering, superseding earlier notions of piling and packing a certain height and width of dirt. In vulnerable areas, concrete
paving was laid on the inner face of the levee to guard against
erosion by waves and boat wakes at various water levels. Below
water level, where the current poses the greatest threat of undermining the levee, revetments were emplaced. At first made of cane
mats, then willow mats, revetments are now fabricated of four-
inch-thick articulated concrete mattresses reinforced with stainless-
steel wire mesh. Sections of these concrete slabs are linked together
by cable connectors, giving the revetment mass the flexibility to

adjust to shifts in the bank's shape. In especially vulnerable places, loose rock called "riprap" is piled atop the revetment to provide additional stability. Revetments are usually laid down during low water by large teams of workers, many of whom come from elsewhere and live on large, floating dormitory ships while the work is being done. With new technology, any undermining of a revetment is quickly detected and repaired. The batture is also recognized as a protection for the levee.

Since the Great Flood, the responsibility for river control has evolved as a complicated interrelationship among various agencies—federal, state, and local. A federal-state partnership, based on 70 percent federal and 30 percent state funding, builds and protects levees, under leadership from the Corps of Engineers. Local levee boards provide oversight and upkeep on the slope and crest of the levee. The Corps of Engineers is responsible for dredging the shipping channel, removing the silt, and maintaining a depth of forty-five feet to enable oceangoing vessels to navigate from the mouth of the river up to Baton Rouge. The U.S. Coast Guard regulates river traffic, maintains buoys and signals to mark hazards and indicate the channel, inspects bridges, and handles most other matters relating to navigation and safety.

Current Mississippi River statistics—Length: 2,350 miles from its Minnesota source to its mouth at the Gulf of Mexico. Drainage area: 41 percent of the United States mainland. Average daily flow: 470,000 cubic feet per second; 304 billion gallons of water pass the New Orleans gauge daily. Sediment carried in the river: 160 million tons annually.

Roads Along the River

A road has been in existence behind the levees on each side of the Mississippi River since the early days of settlement, part of the strictures of colonial land grants. In 1732, French colonists were ordered to build a road wide enough for wagon traffic alongside the levee. The Chemin Royal (Royal Road), as the route was called, was public, but individual landholders were responsible for maintaining it and bridges over any ditches that crossed it. The Spanish were equally demanding. A landholder was obligated to construct a road or highway in the front of his land within three years and to keep the road and any bridges opened and maintained. Despite these injunctions, however, the roads were often impassable.

"Roads generally run on the margins of the rivers; when [they] diverge to any distance . . . they soon touch the swampy soil and in wet weather are intolerably deep, muddy and heavy." Timothy Flint, 1818.

By 1834, a dirt road existed from Gretna to Donaldsonville on the west bank and from below New Orleans to Baton Rouge on the east bank. But these roadways—dusty in good weather and muddy and rutted after rains—primarily served local traffic. Reliable transportation of goods and people continued to depend on the waterways.

The River Road remained a secondary artery until the turn of the twentieth century, its location changing according to the river's whims. Some sections of the original road washed away; elsewhere, the buildup of new front land left the River Road some distance from its namesake.

As automobiles gained popularity, it became expedient to gravel the dirt roads. Suggested the Donaldsonville *Chief* in January 1913: "Let the slogan be 'Gravel Road from Port Allen to Donaldsonville by 1914.'" (By 1928, gravel stretched from Gretna to Port Allen.) In the early 1920s, the east-bank River Road was graveled from Iberville Parish to St. James Parish. To reflect its importance, much of the River Road from New Orleans into Iberville Parish was renamed the Jefferson Davis Memorial Highway, or Jefferson Highway, in the 1930s.

The winding, gravel River Road remained the sole overland route between New Orleans and Baton Rouge until the completion of U.S. 61—the Airline Highway—in 1935. One of the first major stretches of paved thoroughfare in the state, the new highway cut a direct, inland route that shortened the distance between the two cities by forty-one miles and several hours. (Political wags at the time suggested that Huey P. Long wanted the road built in order to expedite his frequent trips to the multiple attractions in New Orleans.)

The Airline Highway was a magnet that reoriented many riverfront towns away from the Mississippi. New business districts developed along this fast road, causing the River Road to lose its status as the area's preeminent roadway.

The River Road in Reserve *circa* 1900. The large building was the Club Café.

Courtesy Venita Cambre and St. John the Baptist Parish Library

Settlement Along the River

The use of the land along the River Road has evolved and changed through the centuries—from wilderness to settlement, from small tracts to large plantation layouts, from plantations back to small landholdings, from natural greensward to agriculture and then to industry, from lowland to communities and from communities to pasture again, and from secure to inundated, or flooded to livable. The entire history of the area is one of continual transformation.

All of the early communities along the wild river were situated along the high ground nearest the bank. Some settlements developed at sites where Indian villages had stood, others at naturally conducive settings such as confluences of waterways, fertile clearings, or locations with a commanding view of the river. Unlike the linear scheme of a plantation layout (see the chapter "Agriculture and Industry"), early river communities developed laterally—a long string of residences and small businesses along the riverfront street, with a parallel lane or two behind. After the Louisiana Purchase, the American township system was introduced, which laid out towns on a square grid.

An optimistic sign of the times, 1930.
Courtesy State Library of Louisiana

During the steamboat era, many settlements built public landings for loading and unloading cargo. Some of these communities expanded to become regional centers for commerce and service, locuses for the surrounding plantations, and workplaces for artisans. When railroads arrived, often laid on the last high ground before the swamp, river communities began to extend inland. Typically, a road was built in a straight line from the river to the rail depot, and a grid of cross streets developed off this important new thoroughfare. Today, many area communities still feature a main street running perpendicular to the River Road.

Among the exceptions to this pattern were communities begun by blacks after the Civil War. These places usually evolved as one long lane or two or three short ones, all perpendicular to the River

Road. Today, many such settlements consist of one or two streets perpendicular to the River Road. On contemporary maps, this arrangement looks quite similar to the layout of the French colonial arpent survey.

Small roads perpendicular to the River Road were often named for the property on which they lay, although many of these names have now been changed. The new names reflect contemporary people or places, but the changes helped speed the loss of the former identities of property and settlements—information that held clues to the history of the land.

Over time, a number of River Road communities have disappeared. Some stood at landings that lost their importance after the steamboat era ended; others had their post office consolidated with another community's and so lost their identity; still others were cut off by levee setbacks or simply overwhelmed by the river.

How People Used the River

Until the late nineteenth century, settlement along the River Road was oriented toward the river. The great waterway was the primary means of transportation, superior to the dusty or muddy local roads. Levees and landings were public areas, centers for socializing. In came news, merchandise, and visitors from the outside world; out went local people and cargo, to be delivered to neighboring plantations, to New Orleans, or to the world. Property owners built stairways up the levee and positioned platforms and benches on the crown. Much visiting took place here. On late summer afternoons the levee became a long promenade, a parklike setting with young couples strolling, children playing, and elders watching it all and chatting. At dusk, the mosquitoes chased socializing inside.

The river also provided food—river shrimp and fish that added to the culinary fare of planters and plain folk alike—and free fuel. In high water, the unleveed riverbanks upstream were susceptible to caving, toppling trees into the swift current. During such times, men and boys along the River Road would drag this driftwood from the batture or even grapple it in midriver and secure it near the inside of the levee. When the river receded, the logs were cut into firewood and hauled off by mule-drawn wagon.

Valcour Aime's plantation diary notes that his slaves sal-

The ferry *Istrouma* at the Baton Rouge landing, 1870. Ferry and steamboat landings were hubs of activity all along the River Road.
Courtesy State Library of Louisiana

vaged ninety-five cords of driftwood during the January–February high water of 1840.

From the St. Charles Herald, January 1884: "Driftwood is running freely in the Mississippi River owing to the recent rise. Now is the time to secure your firewood."

The river was the site of baptisms, especially for black congregations. A special church service was held, then everyone—the sisters of the church dressed in long white dresses and white headpieces—followed the preacher and deacon to the water's edge. Men and women formed two lines, and the baptismal candidates walked between them to the accompaniment of hymns. Standing chest-deep in the river, the preacher and deacon performed the baptism by completely immersing each candidate in the muddy water.

St. Charles Herald, June 1895: "The Canaan Baptist Church of Freetown baptized 38 converts in the river fronting the town, Reverend G. B. Duman officiating. Fully 500 people witnessed the ceremony."

And of course the river was used—carefully—for recreation such as swimming and boating.

> St. Charles Herald, *June 1884: "Attention, parents: Complaint is made by many of the habits and latitude allowed the boys of our village, particularly that of bathing [at] the river front throughout the day in full view of everyone."*

The river and its levees were also a source of intraparish friction—and even conflict—during high water. Residents feared that neighbors from the opposite bank might sneak across the river and sabotage the levee in order to relieve the pressure on their side. From distrust grew the practice of levee patrols in the late nineteenth century, a practice that continued at flood stages until after the Bonnet Carré Spillway opened. Men carrying guns and lanterns walked a mile of levee in six-hour shifts, on the lookout not only for hostile neighbors, but also for weak spots—any fissure, boil, or crawfish hole that might undermine the stability of the levee. When the water rose very high, the patrols might be joined by fearful citizens carrying a statue of the Blessed Virgin, saying the rosary, and praying for safety.

Ports

River landings were the predecessors of modern ports along the River Road. Plantation and town landings served as mooring facilities for loading crops, firewood for steamboat fuel, and other products and for unloading cargo and merchandise. The landings were straightforward wooden wharves worked by manual labor. Inland planters and farmers paid to use a town or private landing.

River commerce has become a far more complicated enterprise, and the vast, highly mechanized, concrete-and-steel port facilities that line the riverbanks between New Orleans and Baton Rouge today bear little resemblance to their rudimentary forebears. Contemporary facilities include not only those for onloading, offloading, and storage of individual and bulk general cargo, but also grain elevators and docks, liquid bulk terminals, barge terminals, and public midstream mooring facilities. The ports accommodate not only towboat-driven river barges, but also large oceangoing ships that require a permanent deepwater docking capacity. In an echo of old times, however, businesses without their own docking and wharfage still pay to use public ports.

The River Road as treated in this book includes parts of three port jurisdictions: the port of New Orleans, which includes the metropolitan area upriver to the Bonnet Carré Spillway; the Port of South Louisiana, from the Bonnet Carré Spillway to the St. James/Ascension line; and the Port of Baton Rouge, an agglomeration of private and public facilities in East and West Baton Rouge, Iberville, and Ascension Parishes.

Recent figures rank the Port of South Louisiana as the national leader in import-export tonnage; the Port of New Orleans ranked third and the Port of Baton Rouge fifth. The Port of Baton Rouge is more than two hundred miles inland, but the river channel has been dredged to a depth of forty-five feet at the port, consistent with the channel depth down to the mouth of the river, to accommodate oceangoing vessels.

Boats

Because so much of the land was low and swampy, and even the most strategic paths and roads were often impassable, the most dependable transportation along the River Road was by boat on the Mississippi River and the network of waterways connecting with it. Even after the advent of railroads in the late nineteenth century and the coming of automobiles and improved roads in the early twentieth century, the vital role of boats in commercial transport along the river remained.

The French explorers noted the Indians' use of dugout canoes—a kind of craft the newcomers called a "pirogue" (pronounced pee-rogue or pee-roh). These primitive boats were traditionally made of cypress; the wood was easily cut, water resistant, and—when cured—light and manageable. André Pénicaut, ship's carpenter with Iberville, described how the Indians fabricated their pirogues: "They kept a fire burning at the foot of a tree called cypress until the fire burned through the trunk and the tree fell; next, [they put] the fire on top of the fallen tree the length they wished to make the boat. When the tree had burned down to the thickness they wanted for the depth . . . they put out the fire with thick mud; then they scraped the tree with big cockleshells . . . and washed it with water."

A pirogue in a Louisiana bayou, 1943.
Courtesy State Library of Louisiana

Pirogues had a shallow draft and could be ridden not only on the river and the bayous, but also in the marshes and swamps and, some swear, on the dew. The design proved highly useful to the French, who created versions up to fifty feet long with room for thirty men and many tons of freight. These large craft were usually propelled by oar, but occasionally one was built with a square stern and provided with a mast and sail. The more common one- and two-man pirogues were always paddled or push-poled. C. C. Robin, traveling in south Louisiana in the years 1803 to 1805, saw French pirogues made of two or three firmly joined logs, as well as skiffs and piroguelike boats made of cypress planks. (Plank pirogues are still commonly used in the swamps and bayous of south Louisiana, although they are too unsturdy for use in the Mississippi River.) Robin noted rounded, flat-bottomed, and keeled designs.

Soon more efficient vessels evolved to transport furs, hides, and other goods downriver from the upper Mississippi River Valley. Called flatboats, these large, rectangular, flat-bottomed craft were essentially floating boxes. They ranged in length from fifty to more than a hundred feet and in width from fifteen to twenty-four feet.

On many, a section of deck was covered by a roof supported by plank sides. Flatboats could be crudely steered by means of a large, tillerlike oar at the stern and two smaller, finlike oars, or sweeps, at the sides. To anchor, the boat was simply tied up to the bank. A captain and crew handled the flatboat and its cargo—four deckhands for loads of less than 75 tons, six or more hands if the load exceeded 100 tons. The early flatboatmen were the first of the stereotypical Mississippi River boatmen with a reputation for rugged character and hard drinking.

Although flatboats were in use by the 1750s, their popularity soared after the American Revolution, when settlers pouring into the Ohio River Valley began to seek a downstream outlet for their farm products. New Orleans became the outlet, and flatboats the means of transport. With the Louisiana Purchase, the already-flourishing flatboat commerce mushroomed. In 1802 New Orleans recorded 265 flatboat arrivals; four years later, there were 1,223; in 1832 the total exceeded 4,000. Not until the 1850s did the large, ungainly boats begin to decline in importance.

Flatboaters usually timed their journeys to coincide with the November–January or March–May high water on the Mississippi. But regardless of the season, the voyage was dangerous. The river's strong, swirling currents, lurking snags, and drifting debris were constant threats. In the early decades, boatmen faced the additional possibility of attack by Indians or river pirates. To gain some measure of security, flatboats sometimes traveled in convoy. The downstream run from the upper Ohio River to New Orleans usually took about four weeks.

There was no upstream run. Flatboats were one-way vessels, incapable of travel against the current (although in later years they were sometimes towed back upriver by steamboats). When their cargo was disposed of, they were broken up and sold for lumber— prompting the sardonic observation that many buildings in New Orleans were part flatboat. Almost a third of the discharged crewmen avoided the problem of getting home by simply staying in Louisiana. Of the rest, the great majority walked, up the River Road and then along the fabled Natchez Trace. (With the rise of steamboats, however, the weary flatboatmen had a relatively swift, comfortable, and cheap means of returning to their farms and villages.)

Despite the difficulty of battling the river's current, a certain amount of commerce flowed upstream from the beginning. The big

A Currier and Ives print of a flatboat adrift on the steamboat-crowded
Mississippi River.
Courtesy State Library of Louisiana

French cargo canoes were one means of moving goods upriver. Another arose in the late eighteenth century—the keelboat. Named for
a keel-like shock-absorbing timber running lengthwise along the
bottom of the hull, these vessels ranged from forty to eighty feet in
length yet drew only two or three feet of water when fully loaded.
Narrow in the beam, with pointed prows and sterns, keelboats offered much greater maneuverability than flatboats.

Both keelboats and their bulkier relatives known as barges could
travel against the current, but it was daunting work for their crews.
The boats could be poled if the riverbed was hard and shallow
enough; more often, the crewmen had to go ashore and haul their
heavy craft upstream by means of towlines. (Keelboats could also
be sailed, but only under rare ideal conditions.) A dawn-to-dusk
journey of fifteen miles was considered good progress. A keelboat
voyage from New Orleans to the upper Ohio usually meant four
months or more of backbreaking labor.

Ironically, some keelboats were adapted as luxury craft for rich
planters in the late eighteenth and early nineteenth centuries. Out-

fitted with a stern pavilion for the master and his family, the boats were oar-propelled by slaves seated on benches on the foredeck. Keelboats might also be appointed for public passengers; John James Audubon traveled quite comfortably aboard one from Natchez to New Orleans in 1821.

Other types of boats plied the river for commerce and personal transport during the eighteenth and early nineteenth centuries, but it was the introduction of the steamboat that revolutionized life along the Mississippi. Larger and faster than flatboats and keelboats, steamboats had the extraordinary advantage of being able to go upriver with dependability and a certain amount of speed (fifteen miles per hour). Their presence very quickly drove the keelboats from the main rivers, although flatboats continued to provide a cost-effective means of shipping bulk goods downstream for several decades. By the mid-1820s, steamboats were the queens of the Mississippi.

Despite popular belief, Robert Fulton did not invent the steamboat; he was only one of many who had experimented with steam engines on watercraft. But with his *Clermont* in 1807, he became the first to design, build, and use a steamboat with commercial success. In 1811 the legislature of the Territory of Orleans granted Fulton and his partner, Robert Livingston, exclusive right to build and operate steam-powered vessels in the territory. Late that year, Fulton's sidewheel packet *New Orleans,* outfitted much like a nineteenth-century oceangoing vessel, with portholes and two masts— just in case sail power was needed—headed downriver from Pittsburgh. Piloted by another of Fulton's business partners, Nicholas Roosevelt, the boat landed at its namesake city on January 13, 1812, carrying three passengers, a dog, and a load of cotton and inaugurating the steamboat era on the Mississippi.

The Fulton-Livingston monopoly was quickly challenged by, among others, the veteran riverman Henry Shreve, whose steamboat *Enterprise* carried supplies for Andrew Jackson's troops in the Battle of New Orleans. The courts overturned Fulton's monopoly in 1824. By then the issue was all but moot: scores of steamboats were operating on the Mississippi. Tonnage carried expanded exponentially, leading to reductions in rates. The luxurious passenger amenities—elegant cabins and staterooms, opulent public rooms, and all the rest—did not enter the world of steamboating until the 1830s, creating what would become its romantic stereotype. By

The main salon of the steamboat *Princess* as portrayed by Marie Adrien Persac.
Courtesy LSU Museum of Art

1840, many steamboats were rightly called "floating palaces" even though the largest and most extravagant—the *Princess,* the *J. M. White,* the *Ed Richardson,* the *Grand Republic,* and others—were not built until the mid-to-late nineteenth century.

Mississippi River steamboats were structurally different from steamboats operating in East Coast and mid-Atlantic states. Narrower and with a much shallower draft, the Mississippi vessels were modeled on Shreve's second steamer, the *George Washington,* with its double engine and sidewheels, not on Fulton's *New Orleans.* Because of their superior maneuverability, sidewheelers remained the norm until after the Civil War, when sternwheelers gradually gained favor for their lower construction cost and better performance in low water and on narrow tributaries. Both designs, however, faced the same hazards on the river: collisions, fires, boiler explosions, sandbars, and snags.

Mark Twain likened the typical tall, multidecked, frothy-looking Mississippi steamboat to "a wedding cake without the complications," and so it appeared. The main deck, or first floor, was the largest. On sidewheel vessels, it extended beyond the hull to include the paddlewheels, as well as the engines, boilers, and other machinery and a vast space for cargo and fuel. (Steamboats consumed great quantities of wood—approximately a cord per hour.) Above the main deck was the narrower boiler deck, which held passenger staterooms. The hurricane deck was the lowest roof deck, narrower again than the boiler deck, with staterooms, officers' quarters, and the boat's office. The Texas deck was the top deck, and atop it was the pilot house.

> Saturday Evening Post. *August 17, 1929: "Atop the Texas deck and in the exact center of the boat is the pilot house, about eight feet square, furnished with a stool, bench, heating stove, steering wheel, and instruments such as bell and whistle pulls and a compass. The pilot sits high enough to see and hear above the noise of the engine, to observe the river and the banks."*

Steamboats operated with their own hierarchy. The captain, the titular head, was principally responsible for handling business and passengers. The pilot commanded the ship on the river, joined by the captain in emergencies. Early river pilots were often former keelboat captains, already inured to the constant challenges of a changing river: shifting channel, disappearing landmarks, collapsing banks, and fresh snags. Such knowledge was always vital, especially before 1875 when there were no buoys or signals on the river. Pilots were glamorous figures, and some became legends for their skill. Mark Twain, who was a river pilot as a young man, used his experiences in many of his famous works.

The steamboat clerk handled bookkeeping. The mate supervised the boat's crew and was responsible for the gangplank and storing freight. Engineers were in charge of the mechanical equipment and were especially watchful of the paddlewheel, engine, and boiler. Disastrous boiler malfunctions were so frequent that in 1838 Congress passed legislation to ensure that steamboats hired qualified engineers.

The lowest position was crewman, or "roustabout," stoker of furnaces and handler of cargo. Before the Civil War, slaves sometimes held this job, although by 1840, many of the roustabouts were immigrants willing to start a new life on low wages.

Saturday Evening Post, June 15, 1929 (an interview with Captain Cooley, a well-known Mississippi River captain who began his career in 1869): "Mark Twain, being a pilot, naturally wrote of the river from the viewpoint of a pilot and gave the impression that the pilot was the whole show. . . . The pilot is highly trained and very valuable . . . but no more so than the engineer, the mate or the clerk. . . . It is just as necessary that the mate moves the freight efficiently, keeps the crew trained and disciplined . . . as it is for the pilot to keep the boat in safe water. [As for] the engineers . . . a carelessly or inefficiently operated engine room will burn up the boat's value in excessive fuel in no time. More than one good steamboat has disappeared up her own smokestacks. . . . A steamboat is a floating business and it costs money to operate a steamboat. . . . The business has got to be kept in good shape, the right freight to the right place. The collections—everything having to do with the money side of it—are handled by the clerk. Even the rousterbouts . . . when he settles the question of wages with the mate, he coonjines down the stage, a willing worker and an obedient seaman, ready to stand by the boat in trouble or disaster. When the Negro rousterbout leaves me, I shall quit steamboating. . . .

"A steamboat man always has two worries: one is, will I get all the freight I can handle this trip? The other is, will I get more freight than I can handle this trip?"

River steamers had no second-class cabins; anyone not traveling first class slept on the deck, with the cargo, luggage, boat crew, and slaves. Often, travelers who could not afford cabin passage could earn part of their fare by joining the crew en route.

First class was usually just that. Certainly some boats were dirty and purveyed bad food and worse service, but on most, cabin passengers traveled in comfort and style, with superb accommodations, food, and service. After a sumptuous meal, passengers could relax on the hurricane deck or take respite in the saloon, an ample, parlor-type room as much as 233 feet long (in the case of the *J. M. White*), decorated in "steamboat Gothic" style with gingerbread tracery and ornate furnishings.

In the August 1878 Louisville Courier-Journal Colonel Will S. Hays described the J.M. White, put in service earlier

that year: "One of the most attractive features of this floating
palace is the stained glass . . . the skylights are very chaste in
drawing and in execution, one of the main features being the
busts and statuary in the center of each light. The statues are
painted in pearly gray on a blue ground enclosed by a wreath
of ivy in gray on a white ground, the whole light surrounded
by a border of purple and gold. . . . One of the bridal cham-
bers is beautifully panelled in mahogany and satinwood, and
the other in rosewood and satinwoods, together with graceful
engraving, illuminated with gold and colors . . . there are
seven, sixteen-burner gold-gilt chandeliers in the main cabin
. . . made of fine brass, highly polished, and then the surface
is covered with pure gold. They are all of Egyptian design."

Formalized gambling entered the world of steamboating early,
as entertainment for the passengers. The legendary riverboat gambler, operating under the captain's rules, preyed on wealthy travelers. Some captains accepted all but the most egregious behavior
by gamblers, and more than one skipper was said to have bought
his boat with the winnings from an unscrupulous game. However,
other tales note card sharps being abandoned on a towhead or
turned over to the local authorities at the next landing stop. (A
Louisiana sidelight: P. B. S. Pinchback, the state's first black governor, appointed during Reconstruction, proudly claimed to have
got his start in life as servant and apprentice to the legendary riverboat gambler George Devol.)

Before the 1850s, in steamboating's less sophisticated era, un-
scheduled stops were common. It was not unknown for a planter
to station a slave at the levee to flag a downriver boat to give the
captain a list of purchases to bring back on the way upriver from
New Orleans. By 1860, more than seven hundred passenger packets
were plying the river, providing efficient transportation as well as
a powerful stimulus for economic development in river towns.
Communities along the River Road built hotels, warehouses, and
landings to service the steamers.

The Civil War dramatically affected the Mississippi River steamboat trade. Union admiral David Farragut's gunboats threatened
any steamers that ran. Some packets were converted into gunboats
or rams, their bows reinforced with iron, their sides armored with
heavy timbers and bales of cotton. (None of the Confederate rams

survived the war.) Other boats were engaged to move troops and supplies. Elaborate woodwork and marble fixtures were stripped away. Even the finely crafted steamboat bells were melted for their copper.

After the war, steamboats enjoyed a brief but brilliant renaissance. Larger and larger boats, improved in design and construction if not in basic technology, vied with one another in decor, service, and speed. This most picturesque era culminated in the now-legendary race between the *Natchez* and the *Robert E. Lee* from New Orleans to St. Louis.

The race, the greatest sporting event of its time in the Mississippi Valley, pitted two renowned captains, T. P. Leathers of the *Natchez* and John Cannon of the *Robert E. Lee*. They had a personal bet of $10,000 on the outcome, and partisans of each boat are said to have wagered millions on the luck and skill of the contest. Late in the afternoon of June 30, 1870, the majestic sidewheelers steamed across the starting line at the Canal Street wharf. Along the River Road, spectators lined the levee to watch and cheer.

Both vessels rammed sandbars but escaped. At Red Church (St. Charles Borromeo Church in Destrehan), the *Lee*'s doctor pump, which fed water to the boilers, sprang a dangerous leak, forcing Captain Cannon to rely on bilge pumps the rest of the way. But he had a tactical advantage: whereas the *Natchez* put in to shore to take on fuel, Cannon had arranged by telegraph for barges loaded with cordwood to meet the *Lee* in mid-channel. Even so, according to legend, the *Lee* ran out of ordinary firewood near the end of the race, and the crew resorted to burning the boat's rosewood and mahogany furniture and mural-painted doors.

The *Natchez* was trailing slightly when fog forced Captain Leathers to halt for several hours. The next morning—the Fourth of July—the *Robert E. Lee* steamed victoriously into St. Louis in the record time of three days, eighteen hours, and fourteen minutes.

Ironically, at this triumphal moment the steamboat era was already nearing its twilight. By the 1880s, the broadening web of railroads was undermining the steamboats' status as the most expedient carriers of freight and passengers. Although steamboats continued to operate on the river until well into the twentieth century, their role was more and more peripheral. By 1931, only two steamboats were still running the lower Mississippi.

A nineteenth-century forerunner of today's towboats, the sternwheeler
May Fisher pushes a barge on the Mississippi.
*By Andrew Lytle; courtesy Louisiana and Lower Mississippi Valley Collections,
Hill Memorial Library, LSU*

Helping to drive the queens of the river into oblivion were their
more prosaic successors, towboats. As early as the 1870s, sturdy
tugboats towing barges were competing with the classical steamboats as haulers of freight. The addition of diesel engines and screw
propellers in the 1930s greatly increased the tugs' power and maneuverability. Today these craft—still called "towboats" even
though they have long since switched to pushing, rather than pull-
ing, barges—are the workhorses of the Mississippi. Engine capac-
ities often exceeding 10,000 horsepower allow them to propel tows
of forty or more barges, each one with a tonnage equaling that of
three or four steamboats of the golden age.

Since the very early days of navigation on the Mississippi, specialized river pilots have been charged with guiding a boat from
one point to another. While the captain remained in charge of his
ship, the on-board pilot oversaw the helm and engine room and
determined how to maneuver the boat along the shifting channel.

Pilots were (and are) well paid to know the river intimately, to understand nuances of the water and interpret bank and channel changes.

Today, three pilots associations divide the river between the Gulf of Mexico and Baton Rouge. The Associated Branch Pilots, also called bar pilots, convey boats from the Gulf of Mexico to Pilottown. The Crescent River Port Pilots are responsible between Pilottown and New Orleans, The New Orleans–Baton Rouge Pilots Association takes over from New Orleans upriver to Baton Rouge. The pilots use the Inland, or International, Rules from the mouth of the river to the Huey Long Bridge in New Orleans, and the Western Rivers Rules above that point.

Nautical rules comparable to land-based traffic regulations have developed to ensure safety for the high volume traffic sharing the river. Before the development of radar, ships on the river were equipped with lights—a green light on the starboard, a red light on the port, and a white light on the masthead. Boats passing at night on the river knew where to position themselves in relation to their direction (heading upriver or downriver) and the color of the light.

Today, the Corps of Engineers keeps the three pilots' associations apprised of river condition, sending updates about dredging, channel changes, and other activity.

Boats in Everyday Life

Before bridges were built, boats were the sole means of crossing the river. Until long after the turn of the twentieth century, many area residents kept small skiffs in order to avoid the inconvenience of traveling to and waiting for ferries—although rowing and even motoring across the river was always a dangerous undertaking.

> From the St. Charles Herald, *April 1885: "Several of our friends ran a narrow escape for their lives while crossing the river on Tuesday. The river was at the height of madness caused by the high wind blowing which made it difficult to cross. When they managed to get to the middle, unfortunately one oar was broken. . . . They finally paddled their way to the nearest shore, right bank, safely."*

Privately owned ferries existed in the early part of the nineteenth century. Travelers were at their mercy in terms of schedules and charges. Eventually, parishes began licensing ferries, thus providing some measure of public oversight. Ferry service became part of the state Department of Transportation after the more recent Mississippi River bridges were built. The state bought out the private entities running the ferries and either continued the operations or closed them down. The ferries along the River Road were considered extensions of the highways—water-borne links between the roads on each bank. Today, three ferries are still in operation along this part of the river. They are at Reserve–Edgard, White Castle–Carville, and Plaquemine–Sunshine.

> *Ferry service existed between Donaldsonville and the present site of Darrow as early as 1846. Required by ordinance for providing the service were "two substantial flatboats (a large and a small one) and two skiffs in good repair, with sufficient persons and necessary apparatus, to cross a flatboat and a skiff at the same time." The ferry had to cross persons at "all hours of the day or night." Toll for foot passengers: 25 cents, double after sunset. Toll to cross a gig and horse: $2. Crossing time: one hour.*

Hand-powered ferries were used until about 1870. The first steam ferry or tug, the *Little Minnie,* ran the river in the 1870s. When vehicles were to cross, a barge was affixed to the *Minnie* to carry them. The *Bella Israel,* a successor to the *Little Minnie,* sank in 1894 and was replaced with the *Grand Isle.*

AGRICULTURE
AND INDUSTRY

To encourage settlement and initiate economic development of the Louisiana colony, the French colonial government made land grants. The Company of the West offered concessions to well-connected Frenchmen, including directors of the company. Some of these holdings were bought merely for speculation and were never seriously developed; others were run by absentee ownership and grew—or attempted to grow—crops on a larger scale, including tobacco, indigo, olives, pineapples, and grapes; there was even an effort to introduce silkworms. The moderate successes of indigo and rice were attributed, at least in part, to the familiarity of Senegambian slaves with these crops, which had long been grown in Africa.

The failure of the concessions to create a strong economic base caused the crown to cancel them in 1728 and reorganize the landholdings, but men of wealth, nobility, or with a record of patriotic service continued to be offered large parcels of land. Meanwhile, beginning about 1720, modest grants of land were made to Germans and others as small farmers, and these small tracts ultimately proved more important to the success of the colony.

After the demise of the concessions, the primary measurement for grants of land was the arpent survey, although this system had been in effect along the German Coast as early as 1724, as revealed by the census of that year. Long used in northern and northwestern France, the arpent survey measured grants by their frontage along the river, the highest and choicest land. The value of a landholding was therefore based on the length of its riverfront, not its total acreage. The customary depth of such a grant was forty arpents— almost a mile and a half—although grants of eighty arpents were also made. Along the River Road, a forty-arpent depth often meant that a land grant included a considerable expanse of swamp at the rear of the property. The arpent system produced a parade of long and narrow tracts that lay essentially at right angles to the river and defined land development along the River Road to such a degree that its effects are very much evident today.

Because property lines ran perpendicular to the river, the position of a plot of land relative to the river's meanderings often affected the size of its acreage. If, for example, a tract was situated on the outside of a bend, its side boundaries fanned out, encompassing additional acreage at the rear. However, property facing the inside of a bend could diminish at the rear because its boundaries tapered inward. Because of such discrepancies, land along the river bends was measured not only in the usual parallel plots, but also in configurations resembling rhomboids, trapezoids, and triangles.

Over time, the vagaries of the river further confused property delineations. River movement could add or subtract substantial frontage, land grants on convex banks being built up by the river while those on concave banks usually suffered land loss due to erosion. Special laws were enacted to define the terms of property ownership along the river.

The Spanish colonial government continued the application of the French arpent survey. Governor O'Reilly's mandate in 1770 decreed that "every family which wishes to settle on the river will . . . receive six or eight arpents de face. The land is to be given out in plots 40 arpents deep so that the settlers will have access to the cypress forests which are necessary and useful to them." Settlers were also required to fence the front of their property within three years and could negotiate with their neighbors about boundary-line fencing.

In 1798 Spanish governor Manuel Gayoso de Lemos issued assorted instructions to his commandants regarding land grants. Settlers without money, slaves, or movable property would not be given grants until they had remained on the post for two years. Settlers with means were required to occupy their grants for specific periods before their title became final: for married settlers, two years; for unmarried mechanics, three years; for unmarried settlers without vocation, four years. No

*land grants were made to traders or speculators. The follow-
ing year, the land code was amended to grant each newly arrived family a tract along the Mississippi River of eight arpents
frontage and forty arpents depth, with the obligation to clear
the property to a depth of two arpents within three years.*

Even after the Louisiana Purchase, land definition continued to
be based on the arpent survey. In 1811 Congress offered holders of
land grants the option of extending their property to the eighty-
arpent line. Some purchased not only the additional forty arpents
depth behind their property, but also other back depths contiguous
to their own—expanding their rear acreage. This offering also provided a valuable opportunity for the young men of a family to acquire property.

Development patterns along the river were affected by French
inheritance laws, under which heirs were entitled to equal portions.
Because the worth of a property was determined by its river frontage, each share consisted of a slice of frontage running to the cer-
tified depth of forty or eighty arpents. Over the years, this system
tended to create a series of narrow, parallel strips.

Questions of land disposition were further complicated by
sloppy and informal surveys and records from the colonial period.
The inevitable title disputes were disentangled only after the federal
government established special commissions in 1828 for this purpose.

The influx of Anglo-Americans after the Louisiana Purchase
brought new money to the River Road. Many smaller tracts and
farms were bought and consolidated into plantations, some of
which commanded twenty-five or more arpents of frontage. After
the financial hardships caused by the Civil War, however, many of
these same properties were once more subdivided into smaller
tracts.

Agriculture

The development of commercial agriculture along the River Road
was an evolutionary process. The old German Coast, settled in the
1720s, was soon known as the "the Golden Coast," reflecting both
the fertility of the land and the Germans' industrious cultivation of
it. They farmed small plots without slave labor and produced garden crops in such plenitude that they furnished food for the tables

of New Orleans. The Acadian Coast settlers, arriving in the latter part of the century, were also productive farmers, but less commercially successful. They grew Indian corn (maize), rice, sweet potatoes, and sugarcane, primarily for their own consumption.

The late eighteenth century also saw plantations supplant concessions as the dominant system of commercial farming along the River Road. (A plantation is defined as a capitalistic form of agriculture in which a large number of laborers work to produce a single crop.) The successful West Indies model of plantations was adapted to the River Road, and before the end of the century, River Road plantations were dedicated to the production of indigo, tobacco, cotton, sugar, and rice in commercial quantities.

Whereas the German and Acadian small farmers generally labored for themselves, slave labor provided the muscle on the large properties. Therefore, large planters were fearful when, on January 1, 1808, a law went into effect that prohibited the importation of slaves into any part of the United States' jurisdiction. The very next year, an exception was made after the Spanish government deported from its colonies—especially Cuba—thousands of Haitians who were living as refugees from revolution in their homeland; about 10,000 of these persons, including whites, slaves, and free blacks in roughly equal proportion, were allowed into New Orleans.

This influx was still insufficient to allay planters' concerns about their supply of slave labor. Despite the new law, however, there remained abundant sources of new slaves for Louisiana. Smugglers were one such source. But the great majority of slaves came from other states—a trade not forbidden by the 1808 law. Slaveowners in older southern states, especially Virginia and South Carolina, sold both males and females "down the river." And, of course, the native population increased simply through reproduction. As a result, by 1860 Louisiana supported more than 326,000 slaves. The state also had a free-black population of more than 18,000—the largest in the nation—some of whom owned slaves themselves.

After the Civil War, planters sought inexpensive labor to replace slaves, recruiting workers from Italy, China, and elsewhere. In 1870, for example, the Louisiana Immigration and Homestead Company was formed in St. Charles Parish to bring agricultural workers from Europe, producing an influx of Italian farmers. For the most part, however, local black populations continued to dominate the labor pool.

Crops Along the River Road

Commercial agriculture in the River Road area developed erratically during the colonial period as the settlers primarily struggled to produce enough food to reduce imports from the mother country. Several kinds of crops were grown commercially with varying success until the advent of the commercial production of sugarcane, which remains predominant in the area to this day.

One of the first important cash crops in the colony was indigo, which was introduced by seed in 1721, although a species of native indigo grew wild. By 1738, large-scale cultivation was well established in the first plantation-style system in the lower Mississippi River Valley. For several decades, indigo was relatively profitable for Louisiana planters, in part because growers in the West Indies had abandoned the market in favor of sugarcane.

Indigo's value was as a dyestuff producing a deep blue. In Louisiana, the plant was processed through a three-vat system thought to have been introduced by African slaves. The resulting moist, caky substance was dried and cut into squares for export. After the colony came under Spanish control in 1763, however, the market for Louisiana indigo diminished because Spain had other sources supplying a higher-quality product. The American Revolution brought economic changes that further reduced the demand for Louisiana indigo. Nevertheless, many Louisiana planters persisted in growing the plant until 1795, when an infestation of insects compounded by a season of bad weather destroyed the crop.

Tobacco was another of the colony's early cash crops, raised on several large concessions. It required neither the capital nor the drainage that indigo demanded. Slaves harvested, dried, and bundled the leaves for export. Tobacco remained commercially important in Louisiana throughout the Spanish administration, peaking in the 1780s. But after the American Revolution, the local product could not compete with that grown in Virginia and elsewhere in the southern United States. Tobacco cultivation survives in Louisiana today in one small and unique form. An indigenous tobacco plant, introduced to the early settlers by the Indians, is ideally suited to the River Road climate. Acadian Pierre Chenet was the first to cultivate and cure this native species commercially, in the 1820s, although it was never farmed on a large scale. The tobacco is known as "perique," allegedly because that was Chenet's nickname (other

Rice mill at Donaldsonville, late nineteenth century.
By Andrew Lytle; courtesy Louisiana and Lower Mississippi Valley Collections, Hill Memorial Library, LSU

archives suggest that the word may be a corruption of *perruque,* a wig with long curls that resembled the tobacco's leaves). Perique is grown on a steadily diminishing acreage in a tiny corner of east-bank St. James Parish. It is primarily used as a blend in pipe tobaccos.

Rice cultivation thrived during the French and Spanish colonial periods, especially along the German Coast. Well suited to the local soil and climate, rice was a favored crop of small and middle-level farmers even after the ascendance of sugarcane because rice demanded much less capital and labor.

Providence rice—so-called because the crop was planted, then nurtured by "Providence," not irrigation—was the French colonists' initial investment. It could be grown on land too wet for other crops. River rice, introduced as a commercial species, was managed in larger plots. Rice fields were flooded when the river was high enough to allow water diversion through the levee. A system of ditches and drainage channels was dug, with controls at the levee and at the rear of the fields to stabilize water levels.

After the Civil War, many sugarcane planters converted their fields to rice because of its lower monetary and labor requirements—and because, ironically, the lack of levee maintenance due to the exigencies of the war provided plenty of water for irrigation. Although rice remained an important commercial crop in St. Charles Parish during much of the nineteenth century, the development of a steam-powered water lifter in 1885 catalyzed the commercial cultivation of rice in previously inhospitable areas, especially the Louisiana low prairie west of Lafayette. At the same time, laws were enacted to regulate (or outlaw) flumes or pipes carrying water through levees from the river to rice fields. The combination of competition from southwest Louisiana and the flume regulations effected the demise of the commercial cultivation of rice along the River Road.

From the St. Charles Herald, *August 18, 1883: "Rice plant-ing is usually carried on among a number of friends, neigh-bors, or relatives in partnership. The heat, perspiration and fatigue incident to rice cultivation are not considered very much in a crowd of friends who are their own bosses and cut their own rice in their own way. But to an outsider, $1.25 per day is demanded."*

Cotton became a profitable crop, grown on a large (plantation) scale, after the invention of the cotton gin in 1793. In the early nineteenth century, cotton rivaled sugarcane in importance along the River Road. Even though much of the land was too low for the best results with cotton, a large commercial crop was grown as far south as St. James Parish. After the Civil War, some sugarcane planters converted to cotton farming, especially along the high ground of East Baton Rouge Parish.

Indigo, tobacco, rice, and cotton, although intermittent contributors to the River Road economy, were nearly inconsequential in comparison with the economic impact of sugarcane—the single most important crop along the River Road and the basis for much that was, and remains, distinctive about this area. For many years, no less than 95 percent of all sugar produced in the United States came from Louisiana, much of it from the canefields and sugar mills along the River Road.

Sugarcane is a tropical grass, thought to have originated in southeast Asia during the neolithic era and propagated throughout the world by cuttings. Its commercial viability is dependent on the ability to transform squeezed cane juice into granulated (crystallized) sugar. From the time of the Le Moyne brothers, sugarcane was planted in the Louisiana colony. The challenge, however, was to find a way to granulate enough sugar from the cane to justify growing it on a large scale.

Sugarcane typically requires at least fourteen months to mature in its native tropics; in Louisiana it is forced to mature in eight months because it is vulnerable to winter freezing. Joseph Dubreuil, one of the first sugar farmers in Louisiana and the first man to erect a sugar mill on the continent (in 1756), is credited with finding a strategy for protecting sugarcane in winter. He discovered that the plant "does not freeze in the ground during the winter if we cover the stalks that have been cut four inches from the ground." Co-operative weather—a warm, dry winter, moderately dry spring, hot, wet summer, and cool, dry fall—can produce an ideal crop in Louisiana. A fall cold snap, however, can be chancy: if mild, it helps the cane reach an artificial maturity; in the form of a hard freeze, however, it ruins the crop by altering its sucrose (sugar) content, so that the juice will not crystallize.

The devastation of the indigo industry drove desperate planters to try their luck with sugar. Almost simultaneously, and certainly serendipitously, a slave insurrection in the French West Indies, a major colonial sugar producer, brought knowledgeable sugar technicians to Louisiana. One, Antoine Morin, was closely involved with Etienne Boré when, in 1795, Boré became the first to crystallize sugar on a commercial scale in the colony. Although others had granulated Louisiana sugar, the ability to do so commercially catalyzed the development of the industry.

George W. Cable, the late-nineteenth-century author of Louisiana fiction, penned this flowery description of Boré's triumph: "The dark sugar house; the battery of huge caldrons, with their yellow juice boiling like a sea, half-hidden in clouds of steam; the half-clad, shining negroes swinging the gigantic utensils with which the seething flood is dipped from kettle to kettle; here, grouped at the end of the battery, the Creole planters with anxious faces drawing around their central figure as closely as they can; and in the midst the old mousquetaire [Boré], dipping, from time to time, the thickening juice, repeating again and again his simple tests, until in the moment of final trial, there is a common look of suspense and instantly

Workers bringing in sugarcane for grinding, *Harper's Weekly,* 1883.
Courtesy Louisiana and Lower Mississippi Valley Collections, Hill Memorial Library, LSU

after it, the hands are dropped, heads are raised, the brow is wiped, and there is a long breath of relief—'it granulates.' "

The sugar industry gained converts as indigo farmers faced ruin, but it expanded dramatically after the Louisiana Purchase. New methods arrived with farmers moving into the region from the upper South and with the 1809 influx of Haitian refugees, many of whom were experienced sugar growers. Also, whereas France and Spain had possessed other sugar colonies, Louisiana was the new American republic's first domestic producer. Sugar soon provided Louisiana's first sound economic base. It was ideally suited to the plantation system and the availability of slave labor.

Intensive experimentation brought new varieties of cane and more efficient milling and boiling apparatus, although harvesting continued for many years to depend on the muscle of men and

Boiling cane juice at a sugar mill, *Harper's Weekly,* 1887.
Courtesy State Library of Louisiana

animals. Cane varieties were a critical factor. Creole cane, available
to Boré, produced strong juice but was not resistant to frost. Ota-
heite, or Tahiti, cane, introduced to the colony in 1797, was slightly
better suited to the Louisiana climate, but not so good as ribbon
cane, which appeared in 1817. Also known as riband, black Java,
and Batavian striped, this species grew quickly, ripened early, and
developed a hard rind that provided added protection from cold
weather. The hard rind also made grinding by animal-powered
mills more difficult, but the introduction of steam-powered grinders
in 1825 solved this problem.

Sugar mills used three vertical wooden rollers to press the cane
and squeeze out the juice, until it was soon discovered that horizontal iron rollers were superior. Early grinding sheds were oval or
circular, configured to accommodate the walking path of horses
and mules (preferred by Americans) or oxen (preferred by Creoles)
harnessed to the arm of the grinding wheels. By the 1840s, most
mills incorporated two successive sets of rollers. By the 1860s,
steam had almost completely replaced animal power for grinding,
transforming sugarhouses into large, rectangular plants from which
the trademark smokestacks rose.

The earliest method for making cane juice into raw sugar was simple. The juice was cleaned and skimmed in cypress boxes, then moved to the boiler, where it was transferred down a series of successively smaller, open, cup-shaped kettles or pans set in a brick frame over a furnace. The heat caused the juice to thicken, then crystallize. Each kettle was named: the *grande* was the largest; the *flambeau* was the one whose base was licked by the flames; the *sirop* was the pan in which the juice boiled to a syrupy consistency; and the *batterie* was the crucial kettle in which the syrup was "struck" or "made a strike"—which, in the vernacular of the sugar industry, means that it formed small crystals. Sometimes a fifth pan was added between the flambeau and the sirop to further clarify the juice. After the crystallized syrup cooled, it was transferred to hogsheads for storage. These were positioned over smaller barrels to catch dripping molasses—uncrystallized sugar.

> *From a mid-nineteenth-century account of sugar processing: "A cane carrier brought the great piles of juicy looking ribbon cane to the crushing rollers. The cane juice flowed in a small river to the row of batteries where the boiling and skimming off of impurities took place. These batteries of open kettles . . . with steam coils underneath were arranged in order. The transfer of the hot juice from one to the other was done by a hand-operated ladling process amid a steamy surrounding, with much sampling and testing to find when the point of proper cooking had been reached. Great long sweeps with wooden buckets . . . carried the boiling cane juice from one cauldron to the other and to the final-process vat before it was transferred to coolers in the cooling room. There the soft sugar mass was left to solidify into brown sugar. Later, men with ordinary spades dug the brown sugar out of the coolers and filled sugar barrels and hogsheads for shipping."* William E. Clement, Plantation Life on the Mississippi.

It was difficult and costly to maintain the constant heat required to boil down the juice, and by this time, steamboats were competing for large quantities of firewood. Norbert Rillieux, a free man of color born in New Orleans and educated in France, provided the solution with his multiple-effect evaporator. Patented in 1843, Rillieux's system produced a higher quality and quantity of sugar

Plaque commemorating Norbert Rillieux, whose inventions revolutionized the sugar industry.

Courtesy Louisiana and Lower Mississippi Valley Collections, Hill Memorial Library, LSU

while using 75 percent less fuel. Sophisticated modern sugar-milling equipment is based on Rillieux's system.

The Sugar Plantation

"[Below Baton Rouge] far as we can see is sugarcane, looking very much as cornfields do in summer with you. The steam from the sugar mills is seen in all directions. Live oak and orange and china trees dot the landscape and there are elegant mansions along the 'coast' so close to one another as to make an almost continuous village." Captain William B. Miller, December 1875, in a letter to his children describing his steamboat journey downriver.

Sugar plantations along the River Road varied greatly in size, and many were much smaller than the myths evoke. But, combining land, labor, and capital, plantations developed an ambiance and culture of their own as quasi-contained communities where owners and workers shared home, farm, and factory.

The antebellum plantation was a social and commercial hierarchy. The property-owning planters were French colonials, Creoles (including West Indian refugees), or after 1803, Anglo-Americans. They administered and supervised their business, facing the risks associated with agriculture and supporting large investments in land and machinery. Most planters lived from year to year, depending on annual loans. It is estimated that before the Civil War, a sugar planter's assets would include a minimum of $90,000 for buildings, equipment, and slave workers—no small sum in nineteenth-century dollars. Until late in the century, most planters were allied with factors (in New Orleans) who supplied credit, marketed sugar, and acted as general business agents.

Many River Road planters, though working incessantly, lived well. With a town house in New Orleans for the social season, occasional travel to Europe, and a reputation for lavish entertainment, the planter's life assumed a romantic (although often unrealistic) aura.

An antebellum guest describes the end of an evening at a Creole plantation ball: "The staircase was garlanded in roses for full three flights. Gentlemen sampl[ed] Scotch or Irish whiskey. . . . About midnight supper was announced. . . . [On

*side tables were] cold meats, salads, jellied galantines; the
main table was set with 'a corsage bouquet at each place.'
Illuminating the whole were candles in crystal chandeliers and
on the table in silver candelabra. . . . [Desserts abounded]—
fruits, cakes, Charlotte Russes, jellies, custards, pies. Various
wines in cut glass decanters, each with its name carved in the
silver grapeleaf suspended from its neck. . . . More dancing
after supper and at dawn when the guests were leaving, a plate
of hot gumbo and a cup of strong black coffee."*

Wives and children of planters had roles of their own. To the
plantation mistress fell oversight of domestic duties, including hospitality, and care of sick and disabled, including slaves—as required
by law. She was aided in her ministrations by slave women who
acted as nurses. Widows often assumed the business duties of the
plantation after their husbands' deaths. Children were tutored by
a schoolmaster; a music teacher and dancing master might also
visit. Young men might be sent east or to Europe for higher education; some went to New Orleans or to Jefferson-College, in east-
bank St. James Parish.

Social life revolved around plantation culture, with much visiting
and lavish entertaining among families when they were in residence
along the River Road. Because of the hardship of travel and the
distance, guests often stayed for weeks.

*From the memoir of William Howard Russell, visiting plan-
tations along the River Road in 1860: "Breakfast is served:
there is on the table a profusion of dishes—grilled fowl,
prawns, eggs and ham, fish from New Orleans, potted salmon
from England, preserved meats from France, claret, iced water, coffee, and tea, varieties of hominy, mush and African
vegetable preparations." This, following at least one, and
sometimes more, mint juleps, "a glassful of brandy, sugar, and
peppermint beneath an island of ice—an obligatory panacea
for all the evils of climate."*

Planters' families lived on the River Road during the April-to-
December growing and harvesting seasons, but many moved to the
city (New Orleans) during the winter social season.

Day-to-day operations of the plantation fell to an overseer—a
critical position but never one that conferred social equality with

the planters. The overseer's job was difficult, a balance between coercing work from slave labor and simultaneously reflecting the planter's good treatment of his slaves. Under the 1806 slave code, only a white man or free man of color could be an overseer, and he was limited in his powers over and treatment of the slaves he administered. The overseer and his family lived in a house usually located between the planter's big house and the utility section of the property. Although much smaller than the planter's, this house was often fenced and surrounded by a garden, plantings, and trees. Overseers were especially vital on plantations with absentee ownership or under the control of a new widow.

Slaves provided both skilled and unskilled labor during the antebellum period, and many stayed on their respective plantations as paid workers after the Civil War. Some worked in the house; some served as blacksmiths, carpenters, masons, or mechanics; many were field hands, tilling the soil, tending the growing cane, digging drainage canals, maintaining buildings, roads, and levees, cutting firewood, manning the grinders, and generally providing the muscle for the large agricultural complex.

Large slaveholders just prior to the outbreak of the Civil War included free blacks and women in addition to white males. Free black slaveholders existed throughout the South but were more common in Louisiana than elsewhere. Women slaveholders, sometimes in partnership with a male associate, were usually the widows of planters.

The physical layout of plantations along the River Road was quite uniform. Plantation property extended from the riverfront to the swamp, following the arpent survey. Many antebellum travelers remarked that each plantation resembled a small village separated from the next by fields and sometimes orange groves, with a neat fence defining its frontage.

"In all the better managed plantations, the arrangement of the little village has a fashion by which it is settled. There is, in large and respectable plantations, as much precision in the rules . . . as in a garrison under military discipline or in a ship of war. A bell gives all the signals." Timothy Flint, 1818.

"Splendid old homesteads dot the road at the distance of a

*quarter of a mile apart, the out-buildings, negro quarters, etc.
forming at each a considerable village, so that the road up the
coast is almost like a street of a vast, thinly built city. The
plantations having a narrow front on the river and running
far back, the houses are thus brought close together and ren-
der the levee road a suburban avenue unequaled in the world,
bordered on one side, as it is, by the unequaled river of the
world, the clustering steamers and other crafts on which give
an animated variety to the changeful scenery." J. W. Dorr,
1860.*

The property began at the river with a landing and, often, a
warehouse. By the latter part of the nineteenth century, a part of
the warehouse or a nearby building might house the plantation
store, which offered credit, easy access to provisions (many new
landholders were too poor to travel), and a center for socializing.
Often, goods were paid for with coins, scrip, or tokens valid only
at that store.

The big house on a large plantation was its most spectacular
structure. Situated on the highest ground behind the River Road to
catch river breezes, the home was spacious, comfortable, and by
the 1830s, usually physically impressive. The early plantation
homes were designed in the Creole style, but many were renovated
with Classical Revival elements to make them more imposing. It
has been said, however, that until the beginning of the twentieth
century, it was easy to tell whether a River Road plantation was
owned by a Creole or an Anglo. The secret was revealed not by
architectural style but by exterior paint colors. The Anglo-Americans adhered to a pristine white, while Creoles painted their homes
in multiple lively colors. (Destrehan Plantation, in east-bank St.
John the Baptist Parish, and Laura Plantation, in west-bank St.
James, are current exemplars of the Creole palette.)

Oak allées were planted between the plantation house and the
river not only for their imposing grandeur within the landscape but
also, it has been suggested, to funnel the river breeze to the house.
The parklike landscape might also include clusters of beech, magnolia, poplar, or cedar trees (according to local folklore, cedars
brought good health and long life). Crape myrtle, oleander, mi-
mosa, acacia, gardenia, magnolia fuscata, yucca, and banana,

lemon, and orange trees were other popular plantings within the formal gardens.

Near the rear of the house stood one or more huge cisterns for collecting rainwater. Off to the side, constructed in a complementary architectural style to that of the main house, were pigeonniers (dovecotes) and, perhaps, a garçonnière—separate living quarters for young men. A detached kitchen stood behind the main house, as did the smokehouse, storerooms, and a ground-level bricked wine cellar. A summerhouse might grace the lawns, along with, on some plantations, a small schoolhouse.

Lyle Saxon, a New Orleans writer in the 1920s and 1930s, remembers a plantation visit from his boyhood: "[We] preferred to sleep in one of the garçonnières. . . . The lower floor . . . was musty and damp but the room above was both charming and comfortable. It was the first octagonal room I had ever seen . . . just room enough to walk between the foot of the bed and the stair rail. . . . One night in the spring when the river was high, we saw a steamboat pass higher than our heads. The river beyond the levee was invisible and the huge illuminated steamboat passed by like a monster in a dream. It was so near that we could hear the negro roustabouts singing on the decks and the puffing of the exhaust pipes. It seemed to come out of nowhere, gliding above the tops of trees." Lyle Saxon, Old Louisiana.

Beyond the overseer's house and garden were various utility buildings: a carriage house, blacksmith shop, stables, barns, tool and storage sheds, and perhaps a dairy.

The quarters was a small community of identical dwellings lining one or more dirt roads where slave families lived. Many slave families had individual, fenced garden plots. On some plantations, an infirmary and a church for the slaves stood near the quarters. (Under French and Spanish law, slaves were exempted from working on Sundays and holidays; Saturday afternoons were often free time as well.) After the Louisiana Purchase, the law was changed so that slaves could work Sundays, but only with compensation. Aside from these restrictions of law and custom, a slave could expect to work from "can see to can't see" (dawn to dark) every day.

The plantation bell, a ubiquitous part of plantation life, was usually located near the sugarhouse or outbuildings, where it clanged

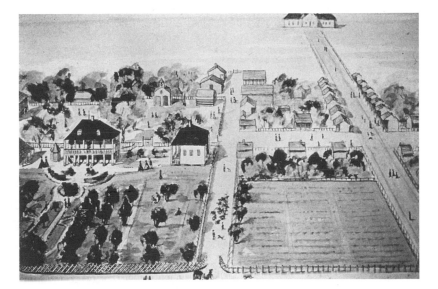

Paret's rendition of Good Hope Plantation shows a layout typical of large sugar plantations along the River Road. The main house faces the road across a large, tree-lined front lawn. Quarters cabins line a lane leading to the sugar refinery in the distance. Not far behind the big house is the plantation chapel.

Courtesy Marcel Boyer from the watercolors of Father Joseph M. Paret

the daily schedule, calling slaves to work and signaling breaks. Between the outbuildings and the fields, in a position of unquestionable prominence, stood the sugar mill, hub of the plantation and by far its largest structure. As early as the 1830s, mule-drawn railcars on narrow-gauge track brought harvested cane from the fields to the mill. After the Civil War, steam locomotives replaced mules. Plantation mills produced raw brown sugar and secondary stuffs—molasses and two distilled liquids, rum and a cheaper grade called tafia, strictly for domestic consumption.

Behind the mill was an expanse of fields. Vast sections of the fertile alluvial plain were cleared, leveled, drained, and planted in a geometric grid of rows (standardized to six feet in width with the introduction of two-mule plows in the 1830s) criss-crossed by drainage ditches. It was especially important to ensure effective drainage so that the sugarcane crop did not flood.

Two types of wooden fencing were most used on River Road plantations. The first, erected to protect fields from free-ranging animals and to enclose barnyards, used *pieux*—spaced vertical posts approximately five feet tall, into which horizontals were set in notched holes. The second type surrounded the house and was made of upright cypress pickets held together and stabilized by horizontal posts.

The antebellum sugar calendar set the duties and activities of work and leisure throughout the year. In late winter and early spring, planting took place, stubble cane was plowed, equipment checked for repairs, and ditches and bayous cleared for drainage. In early spring, ratoon cane sprouted and was tended. During the summer months, fields were tended and—all prayed—adequate rain fell. The end of summer and early fall were dedicated to cutting wood, making hogsheads and barrels, ensuring the repair and maintenance of buildings and equipment, and sometimes planting a new crop. In October, fields were plowed, seed cane was put up, and the harvest and grinding began. The crucial task of getting the crop in and processed lasted until mid-December, with all hands working to beat an early freeze.

On the last day of harvest a special ritual took place. The foreman chose his best worker to cut the tallest stalk of cane from the last row. With the other workers congregated around, the foreman tied the cane with a blue ribbon and brandished the cane knife, singing to the stalk before the laborer cut it. Then the entire group, bearing the last cane, returned to the mill in carts with much song and waving of colored handkerchiefs. The master gave everyone a drink as all celebrated the end of the season.

New Year's Day was also special. The slaves celebrated with dancing and singing. Alcée Fortier, the late-nineteenth-century Louisiana historian, described instruments such as a drum made of a barrel with one end covered with oxhide, and a violin fashioned from two sticks and the jawbone of a mule—with the teeth still on it.

Sugaring to the Present Day

The River Road sugar industry reached its zenith at the outbreak of the Civil War, although little refining (as opposed to milling) was done locally. This prosperity abruptly ended with the Union navy's blockade of the river, subsequent fighting, Federal occupation of south Louisiana, and wholesale destruction of plantations, mills, and equipment. The number of operating sugar plantations fell dramatically, from 1,200 in 1861 to 175 in 1864.

Ironically, many sugar planters had opposed secession. As a group, the planters were politically influential and active and insisted on government protection from cheap imported sugar. Fearing that their economic advantage would disappear if the state voted itself out of the Union, they had fought the idea of secession—although the great majority staunchly backed the Confederacy once the war began.

After the war, the sugar industry was in shambles. Hard assets—land, buildings, mills, and equipment—were critically damaged, capital and credit were virtually nonexistent, the market was diminished, and the slave labor pool had been transformed to one of free wage earners. Although federal officers advised former slaves to continue working on their home plantations for wages or a share of the crop, securing labor became an ongoing problem. Efforts began to attract foreign workers. Many large properties, bankrupted or nearly so, were sold and subdivided; some were farmed by tenants or sharecroppers. Other plantations were eventually bought by syndicates, corporations, or consortia, often from outside the state and run by professional managers. Not surprisingly, these changes also rearranged the social composition of the River Road.

The wartime destruction of many sugar mills and the subsequent subdivision of properties catalyzed the development of centralized, cooperative sugar factories. These facilities were larger and more efficient than the earlier mills and served many plantations and small farmers or tenant growers. Centralization in turn required more effective transportation for hauling cane over distances, which increased the use of railroads and changed both the industry and the landscape.

By the 1870s, the sugar industry was recovering. Land use had been reorganized, and a number of mills were in operation. Mule-drawn plows had replaced men with hoes. But major setbacks challenged the recovery: the national financial panic of 1873 depressed sugar prices; international competition at the end of the decade arose from the German sugar-beet industry; and labor strikes in 1880 in St. Charles, St. John the Baptist, St. James, and Ascension set workers against owners and disrupted production.

Between 1887 and 1910, new agencies and resources dedicated

Feeding cane into a crusher, 1938.
  Courtesy State Library of Louisiana

to sugar production emerged. The formation of the Louisiana Sugar
Planters' Association (which became the American Sugar Cane
League), the opening of a sugar experiment station, the founding
of an academic program dedicated to learning and research in the
sugar industry, the introduction of new varieties of cane, and the
further expansion of centralized mills were all advantageous devel-
opments. After 1910, small farmers gained increasing importance
despite continuing setbacks, which culminated with the catastrophic Mississippi River flood of 1927 followed by the stock market crash of 1929 and a nationwide depression.

As the depression deepened in the 1930s, many plantations along
the River Road were abandoned and many communities disappeared. Small farmers were especially vulnerable. In 1930 there
were more than 10,000 sugarcane farmers in Louisiana; by the
1950s, there were fewer than 3,000, but the average farm size had
increased as larger operators accumulated properties. Research and
development continued, producing new cane varieties such as
Coimbatore, which was resistant to mosaic disease. In 1937 Congress passed the protective Sugar Act, which remained in effect until

1974 (sugar farmers today continue to depend on protective tariffs to remain competitive internationally). When World War II took workers from the industry, it created additional impetus to develop mechanized planting, loading, and harvesting equipment. More recently, advanced chemicals were developed to treat cane diseases and control weeds, and new processes evolved to make hardier and more disease-resistant cane.

The face of the contemporary sugar industry is much changed. Cane knives and open kettles have become cultural artifacts, replaced by machines and technology, including highly computerized milling operations. Unfortunately, a disproportionate number of the men and women who once worked in the sugar fields and factories have also been displaced. In recent years, too, considerable acreage along the River Road has been converted to pasture for raising cattle—a familiar pursuit in the area since the first *vacheries* (cattle ranches) were established in west-bank St. James Parish in the mid-eighteenth century. Yet the volume of local sugar production still contributes greatly to Louisiana's third-place ranking—behind Hawaii and Florida—as a source of domestic cane sugar.

Meanwhile, the sugar calendar has changed very little. Fallow ground is prepared during spring and summer for an August-to-mid-fall planting. Cane stalks are planted in six-foot-wide rows (to ensure sufficient drainage) and covered. Each stalk will reproduce from a series of joints and buds along the stem, giving three or four ratoon crops. Planting occurs from August to mid-October, and cane shoots die back in winter. Soil cultivation and fertilization take place in spring before the cane sprouts. Sugarcane grows rapidly in summer—with sufficient rainfall, more than an inch per day!

Harvesting and grinding begin in mid-October and can last until late December. Two-row mechanical harvesters cut the cane and lay it neatly in heap rows. Plumes of white smoke rise from the fields as leaves and trash are burned off the stalks, which are too ripe with juice to be damaged by the fire. (It is expected that within a few years, the use of cane combines will eliminate the need to burn in the fields.) Mechanical loaders lift the cane into large basket trailers to be trucked to the mill—a journey that leaves a ruff of cane stalks to outline the shoulders of every road between field and mill during season. The trailers, carrying about twenty-five tons of cane per load, go first to a scale house, where the cane is weighed and core-sampled by laboratory computers for sucrose content and purity. Farmers are paid for the quantity of sugar content of their cane, not for its gross weight; typically, sugar makes up about a tenth of total cane weight.

After analysis, the cane is dumped into hillocks in the cane yard and loaded by forklift onto automatic wash tables, where water and sloping conveyor belts remove the field mud. The washed cane is conveyored to the mill, where it is chopped, then put through a hammermill shredder, making a fibrous pulp that resembles garden mulch. Five separate mills squeeze the juice from the fibers with increasing pressure. The released juice is filtered to remove residual fiber, which is run back through the mills for a second pressing. The filtered juice is pumped to a station where lime is added to purify it, then sent on to a clarifier. There the muddy juice, looking much like dark cola, is again filtered to remove impurities.

The mud and other residue collected during all this processing are returned to the fields, where they serve as excellent fertilizer. The bagasse is dried and either burned in the mill's furnaces or sold to make paper, fiberboard, mulches, and other products.

> *Louisiana trivia: The original ceiling tiles in the legislative chambers of the new State Capitol Building in Baton Rouge were made of processed bagasse.*

The clarified cane juice is piped to the evaporating apparatus, where most of the water is driven off as steam, which is captured for use in running the machinery. What remains of the juice is molasses. It is boiled at low temperatures in huge partial vacuum pans under the watchful eye of an engineer who tests the process to determine a "strike." The resulting mass of raw sugar crystals mixed with molasses, resembling sludgy coffee grounds, is called "massecuite" (from the French for "cooked mass"). When the grain of the crystals is right, a whistle or bell announces it, and the massecuite is dropped into a high-speed centrifuge, which separates the crystals from the molasses. Evaporation is a critical step because prolonged boiling can result in all molasses and no crystals.

The new raw sugar, a sandy-colored grit, goes by conveyor into sugar hoppers, where it is weighed before being stored in warehouses. It will be sold to a refinery to be transformed into the familiar white table sugar. The molasses spun off in evaporation is sold as blackstrap, used for cattle food or in the production of alcohol, yeast, citric acid, and vinegar.

The Lutcher and Moore lumbermill *circa* the turn of the twentieth century. *Courtesy St. James Historical Society*

Colonial Sugars, in Gramercy, is the sole sugar refinery along the River Road today.

Industry

The milling of lumber was the first nonagricultural industry of significance along the River Road, a main source of revenue for the Louisiana colony in the eighteenth century. Two cypress mills were in operation in south Louisiana as early as 1716; by 1800, there were as many as thirty, despite the difficulty of floating and hauling the heavy logs to mill. This growth was partially inspired by a Spanish decree specifying that only boxes made of Louisiana cypress could be used to transport sugar to Spain's colonies around the Gulf of Mexico. In addition to packing boxes, local timber was processed into construction lumber, storage tanks and cisterns, ships' masts, barrel staves, and other items. Wood products such as pitch, turpentine, and tar were also made commercially during the colonial period. In the antebellum nineteenth century, many plantations had sawmills, but their use was essentially domestic.

A postcard features two views of Standard Oil's giant Baton Rouge refinery soon after it opened.
Courtesy State Library of Louisiana

Lumbering on a truly industrial scale arrived along the River Road in the late nineteenth century. Passage of the federal Timber Act of 1876 made the area's swamps and lowlands more attractive to buyers at prices ranging from a mere 12.5 cents to $1.25 per acre. By the 1880s, lumber companies had depleted forest resources in other parts of the country and turned to Louisiana, lured by old-growth cypress located on terrain previously considered too difficult (and expensive) to log. New technology such as steam-powered skidders made the task of pulling logs out of the swamps more feasible, while the development of a broad network of railroads facilitated distribution.

Garyville and Lutcher on the east bank and White Castle on the west bank are surviving examples of mill towns built during the lumber booms. These company towns were developed by individual lumber businesses whose employees lived and worked together, accessible to their jobs twenty-four hours a day.

So efficient were these and other lumbering operations that by the early 1930s, the huge stands of virgin cypress had been depleted.

Lumber companies were forced to switch resources or close. By this time, however, another industry was firmly established and rapidly growing along the River Road. In the early 1900s, Standard Oil of New Jersey, the giant of the fledgling petroleum industry, began scouting Gulf Coast locations for refineries that could receive oil from midwestern wells (at the time, the huge oil fields of Texas and Louisiana were only just being discovered). An antitrust case in Texas, the company's first location of choice, resulted in Standard's selection of 213 acres just north of Baton Rouge. The site boasted a dependable water supply, access to rail and water transportation, and terrain high enough to ensure security from floods.

The new Standard Oil (now Exxon) refinery opened in 1909 and began expanding almost from its inception. During World War I, output rose dramatically with increased demand for chemical products made from oil. By 1924, the Baton Rouge refinery was Standard Oil's largest facility—for many years it was one of the largest in the world—with a greatly expanded product line.

The Standard Oil refinery formed the cornerstone for what would become a massive petrochemical industrial corridor along the Mississippi River between New Orleans and Baton Rouge. In 1914 Mexican Petroleum Company purchased the Destrehan Plantation property on the east bank of St. Charles Parish and opened an oil refinery there. In 1916 the New Orleans Refinery Company bought 460 acres between Sellers and Good Hope Plantations in east-bank St. John the Baptist Parish and constructed a marine terminal on the river. Their processing plant became Shell Oil in 1928 and Sellers (later renamed Norco) developed essentially as a company town. Cities Service Company established an oil export terminal in St. Rose in east-bank St. Charles Parish in 1922.

The huge expansion of the automobile industry in the 1920s and 1930s brought a parallel demand for fuel and lubrication products, and during World War II, the need for synthesized chemical substitutes for materials such as natural rubber impelled dramatic growth in the petrochemical sector. The Chemical Products division of Standard Oil went on line in 1941. After the war, the use of oil-based synthetic fibers, plastics, fertilizers, pharmaceuticals, pigments, gasoline additives, asphalt, and pesticides expanded rapidly, as did the new unit, which later became Exxon Chemical.

In the booming postwar economy of the 1950s, oil and petrochemical plants sprouted like mushrooms along the Mississippi.

National companies (many of which became international) were attracted by the access to natural resources, the navigable river, a strong port of New Orleans, favorable taxation policies, and the availability of large tracts of land. Plantation properties, often thousands of acres, were on the proper scale for building a large processing plant, and many River Road landowners were ready to sell. As one giant facility after another bloomed on land previously under cultivation, the petrochemical industry became the major employer along the River Road, luring many residents away from agriculture and small businesses in tiny communities.

During the 1960s, the state initiated aggressive tax incentives and exemptions to attract more corporations to the River Road corridor and to encourage existing plants to expand. The petrochemical plants committed huge sums for capital investment and developed technology to produce their products more efficiently through automation. Today, approximately one-quarter of America's petrochemical industry can be found along the River Road between New Orleans and Baton Rouge, forming the region's most significant economic base and bringing with it problems of pollution and health effects that have only recently begun to be addressed.

ARCHITECTURAL STYLES

The emergence of one distinctive architectural form and the adaptive use of others have combined to produce an interesting mix of building styles along the River Road. Formal architecture adhered fairly closely to the tenets of classical design; vernacular (folk) buildings reflected more concrete demands of function, materials, and resources. Yet both evolved with at least one careful eye on local conditions: prevalent heat and humidity, heavy annual rainfall, an occasional spell of harsh cold, the incessantly flat terrain, and the ubiquitous presence of the Mississippi River.

The earliest explorers found the Indians' hutlike structures primitive but expedient. These buildings varied somewhat in style and materials from one area to another, but a typical construction featured wooden poles thatched with smaller branches and filled with mud and Spanish moss (a mixture the French called "bousillage"), roofed with cypress bark or palmetto fronds. The Europeans used these structures as models, setting *pieux debouts* (upright posts) with cross timbers, filling the spaces with bousillage, and roofing with cypress bark or palmetto.

The newcomers soon realized that life in the alluvial plain would be enhanced if the houses were raised off the ground as they were in the West Indies. Buildings on piers were more able to withstand flooding, offered increased air circulation, and reduced exposure to mosquitoes. The settlers also realized that houses were best situated facing the river, not only for a view of the major traffic artery, but also to take advantage of the river's cooling breezes. Front galleries (porches), standard for both simple and grand dwellings, served as pleasant, shaded, relatively cool extensions of the interior rooms; in the hottest months, they served as outdoor bedrooms.

The use of indigenous materials localized the appearance of River Road architecture, although decorative amenities—paint, glass, and elaborate hardware (luxuries in the beginning)—were imported. Abundant native woods, especially swamp cypress, were readily available for construction. Cypress was valued for its resistance to dampness and insects and could be hewn into posts, timbers, siding, shingles, and flooring. To facilitate using the giant cypresses, a ring was often cut around the base of a tree a year before it was to be logged. This measure stopped sap circulation and dried out the trunk, curing the wood in place and making it much lighter to handle and haul. For a large house, the cypress beams, joists, and planking might be rough-hewn in the swamp and numbered for assembly on the building site—a distant ancestor to modern prefab construction methods. Millwork, however, was done at the building site.

Clay was another important building material. Since stone was nonexistent in the south Louisiana lowlands, colonial settlers substituted brick made from the clays of the Mississippi River or Lake Pontchartrain. Soft-baked brick was used as fill between posts in walls (*briqueté entre poteaux*); finished walls were covered with plaster or weatherboard. Harder bricks, baked hotter and longer, were used on exposed surfaces—walls, floors, and terraces. Shells from the river and lake were ground and burned like charcoal to make lime for whitewash.

Because of the enduring appeal and functionality of historic architectural styles, many contemporary houses are built to resemble eighteenth- and nineteenth-century buildings, at least on the exterior. Often, it is difficult for a nonprofessional to judge whether a structure is original, vintage, or a contemporary version. This is, perhaps, the best testimonial to the timelessness of good architecture, as well as a fitting tribute to the many structures that have been destroyed by forces as disparate as the river, levee movement, fires, and hurricanes.

According to architectural historians, *Creole* or *Louisiana colonial* architecture was the only one of America's colonial building styles that actually emerged in this country. Experts define the Creole style as a combination of elements from several traditions mixed with local adaptations.

The basic Creole residence seems to have evolved from a West Indian adaptation of an Italian style in which the front loggia (a pillared porch open on one or more sides) was replaced with a gallery (a porch open on three sides). A rear loggia was flanked with small rooms, called "cabinets" (pronounced "cah-bee-nay") by the French. The French altered the floor plan to suit their cultural aesthetic, and this was the basic form that arrived along the River Road with the French planters.

In Louisiana, the Creole house received an internal chimney (rather than one located on an outer wall) with a French wraparound mantel; a spreading umbrella roof from Canada; and a braced timber framing from Normandy. The elements were incorporated into the three basic forms of Creole house: the single-story cottage, the raised (essentially, two-story) plantation house, and the town house.

The first permanent Creole houses were simple structures built on piers of cypress blocks or brick. They had two or more lateral rooms—a square parlor and at least one narrow bedroom next to it. Larger cottages had additional in-line bedrooms, lengthening the facade. In many single-story Creole homes, a rear cabinet/loggia row was behind the front rooms. There were no internal hallways; rooms simply opened into each other. A gallery ran along the front of the house. Initially, gallery roofs were attached to the facade; later, houses were built so that the main roof overhung the gallery. Thin, postlike cypress columns rose from the gallery to support the roof. Equal front doors entered each room from the gallery. Walls were of timbers filled with bousillage.

Decorative elements in more elegant Creole cottages included exposed beaded ceiling beams, a diamond-shaped motif called "lozenge," and boxed chimney flues. Exposed exterior walls were covered with clapboard and left unpainted to weather; interior or sheltered walls were plastered, whitewashed, or painted. This unusual treatment of exteriors can still be seen along the River Road on some Creole-style cottages, where three sides of the house are natural, weathered wood and the gallery wall is painted.

With prosperity came grander houses—the raised Creole plantation house. This gracious style utilized but expanded many features of the one-story dwelling. The main living quarters were elevated a full story on tall brick piers. The lower level, usually carpeted with brick, was used for storage and other utility purposes; its contents could be moved upstairs in times of flooding. (In later renovations, this area was often walled and used as basement, pan-

A typical Creole-style cottage set on short brick piers. The walls are plaster and timber.

Courtesy State Library of Louisiana

try, servants' quarters, weaving rooms, wine cellars, or carriage rooms.) On the second floor was the primary living area—parlor, dining room, bedrooms, etc. Its galleries were usually encircled by collonettes, supported by the brick columns of the first floor. Some galleries were finished like interior rooms with chair rails, wainscoting, and cornices. Stairways were placed from the lower floor to the gallery rather than inside the house. Brick walls were stuccoed in a white or wheat color.

The front and rear facades of the second story were broken by elongated double doors. According to some traditions, the central room, a parlor, was never entered directly from the gallery, but rather through the men's or women's sides. (It is said that, in Creole tradition, men's bedrooms were placed on the downriver side of the house—toward the excitement of New Orleans—while the upriver side was for the women.) The parlor's gallery doors served as principal conduits of ventilation, with doors at the rear of the parlor arranged to redirect breezes to other rooms. Cabinet rooms at the

Pierre Chenet's home in Lutcher was a prime example of a raised Creole plantation house. Chenet is remembered for his role in founding Louisiana's perique tobacco industry in the 1820s. The house no longer exists.
Courtesy St. James Historical Society

rear were sometimes added as offices or as sleeping quarters for children or servants.

Pigeonniers, small towers for doves or others birds, were positioned on the grounds near the main house as part of the formal landscape design. The lower level of the pigeonnier was sometimes used as a garçonnière or office.

Creole town houses, as the name implies, were built in urban areas such as the New Orleans Vieux Carré. Farther up the River Road, modified versions are found only in Baton Rouge and Donaldsonville. Town houses were two-story brick structures, with a commercial space and a wide, gated carriageway on the first floor and living quarters on the second. The carriageway led to a landscaped courtyard enclosed by utility rooms; a rear gallery overhanging the courtyard furnished exterior living space off the busy urban streets.

Louisiana *Acadian* style is a relative or modification of the small Creole raised cottage. Chief among its distinctive features is a lean-to extension on the rear of the cottage, covered with a roofline defined as a broken gable. A steep, narrow stairway rises from the

A pigeonnier at Uncle Sam Plantation before the property was demolished in 1940.
Courtesy State Library of Louisiana

front gallery to the attic space, or half story, used as a garçonnière or sleeping loft. (Daughters' bedrooms, however, were usually located behind the parents' room, with no direct access from outside the house.) The front gallery was used for work and storage; chimneys were located on end walls, rather than within the house.

The architectural style known as *Greek Revival* can more precisely be called *Classical Revival*—a combination of elements derived from both Greek and Roman formalism. This influence arrived along the River Road from the East Coast and mid-Atlantic states when Anglo-Americans poured into the area after the Louisiana Purchase. From this style evolved the stereotypical white, colossal, columned, Gone-with-the-Wind plantation mansion.

The Anglo-Americans brought different aesthetic tastes and cultural backgrounds, new talent, and new money to the River Road. Classical Revival was a grander style than Creole and, because of its reference to ancient republics, seemed to suggest the political philosophy of the new American Republic—adherence to the classical principles of democracy and liberty. Classical Revival dominated River Road architecture from the 1820s through the 1860s, with its high point from the 1830s to the 1850s. Its most prominent south Louisiana practitioners were the architects James and Charles Dakin, James Gallier, and Benjamin Latrobe.

Classical Revival, unlike Creole, valued symmetry. Houses were large, two-story structures with gable ends, a large center hallway behind a central front door, and imposing columns extending from the ground to the ceiling level of the second floor. Living quarters were one or two rooms deep and two rooms wide, in a balanced arrangement on either side of the hall. The interior stairs were usually located in the central hallway.

The Classical Revival style utilized both floors for living quarters. The house was slightly elevated on short piers (in contrast to the story-high piers of Creole plantation houses) to protect the first floor from dampness, and chimneys were positioned at the ends of the house. Classically inspired decorative elements included pediments, ornate column capitals, massive pillars, and entablatures. The austerity of the classical form was softened with a broad front gallery, and in many cases with galleries at the rear or on all sides. In Louisiana, squared pillars were sometimes used instead of round columns. The formal symmetry of the house was extended to the grounds with carefully positioned garçonnières, pigeonniers, and other outbuildings.

Anglo-Creole is a term contrived to describe houses built in the Louisiana colonial style but later renovated to incorporate the grandeur of Classical Revival elements. Central hallways and symmetrical room arrangements, as well as the decorative embellishments

A line of quarters houses, 1940.
Courtesy State Library of Louisiana

of Federal and Georgian styles—elliptical transoms and sidelights, cornices, brackets, and mantels—were added to raised plantation homes and more modest cottages. Stairways were moved front and center and rooflines altered. Faux bois and faux marbre (false wood and false marble, effects achieved by special painting techniques) transformed cypress doors, mantels, and millwork into surfaces resembling more expensive woods and imported stone. Hand-painted designs added decorative touches.

A modest architectural form was found in the *quarters,* built for slaves during the antebellum period or for tenant workers after the Civil War. Although a few River Road quarters were constructed of brick, most were made of wood. The earliest quarters had *bousillage entre poteaux* walls, with roofs of palmetto thatch or cypress shingles. Later cabins used plank siding on the exterior, and most roofs were replaced or covered with corrugated metal sheeting.

One of the most common River Road quarters designs was similar to a Creole cottage—one room deep, two rooms wide, with a small porch and overhanging roof. But the rooms were separated by a central, double-faced fireplace. Two front doors led from the porch to separate small living areas, each for an individual family.

A gingerbread house photographed by Walker Evans in the 1930s exhibits numerous neo-Gothic features.
Courtesy State Library of Louisiana

A single window—with board shutters, not glass panes—was placed in each side wall. No interior doorway connected the two sides of these two-family dwellings, called "double-pen cabins." Sometimes, a shedlike addition would be added on the rear.

The *romantic* style arrived in the mid-nineteenth century, primarily influenced by Gothic and Italian architecture. *Neo-Gothic,* or *Gothic Revival,* emerged in south Louisiana after 1845, a less imposing alternative to Classical Revival architecture for houses, churches, and schools (although Classical Revival elements were often incorporated). A variety of rural churches were built in this style, with prominent vertical lines, gables, arches, spires, usually constructed of wood. The Old State Capitol in Baton Rouge is a fine example of another expression of Gothic Revival. The building resembles a medieval castle, complete with imposing octagonal and square towers, pointed arches, and a crenelated roofline. Neo-Gothic was also a popular style for tomb architecture and can be seen in some of the cemeteries along the River Road.

A sprinkling of River Road mansions were built in grand romantic styles, including the "steamboat Gothic" San Francisco in east-bank St. John Parish and the Italianate Nottoway in west-bank

Iberville Parish. The Italianate style was considered lighthearted and expressive. Its peak popularity ran from about 1850 into the 1880s, although it continued to be adopted for smaller houses and business buildings long after that. Columns, arched windows and doors, decorative brackets, and intricate moldings were among the elements of the Italianate style that were sometimes added to even simple Creole cottages. Commercial buildings, too, showed Italianate influences, with exterior pilasters, arched windows, and pediments capping central doorways.

Queen Anne and *Eastlake* are late-nineteenth-century styles in which ornamental eccentricities abound. Half-octagon rooms or room-additions, many-gabled roofs, and an overall appearance that mingles grace and asymmetry characterize these Victorian expressions. The Eastlake variation can feature multicolored, many-textured exteriors, bay windows, towers, and elaborate gingerbread moldings and trim.

Shotgun houses and *bungalows* are modest vernacular forms, highly regarded for offering maximum interior space with minimal use of materials. One historian of vernacular architecture believes that the shotgun style was brought to New Orleans *circa* 1800 by immigrants from Haiti and that its use drifted upriver through the century; others suggest that it evolved from temporary or camp housing. A shotgun is a long, narrow frame structure, raised on short piers, a single room wide and at least three rooms deep, with a front-gabled roof overhanging a small front porch. The name "shotgun" derives from the straight-line arrangement of the rooms and doors; supposedly, a shot fired through the front door would pass out the back door without hitting a wall. Their narrow width and inexpensive construction have made shotgun houses a standard choice for workers' quarters, tenant cabins, and low-income housing where multiple units share a single lot.

The bungalow developed at the turn of the twentieth century. A simple, one-story house with a small, gabled front porch supported by a column-over-pier, it resembles a double shotgun, two rooms wide and at least three rooms deep. Each of the two front rooms has its own porch entry.

Small-town and country stores form a special subcategory of buildings along the River Road. From approximately 1840 to 1940, most rural stores in the area were built in similar style, a simple and straightforward version of Classical Revival. Interiors were longer than wide, and a gabled roof ran the length of the building and overhung the front porch. During modernizations, the front gable has often been hidden behind a stepped roof facade. Shed additions on the sides or rear of the building offered additional usable space. A second story might serve as a residence, office, storage area, or small meeting room. The extant River Road country stores date from the great lumbering era, the 1880s through the turn of the century.

THE NATURAL SETTING

The landscape along the lower Mississippi River looked very different when the first Europeans arrived than it does today. Except for a few widely scattered Indian villages, there was little cleared land anywhere. The river's vast floodplain, a network of old stream channels and terraces, flatlands, lakes, and backwater swamps, harbored a great variety of natural communities, separated and determined by differences in the soil (ranging from sand to clay), in elevation (sometimes literally a matter of inches), and in drainage.

On the highest ground—the riverbank or relic terraces—grew oaks, pecan, honey locusts, shagbark hickory, and sweet gum. Back in the bottomlands and swamps—under water part of the year—were bald cypress, tupelo gum, red maple, ash, palmetto, Virginia willow, and button bush. Between these two areas lay belts of poorly drained land—lower than the bank, but drier than the swamp—hosting species such as overcup oak, bitter pecan, green ash, willow, water oak, and hawthorn. Along the batture and sandy frontlands of the levee grew willows, cottonwood, red gum, locust, and cane groves. (Of the latter, Iberville observed that "both riverbanks are, almost without exception, so densely lined with cane of all sizes, one, two, three, four, five and six inches in circumference, that it is impossible to walk along the riverside. . . . Most of the foliage is dry; setting it afire, it burns easily and makes as much noise while aflame as a pistol shot. A person who was ignorant of this and did not see them burning would think it was a skirmish." The same cane is still used at the Bonfires on the Levee festival.)

In his 1735 journal, Antoine Simon Le Page du Pratz mentioned a trove of indigenous flora: wild mulberry trees, indigo, native tobacco, white and red cedar, cypress, pine, laurel, magnolia, sassafras, maple, wax myrtle, poplar, locust, mangrove, red and white and black oak, live oak, ash, elm, beech, lime, hornbeam, aspen, willow alder; also grape, box elder, yaupon, prickly ash, palmetto, birch, and Spanish moss. Even after statehood, long stretches of the riverbank remained heavily wooded. Traveling the Mississippi in 1818, the Reverend Timothy Flint noted "the prodigious growth of timber, luxuriance of cane, tangle of vines and creepers, astonishing size of the weeds and the strength of vegetation in general."

The Europeans were fortunate to encounter a hospitable native population that was knowledgeable about this varied and prolific environment of plants and animals unfamiliar in the Old World. The Indians used indigenous plants not only for food, but also for medicines, dyes, construction materials, utensils, and much else. They gathered berries, mayhaw, and muscadine, dried and ground seeds into meal, harvested wild rice and swamp potatoes, powdered dried sassafras leaves for thickening stews, and cultivated native tobacco. They used the hard stalks of short cane for eating utensils and small knives and crafted furniture from larger cane. They wove palmetto leaves into roofs and baskets and made wall fill with Spanish moss. Le Page du Pratz observed the Indians' use of swamp maple, or "stinking wood," for yellow dye, and Father Paul du Ru, while attempting to convert the Houmas and other tribes to Christianity in 1700, complained that the Houma women brewed yaupon into an intoxicating liquor that they "drank in excessive amounts at the funeral ceremony" of a chief.

As plentiful as the plant life were the native animals. In his 1758 *Histoire de la Louisiane,* Le Page du Pratz graphically depicted unusual creatures: alligator, rattlesnake, porcupine, flying squirrel, pelican, paddlefish, alligator gar, wildcat, and opossum. Explorers found the native peoples hunting deer, bear, rabbit, squirrel, gray fox, opossum, turkey, and beaver, as well as muskrat, raccoon, mink, otter, and skunk. Bison may have roamed the area into the nineteenth century. Seasonal migrations of ducks, geese, ibis, and other waterfowl darkened the skies. The passenger pigeon, now extinct, roosted by the thousands in the trees; it is said that the Indians hunted them by night, blinding them with torchlight and simply knocking the birds from branches with long poles.

Turtles, frogs, snakes, and alligators populated backwaters. Swamps, lakes, and the river itself abounded with alligator gar, choupique, freshwater drum, buffalo fish, catfish, and other species.

Among the animals sketched by the early Louisiana historian Le Page du Pratz were a "chat sauvage" (wildcat), a "rat de bois" (opossum), and a "bête puante" ("stinking animal"—obviously a skunk, even though the artist got the stripes wrong).

Courtesy Louisiana and Lower Mississippi Valley Collections, Hill Memorial Library, LSU

The river also offered a particular treat, as Father du Ru discovered when he was received at the village of the Bayougoulas with "an excellent mess of brill." These were the indigenous river shrimp, which became a staple of the River Road diet. They were caught in box traps sunk in the river during the season—late spring into the fall; swimming out to pull in the traps was a boyhood chore. During the 1960s, however, the river shrimp population disappeared—destroyed, it was surmised, by pollution.

Many other aspects of the River Road environment have vanished or undergone great change. As the population increased, lands were cleared, bayous dammed, and the river lined by levees, forever altering the natural dynamic of the river system, the landforms, and the flora and fauna. Yet as George Washington Cable wrote in 1884, "The scenery of this land, where it is still in its wild state, is weird and funereal"—and so it remains today where pockets of swamp and stands of dark oak forest can be found. Such places include cypress swamps at old crevasse locations and abandoned fields or house sites reclaimed by bottomland hardwood overgrowth.

Faint reflections of the past can be seen elsewhere as well. The batture is still a willow farm, and crawfish run in roadside ditches. Snakes and turtles, squirrels, rabbits, raccoons, and possums still inhabit the woods and fields, and ducks and other waterfowl still arrive in considerable numbers each fall. And two nonindigenous animals have recently taken up residence: The plated armadillo, an émigré from Mexico via Texas, arrived in this area in the 1940s and has been used in research for treatment of Hansen's disease. The cattle egret, a small, white wading bird that migrated from Africa to South America and thence to Louisiana, has been seen flocking around cows in pastures and stalking about in shallow water since the 1950s.

Though the natural setting of the River Road has changed dramatically from the scene that Iberville encountered, it still retains a certain flatland beauty, accessible to all who care to look.

The following are a few of the most prevalent local flora:

Bald cypress (Taxodium distichum). Called "wood everlasting," cypresses are large, slow-growing trees with flared bases and vertical protrusions from the roots called "knees," which vary in size. Although some botanists theorize that the knees are air roots, the most widely accepted explanation of their function is that they balance and stabilize the heavy trees in soft soil. The wood, soft and easy to craft, has been used through the centuries for shakes (shingles), fenceposts, construction timbers, paneling, doors, shutters, furniture, fine cabinetry, and barrels. It was, and continues to be, a wood of choice for exterior uses subject to weather or soil. Because it was a primary lumber resource, little virgin cypress remains in Louisiana. *Pond cypress* differs slightly from bald cypress and prefers more alkaline soil conditions.

Live oak (Quercus virginiana). Indians looked for live oaks because their presence indicated a ridge or other high ground. In Louisiana folklore, the live oak has provided the setting for lovers' liaisons, duels, hangings, the burying of treasure, and other colorful events. The live oak is distinctive, noted for the low spread of its limbs; very old trees often have limbs that rest on the ground. Live oaks can have a branch spread that is twice the height of the tree, making them appear very gracious and expansive. The tree sheds leaves all year but remains green even in winter. Its wood is very heavy, hard, and close-grained, making it difficult for cabinetmakers to use but excellent for shipbuilding. Hurricanes are the nemesis of live oaks. The Live Oak Society, founded in 1934, celebrates the grandest examples of the species. The philosopher and writer William Darby, traveling the river in 1816, said of the oak trees: "The size, majesty, and productive qualities of the oak in Louisiana have been the subjects of admiration to all men who have travelled the country."

Spanish moss (Tillandsia usneoides). *Itla-ogla* ("tree hair") to the Indians of Iberville Parish, this plant was derisively called "Spanish beard" by the French and "Frenchman's wig" by the Spanish. A local legend says that the moss is the hair of an Indian princess killed by enemies during her wedding ceremony. Her hair was cut off and hung on the large oak tree under which she was buried. Over time, the hair was blown to other trees, where it turned gray. Other myths about Spanish moss were that it both spread malaria and purified the air. Contrary to popular belief, the plant is neither a parasite nor harmful to the trees it inhabits. Rather, Spanish moss is an epiphyte, drawing its nourishment from the air. It is a member of the pineapple family.

Indians and early settlers used moss with mud or clay to make bousillage for filling walls. The Europeans later developed the process of retting (curing) moss through drying, washing, and ginning

Quintessential Louisiana—cypresses draped with Spanish moss.
Courtesy State Library of Louisiana

to use for mattress and furniture stuffing, horse collars, saddle pads, and packing material. About six pounds of fresh moss are required to produce a pound of cured moss, which is black and wiry, resembling horsehair. This practice is nearly extinct. In 1940 approximately fifty moss gins existed in south Louisiana; today there are none. Moss grows on many trees besides oaks—cypress, pecan, persimmon, ash, gum, even crape myrtle, which is an introduced species.

Willow (genus Salix). These familiar trees flourish along stream banks and on the batture of the river. Certain species quickly spring up along temporary locations such as sandbars and borrow pits. Thomas Drummond, a collector for the Royal Botanic Gardens at Kew, included willow in the plant matter he shipped to England in 1832. Willows grow in clumps or loose rows on the batture, and their feathery green tops can be seen over the crest of the levee from the road. Willow is the wood of choice for building the bonfire structures that are the centerpiece of the Christmas Eve festival, Bonfires on the Levee.

UPRIVER ALONG
THE EAST BANK

~~~~~~~~~

Note: This linear route along the River Road from the Jefferson/St. Charles Parish boundary upriver to Baton Rouge, with occasional side trips, offers the traveler a pleasurable outing into the area's history, culture, and lore. Numbers indicate mileage as measured beginning at point 0 0—the sign indicating the Jefferson/St. Charles Parish line on the River Road. A new set of mileage numbers begins after the Bonnet Carré Spillway.

0.0 Jefferson/St. Charles Parish line.

0.3 The water tower indicates the community of St. Rose, one of the oldest settlements in the area. The name comes from St. Rose Plantation, which in turn was named for the first and patron saint of the Americas. The Cities Service Oil Company opened an oil export terminal in St. Rose in 1922.

0.5 Fairfield subdivision and Riverbend Business Park are both on property that was part of the extensive Fairview Plantation of H. Frellsen, according to Persac. A small community called Frellsen was located here in later years.

1.9 Charlestowne subdivision is the site of Patterson Plantation, once a part of Fairview Plantation. Roadwork to straighten out a bad curve exposed the foundations of two houses. One, owned by Louis Augustin Meuillon, burned during the 1811 slave rebellion that started upriver in St. John the Baptist Parish. The other belonged to Jean François Piseros, a French settler who established a successful trading company that operated between New Orleans and Natchitoches. The house, built after the destruction of the Meuillon house, stood on what was called Piseros Plantation, according to Persac.

2.1 A Creole raised cottage and small outbuilding.

2.3 It is said that the line of large oaks along the River Road was planted for road beautification by George Kugler in the late nineteenth century. Kugler worked for Judge Pierre Adolphe Rost at Destrehan Plantation and owned a property called Hermitage where the Bonnet Carré Spillway is now located, upriver in this parish.

2.5 LaBranche Plantation Dependency. The German von Zweig family settled here sometime after the establishment of the German Coast. Their first substantial house, built about 1792, burned during the Civil War. The sole building remaining on the property is the Creole garçonnière, which boasts Federal-style woodwork and consists of four symmetrical square rooms, each with a mantel and fireplace. Though most Creole houses of this size were built as independent single homes, the LaBranche Dependency was built as an ancillary to a big house. In the 1940s, this property was renamed Idle Hour Farms and became a breeding farm for racehorses. A curiosity: Adolf Hitler's horse, Nordlicht, is buried here. Open to the public.

> *It is said that Johann von Zweig arrived in the Louisiana colony from Germany and approached the Ursuline sisters in New Orleans to select a wife for him. They introduced the young man to Suzanna Marchand, and he pledged his troth. But the local French official and the French Catholic priest had great difficulty with the pronunciation of von Zweig's name. The notary determined that, as the German would live in a French province with a French Creole wife, he should instead have a French name. Since* Zweig *translates from the German as "branch," Johann von Zweig became Jean La-Branche.*

3.0 Junction La. 626, St. Rose Street. In this area was the site of St. Rose Plantation house, a raised Creole plantation home with neoclassical additions. The house survived until 1904 (with, at some point, the second floor lowered to ground level).

3.1 The Elfer House, a Creole-style cottage, dates from the late nineteenth century. It was the home of prominent local resident Charles Elfer, on old family land—the Elfer family came to the area in the 1760s as Helfer. The front facade is faded green, and the sides are weathered and unpainted, reflecting the Creole tradition.

3.4 The St. Rose Tavern is a longtime landmark, built in 1922 as the St. Rose Hotel to meet the demands of the burgeoning oil industry and serve travelers going from New Orleans to Baton Rouge along the River Road. The tavern won additional local notoriety when rock star Bruce Springsteen played pool here while visiting in the area.

3.5 The original Cities Service refinery was located on the current IMTT site.

4.9 The community of Destrehan was named for Jean Noël Destréhan, who owned the eponymous plantation. In this area was the plantation house of Octave LaBranche, shown in Father Paret's sketch with an orchard and gardens extending across the front yard. The Creole house was renovated with Classical Revival influences, although the stairway remained under the front gallery.

> *From the journal of Dr. John Sibley, 1802. "Just at sundown, there came into the gate [of the plantation where he was spending the night, several children] the Gentleman presented them to me and told me they were his children who had been to dancing school. . . . They spoke no English and I did not speak French enough to converse with them."*
>
> *(On board a barge all day, upriver from Destrehan): "We ascend the river—the country exhibiting on each side of the river a beautiful appearance, interspersed with sugar and cotton plantations, ornamented with orange groves, gardens, etc and large numbers of cattle, horses, mules and sheep covered the banks of the river which is a most luxuriant pasture from the edge of the water to the fences within the levy [sic]."*

5.0 Bunge Grain Elevator is the former site of Pecan Grove Plantation, owned by the Elfer family. A two-story raised cottage with front gallery and plastered facade was built in a grove of pecan trees. One particular tree near the house was alleged to possess supernatural powers—animals that strayed or were tethered beneath its branches would die. Sad to say, according to local lore, friends from New Orleans rode up and unknowingly tied their horses to the tree. When the host learned where his guests had left their mounts, he raced out to move them, but the animals had already died. Subsequent levee setbacks destroyed the trees, including the allegedly malevolent one.

5.4 Gordon Street, formerly Modoc Lane, marks the site of Modoc Plantation, another Elfer holding. The house was a two-story Classical Revival mansion with galleries along all sides. An orchard of oranges, plums, figs, and cherries grew in the front of the house. The 1893 Sarpy crevasse destroyed Elfer's crops, and after he moved downriver to St. Rose, the house was demolished.

5.7 This line of oaks may be from Modoc Plantation property or possibly from the plantation of P. Soniat, as identified by Persac.

6.0 On the left, a road up the levee flank leads to the former eastbank landing of the Luling–Destrehan ferry, which served the area until the Hale Boggs Bridge opened just upriver in 1983. Here, at midriver in 1976, a Norwegian tanker collided with a fully-loaded vehicle-and-passenger ferry, killing seventy-one people—one of the worst navigational accidents to occur along this stretch of the river.

6.1 An allée of oaks announces Destrehan Plantation, the oldest documented plantation house in the Mississippi Valley. The raised Creole mansion was built over the years 1787–1790 for Robert Robin de Logny by a talented free mulatto named Charles (Pacquet?). By 1810, when the symmetrical wings were added, the house was owned by Jean Noël Destréhan, Robin de Logny's son-in-law (Jean Noël was also the brother-in-law of Etienne Boré). The extended Destréhan family, very prominent in the area, controlled the property until 1910. During the Civil War, Federal troops used the plantation to house freed slaves. It was returned to Judge Pierre Adolphe Rost, a Destréhan son-in-law.

Architecturally, the house reflects both its origins as a late-eighteenth-century colonial cottage and the 1840 addition by Rost with its grander Classical Revival features on both the exterior and interior. By the late 1950s, Destrehan was abandoned, badly vandalized. It was on its way to destruction when Amoco Oil, responding in 1971 to local preservationists, donated the house and four acres to the nonprofit River Road Historical Society, which is responsible for its restoration. An introductory video and interpretative architectural room show attic construction, bousillage, and other original structural elements. Open to the public.

Jean Noël Destréhan.
Courtesy State Library of Louisiana

Local lore says that the famed pirate Jean Lafitte was a frequent guest at Destrehan and buried part of his treasure on the grounds. Lafitte's shadow is said to haunt the house, appearing on stormy nights to point its finger at the hearth before vanishing. It is also said that the ghost of Nicholas Noël Destréhan, Jean Noël's son, is in residence. A particularly eerie tale concerns the relative who came to call and, while awaiting her hostess in the parlor, saw a distinguished old gentleman with a long white beard enter the room, wander about, and leave by the same door, all wordlessly. The visitor told her hostess of the old man's appearance; she responded with disbelief as the gentleman described was very ill in a New Orleans sanitarium and could not have been in the parlor. Shortly thereafter, a message came telling of his death, which corresponded with the time of the vision.

6.5 The Hale Boggs Bridge crosses the Mississippi River as I-310 and leads to Luling on the west bank and points south via U.S. 90. The bridge is named for the late Louisiana congressman whose plane disappeared in Alaska in 1972 (Boggs was declared dead by an Alaskan court). It opened in 1983 after nine years in construction. The structure employs a cable support system that is found in fewer than ten other bridges in the country. I-310 east links with Interstate 10 to New Orleans and Baton Rouge.

> *A ride across the elevated route of I-310 north from the River Road offers a perspective on the topography of the alluvial plain. For less than a mile, the land is high (relatively speaking); then, almost abruptly, it gives way to swamp filled with young cypresses, willows, and tupelo gums standing in shallow, dark water. In spring, the cypresses are plumed with lime-green feathers; in the fall, their boughs turn rust-and-olive. The swamp is a beautiful but harsh environment that early settlers learned to treat with respect.*

In this area was located the presbytery of the Church of St. Charles Borromeo. In the mid-nineteenth century, according to Father Paret, it was a raised Creole log cottage with a single chimney and front and rear galleries with cabinet rooms; in the backyard were outbuildings and a garden.

6.8 Although the current St. Charles Borromeo Church was built in 1921, this is the site of the first church parish established on the east bank, beginning from a log church built *circa* 1740. It was named for a sixteenth-century counter-Reformation Italian cardinal who was canonized in 1610. A frame church, painted red, replaced the original in 1806 and became known as the Little Red Church, a famous riverboat landmark: twenty-five miles upriver from New Orleans, it was the point at which captains on downriver voyages paid off their crews. The present church was built in mission style with a red tile roof. Inside the church are nave paneling and balcony railings made from the cypress pews of the 1806 church. Open to the public.

Unfortunately, an arsonist set fire to the rectory in 1877 and all of the church records accumulated from its inception burned. The cemetery was established in 1740, the oldest existing cemetery of the Germans along the river. The Trepagnier family donated a statue of Saint Charles, which stood in a part of the cemetery that is now in the river, as are some of the earliest gravesites. Extant tombs date from the early nineteenth century and carry French inscriptions. The tomb of Karl d'Arensbourg was among those in the cemetery, but no marker remains. The monumental tomb of Nicholas Destréhan still exists, as does the burial place of Jean François Trepagnier, who was killed in the 1811 slave insurrection. Zeringue, Lambert, Kugler, Hymel, Webre, and Montz are among the native-German family names represented here. The grand tomb of Amelie Perret Rixner, who died young, is said to have been built with money her husband, George, had earmarked to build her a beautiful plantation home. Two large live oaks on the grounds were planted in the mid-nineteenth century.

> *Local lore tells of a gang of robbers who operated in the vicinity of the church in 1806. They set upon a traveler who was camping on the church tract under an oak tree, killed him, and stole his money. In the 1890s townspeople found a stranger, an old man, digging in front of the church. When confronted, he said he was searching for buried money—he had been in a St. Louis prison with one of the robbers, learned of the buried loot, and came to claim it for himself, as the robber was still jailed. (The fact that the jailed robber would have had to be at least 100 years old would never stand in the way of a good story.)*

7.4 This grove of oaks was likely part of Ormond Plantation property. The broad land formation here is called Twenty-Six Mile Point, thought to have been named for its distance upriver from the Canal Street wharf in New Orleans. (Although the distance today is closer to twenty-eight river miles, it is surmised that the difference is owed to river movement.)

7.5 Ormond, a two-story Louisiana colonial plantation home, was built *circa* 1790. The house is cypress-timbered *briqueté entre po-*

teaux and bousillage; the two-story wings, added between 1811 and 1820, are stuccoed brick. Pierre Trepagnier, an officer of the Louisiana militia under Spanish governor Bernardo de Gálvez, was deeded a tract running from the river to Lake Pontchartrain in gratitude for his service.

> *Legend has it that Pierre Trepagnier became quite wealthy and involved in local intrigue. One morning during breakfast, a Spanish* carroza *(state carriage) arrived bearing an important person who delivered a secret message to Trepagnier. Trepagnier bade his family good-bye and left with the stranger, never to return. Investigation proved that the stranger in his official carriage had not been sent by the Spanish government. After months of waiting, a disconsolate Mme Trepagnier sold the plantation and moved back to New Orleans.*

The property was named Ormond in 1805 after the Irish ancestral castle of second owner Richard Butler, a well-respected soldier from George Washington's army. It was Butler who added the wings. In the 1820 yellow fever epidemic, the Butlers fled, but died of the disease shortly thereafter anyway. Butler's sister, Rebecca McCutchon, and her family inherited the property, which was successfully operated by her son and family until the mid-1870s. They grew indigo, sugarcane, and rice. A man named Laplace owned it subsequently and disappeared as mysteriously as Trepagnier, which contributed to a bad-luck reputation for the house. Open to the public.

7.8 Ormond Estates subdivision occupies part of what was Ormond Plantation property.

In the area just upriver from Ormond was Victoria Plantation; between Victoria and its upriver neighbor Sarpy Plantation—where the Sarpy crevasse occurred in 1893—was the alleged hideout of the infamous Little Red Church killers of 1806.

8.7 In 1722 a tiny settlement here was called L'Anse aux Outardes—Coast of the Bustards, or Bustards' Cove. (A bustard is a large Old World bird resembling a goose; probably the "bustards" were Canada geese passing through the area on their migrations.) The original settlement was inhabited by French-Canadians and Indians; the development of the Second German Coast increased the population. The site was the western terminus of a series of waterways and canals connecting the Mississippi River and Lake Pontchartrain—a much-used transportation route.

New Sarpy town limits. The post office was established here in 1937 and given the name New Sarpy—the original settlement of Sarpy, just upriver, having been renamed first Sellers, then Norco. The name honors planter and entrepreneur Leon Sarpy, a Tennesseean who fought at the Battle of Shiloh during the Civil War and purchased his first property in St. Charles Parish in 1869. His plantations—Prospect, Good Hope, and Sarpy (Crevasse)—became the communities of New Sarpy, Good Hope, and Norco.

9.1 Arterbury Memorial Building is the approximate site of Sarpy Plantation house, which was ultimately devastated by the Sarpy crevasse in 1892—caused by a crawfish hole that weakened the levee.

10.1 The Good Hope town front is at the junction with La. 627, called Prospect Street. La Salle noted the presence of Quinapisa Indians in 1682 in this area and across the river, but by 1700, according to Iberville, they had moved elsewhere.

Prospect Street denotes the site of Prospect Plantation. The house, built *circa* 1815 as a Creole cottage, was remodeled in Classical Revival style and became a grand two-and-a-half-story mansion. The property was owned in the mid-nineteenth century by Edgar Labranche and the Widow Norbert Fortier and extended to Lake Pontchartrain. Leon Sarpy purchased it in 1869. The house was either destroyed in the 1927 flood or demolished in conjunction with levee work. The Good Hope Baptist Church, a black congregation, was established in 1869. The building was replaced in 1881 when a levee setback left it on the batture; in 1930 the church was rebuilt at its present site, on East Street about a half block off the River Road. This small rural church has two miniature belfries. Churches such as this one served as the first schools for the area's black children.

The Good Hope School, built in 1930, is the former public school for the community of Good Hope, and a fine example of Spanish Colonial architecture.

GATX (General American Transportation Corporation) is at the approximate boundary line between Good Hope and greater Norco. Just upriver was the site of Good Hope Plantation, a huge property that extended to Lake Pontchartrain during the mid-

A Paret watercolor of Prospect Plantation in the antebellum years shows spacious grounds and allées fronting the house. A photograph taken *circa* 1880 reveals the results of levee setbacks: the house sits virtually astride the River Road. The residence eventually fell victim to the river.

Watercolor courtesy Marcel Boyer from the watercolors of Father Joseph M. Paret; photo courtesy Dorothy D. Keller and St. John the Baptist Parish Library nineteenth century, when it was owned by T. Oxnard and B. S. LaBranche.

10.6 Norco is an acronym for the New Orleans Refining Company, which in 1916 bought 460 acres of land between Sellers (now merely the name of a small area where the railroad enters the Bonnet Carré Spillway) and Good Hope Plantation. Norco was first known as Sarpy in 1886, then changed to Sellers in 1894. The Sellers postmistress and the refinery manager renamed the post office Norco because of the confusion caused by both the Sellers and Good Hope post offices receiving the refinery's mail. Shell Oil Company bought the refinery in 1922 and changed the name of the town to Norco in 1934. Behind Norco was Bayou Trepagnier—called "Tigouyou" by the Indians—which ran from the river to the lake. The bayou is said to have been one of the primary routes along which the farmers of the German Coast returned in their pirogues from selling their produce in New Orleans. They came home "the back way" as it was too difficult to paddle upstream in the Mississippi River.

11.2 La. 48, also called Apple Street, turns right and links with U.S. 61, the Airline Highway. This is the route to take to reach the other side of the Bonnet Carré Spillway (located just upriver) when the road through the spillway is closed to traffic, which occurs when any of the floodgates is open. To follow this route, take La. 48 to the Airline Highway, turn left, and cross the spillway to La. 628; turn left on La. 628 and follow it to the River Road. The distance is approximately 7.4 miles.

11.5 Diamond Street recalls the site of Diamond Plantation, one of the large plantation properties sold to the federal government for construction of the Bonnet Carré Spillway. The Widow Trepagnier sold Diamond to Thomas Sellers *circa* 1876, but the Bonnet Carré crevasse ended Sellers' prosperity. The plantation had a noted stable of racehorses, and Sellers' friend Samuel Clemens (a.k.a. Mark Twain) was known to visit occasionally. In 1886, the Roseland and Trepagnier plantations were bought and consolidated to form Diamond, which was sold to Leon Godchaux in 1897. Godchaux held it until 1926, when the federal government bought it in preparation for building the spillway.

Myrtleland Plantation as seen by Paret.
Courtesy Marcel Boyer from the watercolors of Father Joseph M. Paret

The Bonnet Carré Spillway and Floodway also consumed parts of Myrtleland, Roseland, Hermitage, and Delhommer Plantations.

Trepagnier Plantation, later known as Myrtleland, was built *circa* 1770 by Jean François Trepagnier, a brother of Pierre Trepagnier, who built Ormond. The house was said to be somewhat similar in design to Ormond. Jean was one of two white men killed in the 1811 slave rebellion, in which one of his slaves was a ringleader. The original house was a raised cottage, but the Myrtleland home, two stories with dormers, was a modified raised Creole plantation. It was in ruins in 1957 when Shell Oil demolished it.

Just upriver from Myrtleland in the mid-nineteenth century was the home of Jules Trepagnier. According to Father Paret, it was a raised Creole house with an enclosed first floor. Its looks were not much enhanced by an enormous cistern at each of the front corners in Father Paret's rendering.

Roseland, directly in the lie of the spillway, was first known as Oxley Plantation. Charles Oxley, an Englishman, built an imperiously Classical Revival house with large Doric columns, a round front garden, and two peaked garçonnières to the rear. Several slaves from Roseland and Myrtleland Plantations served in the Union army during the Civil War. After the war, the area became a popular settlement for freedmen who returned to work on the plantations and resided in the former slave quarters.

The Hermitage was the property of Pierre Adolphe Rost, who also owned Destrehan. The house, according to Father Paret, was an unimposing raised Creole cottage, later renovated with Classical Revival elements, including a front stairway and central doorway. The United States government confiscated the property in 1864 because Rost was an active supporter of the Confederacy, but returned it to him in 1866—supposedly after discovering it to be too expensive to maintain.

Delhommer, the farthest upriver of the spillway tracts, is thought to have been part of the concession given to Karl Friedrich d'Arensbourg, commandant of the German Coast. The house was a raised Creole cottage with impressive outbuildings in Father Paret's depiction. Widow Delhommer, née Louise Destréhan, was d'Arensbourg's granddaughter. She eventually was remarried to Judge Rost, and they combined Delhommer and Hermitage Plantations in 1856. The house was destroyed during the Civil War by naval attack. Part of the consolidated Delhommer-Hermitage property was sold by Rost's son to his overseer, George Kugler, in 1906. The Kugler cemetery is located behind what was the quarters area of Hermitage.

The Bonnet Carré Spillway, built to protect the downriver levees and New Orleans, covers 7,824 acres comprising thirty-eight separate, privately owned tracts. All inhabitants were required to move when the spillway was built. Completed in 1935 at a cost of $14 million, the project took advantage of the short distance here—about 5.7 miles—between the river and Lake Pontchartrain. Water released through the gates flows across a broad, fan-shaped flatland widening from 7,700 feet at the river end to 12,400 feet at the lake. Guide levees along each side of the runoff area contain the outflow.

The spillway's control system was something of an engineering feat. The main structure resembles a combined bridge and dam approximately a mile and a half wide. Made of reinforced concrete, it rests on a base of steel pilings sunk forty-five to fifty-five feet deep. In its face are 350 bays, each twenty feet wide and made of vertical timbers. The bays can be opened singly or in combination by a crane that moves across the structure on a track. It takes thirty-six hours to open all 350 bays. When all are open, as much as 250,000 cubic feet (1,875,000 gallons) of water per second can be released—more than half of the river's average flow.

Behind the main structure is a set of weirs and baffles to dissipate the force of the water, as well as articulated concrete mats laid along the bottom to keep the water from gouging the floor of the spillway. The control structure automatically closes when sinking water levels trigger a mechanism in each bay. A tile gauge on the floodgates measures up to twenty-six feet. The floodgates were first opened in 1937 and successfully alleviated the danger of a potentially disastrous flood.

Two elevated railroad bridges and two elevated highways traverse the floodway, which is used for recreation when the gates are closed. A narrow road crosses the low land just behind the gates and is accessible when the control structure is closed. It leads across the spillway and rejoins the River Road. If this roadway is closed, return to Apple Street.

The east-bank River Road route begins again at the junction of La. 628 at River Road. The route numbering begins again at 0.0 at this point.

0.0 Montz, the name of this community, is a transmutation of Manz, the surname of a large family of German farmers who settled here. Land transactions in this area have been documented since 1760.

0.6 Virginia Town, an Italian enclave within the present site of Gypsy Power Plant, is located on what was the upriver portion of Hermitage Plantation from 1859 to 1887. Between 1887 and 1895, Virginia Town was part of the Charles Lagroue property, later New Hope Plantation. The black community lived in an area called Coffee Town, just downriver from the original Montz settlement. Before the Civil War, a single arpent of the New Hope property was sold to Achille Hawkins, a free man of color. Hawkins became a community leader and in 1889 helped found the Sons of Levi Benevolent Association through the Good Hope Baptist Church in Norco. Many of the families in the community were freedmen from Hermitage (Roseland) and Diamond (Myrtleland) Plantations.

In 1912 an excursion train traveling from New Orleans to Woodville, Mississippi, collided with a freight train here, killing fifteen people and injuring hundreds. For many years the wreck was

The O. Montz and Bro. Store, Montz, 1909. Co-proprietor Octave Montz
and his daughter pose on the porch.
  Courtesy Joanne M. Montz and St. John the Baptist Parish Library

listed among the worst in history. During the flood of 1973, a caving riverbank threatened the levee, and the Corps of Engineers determined the need for a levee setback. Many homes were relocated,
some were demolished, and Montz, like many other river towns,
was redefined.

> *On a point along the Montz levee is a Coast Guard light
> that, until electrification in the 1950s, was tended by local
> residents, who kept it filled with kerosene. Many locals along
> the river were paid keepers of navigational lights until the
> system was electrified.*

Gypsy Power Plant is located on part of the Gypsy, or Gipsy,
Plantation, thought to have been named for bands of gypsies who
traveled along the river, stopping to camp and entertain where there
was a settlement. According to Persac, the property was owned by
S. Labranche in the mid-nineteenth century. Father Paret shows
a dilapidated sugarhouse in the background, indicating that Labranche, a sugar planter, may have had to send his cane to someone
else's mill.

Gypsy (or Gipsy) Plantation as depicted by Paret, who identified the property by the name of its owner, Similien LaBranche.
Courtesy Marcel Boyer from the watercolors of Father Joseph M. Paret

1.2 Montz water tower.

Food along the River Road: Creole cooking developed as a result of cultural interchange and local ingredients. This unique cuisine utilizes spices and herbs derived from French, Spanish, African, West Indian, and Indian traditions. The ubiquitous gumbo, a stewlike soup, is thickened and flavored with filé (from the French filer, "to twist"), a powder made of dried sassafras leaves. (The indigenous sassafras tree is a member of the laurel family; its root is used to make root beer.) To make filé—the use of which the French learned from the Indians—the leaves are gathered and dried, then pounded fine into a dull green powder. The word gumbo itself is thought to be derived from the African Congo, where quingombo is a word for okra, another favorite gumbo ingredient; okra seeds were brought to the New World by African slaves.

Creole specialties include maque-choux (corn off the cob smothered in onions), turtle soup, shrimp stew, and every sort of gumbo. Jambalaya, a Spanish-Creole dish perhaps descended from paella, is made with rice and one or more other *main ingredients—shrimp, sausage, chicken, or game. Daube glacée is jellied veal, and calas tout chaud are fried rice cakes. Slaves from the West Indies and Africa contributed a knowledge of spices in cooking produce and native game. Africans also introduced the use of heavy iron cookware. German settlers contributed the winter hog butchering (boucherie), hog's head cheese, and the Cajun smoked sausage known as andouille, made from the neck and stomach of the hog.*

On sugar plantations, molasses or syrup was a staple of the working man's table—twice a day, every day. Pralines, a favorite delicacy of the sugar culture, may have been invented when someone dipped pecans in cuite coolerhouse molasses.

2.6 The raised frame house with interesting turretlike elements above the second story is in the community of Gypsy.

2.7 St. Charles/St. John the Baptist Parish line.

Bouligny Plantation, on the St. Charles/St. John the Baptist boundary, was flooded out several times. In Father Paret's drawing, no big house remained on the property, only quarters and outbuildings. The 1850 flood destroyed many structures, which were replaced by temporary ones; again in 1859, flooding ravaged the property.

The community of LaPlace begins at the parish line and extends upriver to the community of Reserve (neither town is incorporated, so no official marker delineates their jurisdictions). LaPlace was first settled around 1728 by members of the Karlstein community who came across the river from Bonnet Carré Point after severe flooding following a hurricane. The new settlement became known as Bonnet Carré. As French and Acadians moved into the area, their culture subsumed that of the Germans. (It was a condition of intermarriage, according to records, that German not be spoken by the newlyweds.) In the early 1800s, Jean Lafitte reputedly sold smuggled West Indian slaves to plantation owners in this area.

The community's present name was taken from the plantation of Basile LaPlace, a Frenchman who immigrated to New Orleans and became a pharmacist and successful manufacturer of a popular medicine, LaPlace's Indian Turnip Syrup. He moved to St. John Parish in 1879 and purchased large tracts of land. Four years later, he granted the New Orleans–Baton Rouge Railroad (later the Yazoo and Mississippi Valley Railroad and now the Illinois Central

Gulf) right of way on his property for a depot, which was named LaPlace. The town grew around the depot, and the post office, previously known as Ory, was renamed for LaPlace in 1892.

3.0 Bayou Steel is on property that was part of the Bonnet Carré crevasse site.

LaPlace was the birthplace of Edward "Kid" Ory in 1886. Ory became one of the great jazz trombone players and played in the first recording session outside of New Orleans featuring a black jazz band.

3.7 Crevasse Street memorializes the recurring levee breaks for which this area was once notorious. Located on the outside of the sharp Bonnet Carré bend, this spot remained one of the most susceptible to breaks and flooding until installation of the spillway. A destructive crevasse occurred in 1844. In 1850 another breach, nearly a mile wide, stayed open for more than six months. In 1859 another mile-wide break occurred in the same place. The flood of 1871 brought yet another crevasse, and the levee was moved back, but the very next year it broke again, not to be fully repaired until after 1883, when the federal Mississippi River Commission provided funding. Another break inundated the area in 1892. It had been suggested before the Civil War that the crevasse area be opened permanently to serve as a floodway, but the site ultimately chosen for the control was five miles downriver.

An eyewitness account of the 1872 Bonnet Carré crevasse by Ralph Keeler and A. R. Waud, from Every Saturday *newspaper: "Following the levee down toward the crevasse, the scene became simply horrible. Everything but a few trees and here and there a tottering house, had been swept away. Then we reached the edge of the crevasse itself. Here with a fall of from fifteen to eighteen feet the water was pouring and boiling and roaring down into the land through a break from six to seven hundred feet wide. It has opened right into a planter's front yard and his house and all his little village of shops and negro quarters had been swept before it."*

Relic sloughs, low and now wooded, are visible on both sides of Crevasse Street; a left turn on Grand Coulee Street reveals a large relic pond. Dirt gouged out by the force of the river formed mounds on which area residents subsequently built houses. Most of the other ponds created by these crevasses have been filled.

4.2 This Victorian cottage, built *circa* 1897, is attributed to Jules Albert Pastureau, an architect and builder in St. John the Baptist Parish in the late 1800s and early 1900s. His houses are noted for their fine craftsmanship and distinctive ornamentation.

4.4 On the corner of Augustin Lane is the Augustin Lasseigne House, built in 1918 by Pastureau. The faded green frame house, though in some disrepair, has an interesting front dormer with arched window.

4.7 Elvina is a trim raised Victorian cottage built in 1898 by Jules Pastureau for Charles Montegut, who named it for his wife. The fence is an old-style River Road cypress picket.

4.9 The Joseph Jules Keine House, built by Pastureau *circa* 1899, is thought to be the Montegut overseer's cottage. Several massive oaks remain on the site. A tiny white frame Acadian-style cabin on the left side of the road is thought to have been the first schoolhouse in LaPlace.

5.0 Amelie, also known as the J. O. Montegut House, is considered an important example of the raised Creole cottage despite alterations. The house was built in 1815 and bought from Zenon Boudousquié (pronounced locally as "Boo-DUS-key") by the Montegut family in 1852.

5.1 At 1128 River Road is Woodland Plantation House, built *circa* 1832. Originally a two-room Creole cottage, it has been expanded and altered, now appearing as a Victorian cottage with a double stairway. The plantation property was acquired in 1793 by Manuel Andry, later a commandant of the German Coast. The slave rebellion of 1811 supposedly was organized here, and Andry was wounded and one of his sons killed in the uprising. Ory Brothers and Lasseigne were the last owners of the plantation, which was subdivided in 1923. Highway 51 was known as the Ory-Hammond Highway.

5.2 Cardinal Drive to the right follows Woodland Canal, formerly the Woodland Plantation Road. The River Road, following the levee, turns left on Cardinal. La. 628 continues to the left as West

Fifth Street just beyond the railroad tracks. Fifth Street was the original River Road, part of the Jefferson Highway. The shift of the River Road to Cardinal reflects buildup of land approximately a quarter mile wide when the river altered its course.

5.4 Woodland Plantation Store, *circa* 1890, now a labor hall, was the mercantile hub of the large and historic plantation. Next door is the store manager's home, also late 1800s. On the left side of the street, the slight rise indicates the remains of the old levee.

5.5 On the plantation property formerly belonging to A. Montz are a few turn-of-the century cottages.

On the left side of the road, on land donated by Woodland Plantation, is the former St. Joan of Arc Catholic Church, a red frame country Gothic church—now in secular use—built in 1922 by Pastureau. When it was a church, a statue of Jeanne d'Arc was prominently displayed atop the tower with a cross below it, but the statue has disappeared.

5.7 Ice Factory Lane on the left leads to the old site of A. Montz's packing company. In 1905 Montz successfully marketed vegetables to buyers in the eastern United States. In 1914 he augmented his operation by building an ice-making plant, complete with diesel generators, producing enough excess power to service his neighbors and, ultimately, customers as far away as downriver St. Rose and upriver Garyville. In 1927 Louisiana Power and Light bought out Montz's electricity enterprise. A tornado from Hurricane Andrew in 1992 destroyed much of the site; one original tin shed remains as well as some rusty generators and evidence of deep-well drills.

Hemlock Street was the main entry to Panis Plantation, which Basile LaPlace purchased in 1870. The plantation held a half mile of river frontage fanning to three miles in the rear, and totaled 3,900 acres. A levee completely surrounded the property. The plantation store, located at the present corner of Hemlock and Fifth, burned in 1938. The LaPlace Plantation sugarhouse was destroyed in the 1909 hurricane. The main house burned in 1917. When the railroad was built in 1885, it crossed LaPlace Plantation between the Jefferson Highway and the river. The plantation was sold to the Montegut family in 1905 and to Leon Godchaux in 1918.

6.9 Jacobs General Store, built *circa* 1890, was formerly the

Maurin property; the store owners lived in the attached house. This area was formerly known as Mylesville.

7.6 The road veers left, returning to the levee.

At the junction with La. 44 is the approximate site of Sunnyside Plantation, called Similien Labranche according to Persac. The property extended to Lake Maurepas.

In the open field before the DuPont Plant are two outbuildings of the former Belle Pointe Dairy.

8.4 DuPont Chemicals is located on the site of Belle Pointe and Sunnyside Plantations. Belle Pointe was owned first by André Deslonde, an officer in the War of 1812; two of Deslonde's daughters married, respectively, U.S. Senator John Slidell and Confederate general P. G. T. Beauregard. It is thought that the name Belle Pointe was given to the plantation because it was just opposite the upriver end of the long point of the Bonnet Carré Bend. Belle Pointe was one of the holdings of sugar magnate Leon Godchaux in the 1890s. The Belle Pointe plantation house was a raised West Indian house on brick columns; the front gallery had cabinets at each end. The Belle Pointe Dairy, built by Leon Godchaux in 1915 on land too low for sugarcane, included a bottling plant and the finest equipment the era could offer. It operated until 1947.

8.8 The Englade House, a small white galleried cottage, *circa* 1890, is similar in construction to the Woodland store manager's house, with two rooms, a central fireplace, and an interior staircase.

East Thirtieth Street is within the community of Reserve, which is considered to include all settlement along the river from Belle Pointe Plantation upriver to Reserve Plantation. The community was part of the Bonnet Carré settlement. The Bonnet Carré post office was established in 1870. It stood on property belonging to St. Peter's Church, and for that reason the town was often called St. Peter. When the railroad built a depot, also on church property, in 1883, the name St. Peter was officially adopted. The depot was moved to Reserve Plantation in 1916, and the name changed again. One of the earliest property owners was Balthazar Vicner—which became Vicknair—whose land became the center of the town of Reserve. The property on which St. Peter's Church was built in 1868 belonged to descendants of Vicner.

Alcée Fortier, in his 1914 handbook on Louisiana places, calls

Reserve one of the largest and most important towns in St. John the Baptist Parish—a major steamer landing and business center, population 475. With the establishment and expansion of Leon Godchaux's sugar business, Reserve became a company town, with many residents working for Godchaux's Sugar.

Numerous older cottages remain in Reserve. When narrow strips were created by dividing land among family members, houses constructed both in front of and to the rear of the original homesite were built facing the river. This is why certain older cottages along streets perpendicular to the River Road face the river, not the street on which they are located.

At River Road and East Thirteenth was Voisin Plantation house, a raised Creole cottage built in 1785 by Jean Baptiste Voisin. The house had mortise-and-tenon construction and overplastered bousillage walls; it had three rooms upstairs, three down, and an outside stairway connecting the galleries. The house remained in the Voisin family and was rescued from the river twice; it was irreparably damaged by Hurricane Betsy in 1965.

10.0 This area of Reserve is called Jacobtown. A large tract owned by Adam Jacob was subdivided into lots bought primarily by members of his extensive family, among them Prentice Jacob, whose store and house date from the late 1800s. The Prentice Jacob Historical Museum, at River Road and East Fifth, occupies the old store and displays turn-of-the-century merchandise. Open to the public.

10.2 La. 53, or Central Avenue, divides Reserve's east and west numbered cross streets. Central Avenue was once Cornland Street, named for the plantation located here, which in turn was named for its excellent corn crops. (Corn was once grown in large quantities along the River Road for domestic consumption by both workers and livestock.) At the levee is the Reserve–Edgard ferry. Until the 1950s, a foot ferry—the boat was a small cabin cruiser— also operated here, taking pedestrians across to the parish seat in Edgard.

10.6 At the corner of River Road and West Fourth was the Liberty Theatre, built in 1897 and moved by Fortune Maurin as the New Sugar Belt Club, first to a location near St. Peter's Church in 1908, and then to this site sometime after 1917. Maurin renamed it the

Liberty Theatre. In 1926 it housed a downstairs restaurant and upstairs theater. The building burned in the 1970s. Just off River Road on West Fourth is the Civic Center of St. John. Formerly the St. John Theatre, the building was originally the Maurin Theatre, which opened behind the Liberty Theatre in 1931.

The LeBrun House, a pink raised cottage facing River Road, was designed by Pastureau in 1885. It is said that Mr. LeBrun fully utilized his levee, building a platform and bathhouse with a swimming pier atop it.

10.8 St. Peter's Church was established *circa* 1864. Before that, residents of Bonnet Carré crossed the river on oar-propelled barges to attend church in Edgard. St. Peter's reputedly was named for the local priest's favorite saint. The church grounds were acquired from Widow André Madère. The church ministered to both white and black parishioners. The first church building, a Gothic frame structure with a small graceful steeple, was replaced by a stone edifice with an impressive rose window memorializing Edward Godchaux. The present building is the fourth on the site, dedicated in 1967 after its predecessor was destroyed by Hurricane Betsy. The cemetery at the rear of the church is original to the site.

> *Toussaint—All Saints' Day—is November 1, the day that Catholic River Road residents traditionally clean the family gravesite. In the old days, before Perpetual Care, families went en masse to their family plots and spent much of the day cleaning, whitewashing, and manicuring the graves before placing flowers on the site. Even today, much cemetery activity takes place on All Saints' Day, and visitors bring flowers.* .

10.9 Leon Godchaux High School is a gracious brick building built by the sugar magnate for the community; it is no longer in use. Next door, on the downriver side on West Tenth Street, is the Godchaux-Reserve Plantation house, a large colombage raised Creole house built in several stages. Its current architectural appearance reflects an 1850 renovation. The house has been relocated twice— once before 1900 and again in 1993, when it was moved about three-quarters of a mile from its site within the Godchaux sugar mill complex. The property was settled in 1764 by Jean Baptiste Laubel and his wife on a tract of six arpents by forty. Laubel's sons split the land in 1809 and sold it. Brothers François and Elisée Rillieux, free people of color, bought the house in 1822 and are credited with adding the unusual eighteenth-century French millwork. They amassed greater landholdings and eventually held a plantation with fourteen and one-quarter arpents of frontage. In 1833 Antoine Boudousquié bought the property and called it Reserve Plantation. It was among the best-producing sugar plantations in the area. When Widow Boudousquié sold it to Leon Godchaux in 1869, it had nineteen and a quarter arpents of frontage and a depth of eighty arpents. The plantation house, which fell into disrepair, is now the property of the nonprofit River Road Historical Society, which is restoring it to its nineteenth-century appearance. Federal mantels still extant reflect a remodeling *circa* 1825, and the galleries and roofline embody renovations in 1850. When completed and open to the public, the house will showcase a sugar industry museum and furnishings and artifacts from previous owners.

Legendary local businessman Leon Godchaux immigrated from France to New Orleans around 1840 and became a successful peddler along the River Road, selling both notions and quality merchandise. He amassed capital and opened a store in Convent, upriver in St. James Parish, and soon a larger one in New Orleans. He extended his holdings to include sugar property along the river. By 1893, he owned more than thirty thousand acres on twelve plantations and had his own sugar refinery. In addition to Reserve, he owned Star, Belle Pointe, LaBranche, Sunnyside, Diamond (in St. Charles Parish), and others. In 1909 President William Howard Taft, on a steamboat trip down the Mississippi to investigate ways of improving the river, addressed a crowd from the gallery of Reserve Plantation house. For many years, Reserve was organized largely around the Godchaux Sugar Refinery. In the mid-1950s the refinery was sold and became Godchaux-Henderson Sugars Company. Down La. 637 is a pink two-story building formerly used as a clubhouse for Godchaux Sugar Refinery employees. The clubhouse was surrounded by a park with a variety of recreational facilities, including the swimming pool across the street.

11.1 Behind the chain-link fence is the Godchaux guesthouse, a two-story white Classical Revival/Victorian house built in 1906. Formerly, private bathhouses were situated along the river here.

Just beyond the guesthouse and overhead are the remains of the walkway of the Godchaux-Henderson Sugar Refinery, which is seen to the far right. The Reserve Refinery that Godchaux bought from Mrs. Boudousquié milled sugar; after 1919, Godchaux re-tooled the factory to do refining as well. The refinery was owned by the Godchauxs until 1958, when it was sold to National Sugars. National converted the plant to refining only. It closed in 1985. One of the narrow-gauge locomotives used for hauling sugarcane from the fields to the refinery was given to Disneyland and used in the California amusement park. The property is now part of the Port of South Louisiana under the name Globalplex.

11.9 At West Twenty-fourth Street, the Lions Water Treatment plant indicates the village of Lions, named for Frank Lions, the community's first postmaster in 1894. When Mr. Lions requested a post office permit, he suggested the name Willow Bridge. For some reason, postal officials considered that name was too long, and sub-stituted Lions. The post office closed in 1954.

Originally this area was known as Terre Haute ("High Land"), for Terre Haute Plantation, owned by Tregre and Deslondes. Sup-posedly the entire plantation was high ground, very conducive to raising sugarcane. Leon Graugnard bought Terre Haute in 1904, and it remained in his family until Cargill, Inc. purchased part of the property in 1972.

12.4 Just beyond the Cargill grain elevator is the Graugnard House, a white Classical Revival cottage with Victorian trim, built *circa* 1904. A nearby cottage and outbuilding are also thought to be from the Terre Haute plantation complex.

12.6 Marathon Oil Company, present owner of San Francisco Plantation, is on property that was part of Terre Haute and later within the community of Lions.

13.3 San Francisco Plantation house was completed in 1856 by Edmond Marmillion and was known as St. John de Marmillion. Its unusual romantic architecture reflects Anglo-American, Classical Revival, and Bavarian influences, but no information is available on how Marmillion selected it. Edmond Marmillion died not long after the house was completed. His son Valsin, who was traveling in Europe at the time, was welcomed home by a house full of flow-ers; Valsin thought they were for his homecoming, as he had not yet learned of his father's death. As the oldest son, Valsin stayed to manage the plantation, and he and his young wife decided to redecorate. The project was completed in 1860, and the couple began calling the plantation "Sans Frusquins," a French colloquialism meaning approximately "down to my last red cent" or "with nothing but the shirt on my back"—a joking reference to the cost of the renovation. Marmillion held the plantation until his death in 1871; his widow sold it in 1879 to Achille Bougère, who anglicized the name to San Francisco. Originally the house was separated from the levee by a broad sweep of garden, but several levee setbacks have stolen the front yard.

The property was owned by the Ingraham Oil Company, which had set preservation of the house in motion before it was sold to the Marathon Oil Company in 1976. The house has been fully restored to its 1860 grandeur with five ceiling frescoes, original paint colors, faux marbre, and faux bois. An original cistern is located on the grounds. Antebellum Street, on the upriver side of the house, was formerly called Sugar House Lane and led to the San Francisco sugar mill, which closed in 1974. The house is open to the public.

13.8 Emilie Plantation was built for Cyprien Chauff in 1882 and named for his daughter. The house is a frame Italianate raised cottage—a Creole cottage with an Italianate cupola crowning the roofline. The cypress for the house was milled in Plaquemine and shipped across the river on flatboat; the bricks were made on site. Inscriptions in the house identify the contractor, carpenters, and mason by name. Emilie had fallen into disrepair but was rescued and restored in the 1960s. To the rear of the house is a vintage building said to have been moved from neighboring San Francisco Plantation.

Next door to Emilie is the Tregre cottage.

14.1 The center of Garyville is several blocks back from the river. Garyville was a company town erected by the Lyon Lumber Company of Illinois in 1903 on the property of Glencoe Plantation, bought for its old-growth cypress forest. At the time, Glencoe was owned by French immigrant Leon Graugnard. As the story goes, Garyville was named for a director of the Lyon Cypress Lumber company, John Gary, who happened to be Mr. Lyon's son-in-law and was not in the meeting when the committee deciding the town's name made its selection. Garyville is said to have been the largest town between New Orleans and Baton Rouge during the lumber boom. Lyon built a sawmill and a complete town, one of the first "planned communities" in the state, including a rail depot, commissary, hotels, boardinghouses, community center, workers' and executive housing, livery stable, church, and commercial district. By 1915, with the cypress resources depleted, the company remodeled their mill, purchased pine stands in Livingston and St. Helena Parishes to the north, and extended their railway. In the late 1920s two fires destroyed millions of board feet of lumber and the company's pine holdings were playing out. According to records, Lyon cut one last cypress tree in 1931—estimated to be 1,283 years old, one of the oldest in the state—and closed their doors. Shortly thereafter, W. J. Stebbins, a former manager of the company, bought the equipment and houses; in 1945 he opened Stebbins Lumber Company, a lumber and salvage business.

The town is laid out on a grid. Some of the workers' residences remain, although altered, as well as a few commercial structures. The Lyon Company headquarters building at North Railroad and Main Streets was designed to resemble a Creole plantation house to disguise the company's Yankee roots. It now houses the Timbermill Museum. Open to the public.

14.4 Hope Plantation house, just off the corner of River Road and La. 54 (Church Street), was built in 1857 by David Adams. Also known as Esperance (French for "hope"), this Creole raised cottage was originally one room wide and a room deep but has been elongated. A gallery once encircled the house, but parts of it have been removed. The area's railroad depot was originally on Hope Plantation and called Hope Station but moved when Garyville was built. Hope Plantation property is now subdivided as part of the town of Garyville.

15.5 Nalco Company is on the site of Angelina Plantation. In 1852 the Trosclair family built the two-and-a-half-story brick house at the end of a cedar allée. An unusual pair of octagonal pigeonniers with pointed cypress-shingled roofs and wrought-iron weathervanes were among the outbuildings, as was a dollhouse or playhouse erected as a small-scale mansion complete with a five-foot-wide fireplace. They were moved in 1930 after the river consumed the big house.

Sport Plantation, date unknown.
Courtesy St. James Historical Society

15.9 The community of Mt. Airy took its name from the local plantation in 1884. Joseph LeBourgeois supposedly had attended college in the North Carolina town of Mt. Airy (some accounts say the town was named Monterey). In 1850 LeBourgeois built a raised Creole cottage, a story and a half, with dormers, multiple chimneys, and a belvedere enclosed by a wrought-iron railing. The front staircase and gallery railings were cast iron. The house was occupied by Union forces during the Civil War. Felicien Waguespack bought the property and sometimes called it Little Mt. Airy to distinguish it from a house he built on Sport Plantation. Little Mt. Airy was moved in 1929 to accommodate the levee. Kaiser Aluminum demolished the house in the late 1950s.

16.0 The story-and-a-half raised Camellia Cottage, built *circa* 1850, is not the LeBourgeois house.

16.7 Petroleum Fuel and Terminal tank farm is on part of the Mt. Airy property.

17.6 St. John the Baptist/St. James Parish line.
    The LaRoche Chemical plant is on the site of Sport Plantation.

Felicien Waguespack, a prominent west-bank resident, bought Sport (a part of the Golden Grove Plantation property) in 1886; nine years later, he bought contiguous upriver property—the rest of Golden Grove, including its Big House. In 1902 a federal official warned Waguespack that his levee was insufficient to withstand the spring high water. He responded by augmenting the levee but, hedging his bet, also removed the contents of his house and its architectural embellishments—gallery ironwork, widow's walk, millwork, etc.—to storage. When the river did destroy Golden Grove as predicted, Waguespack built a new mansion on his Sport property using the materials and architectural elements he had saved.

18.1 Waguespack called the new big house at Sport "Mt. Airy." It closely resembled the late edifice from Golden Grove with the addition of a porte cochère (a covered entrance, usually on the side of a house). Completed in 1906 and one of the last of the Classical Revival mansions built in this area, the house burned in 1944.

The town of Gramercy occupies the site of a Colapissa Indian village that was part of a concession granted to the marquis d'Ancenis *circa* 1720. The tract was owned by Pierre Joseph Dupard from 1739 to 1776. Subsequently, this and several other properties were joined to form Golden Grove Plantation, so called for either the fall coloration of a grove of sycamore trees or an entrance allée of orange trees. Golden Grove was bought by the Shepherd family in 1817; its Classical Revival mansion, dating from the 1840s, may well have been a remodeled raised Creole plantation with ironwork balcony railings, dentil molding on the frieze, a lacy belvedere, and graceful Doric columns on the front and rear of the home. The house, destroyed by the 1902 flood, would have been under or just upriver from the Gramercy–Wallace bridge. A small settlement behind Colonial Sugars is still called Golden Grove.

In 1895, the portion of Golden Grove not sold to Felicien Waguespack was bought by a group of New York businessmen to build a sugar factory and company town. It was named Gramercy, perhaps wishfully, by one of the New Yorkers who had moved from the fancy Gramercy Park residential neighborhood in Manhattan.

18.5 The Veterans Memorial Bridge, connecting the Airline Highway (La. 61) and the town of Gramercy with Wallace on the west-bank River Road, was completed in 1995 after fourteen years, numerous lawsuits, a barge accident, and the exigencies of state bureaucracy. It replaced the Lutcher–Vacherie ferry. The bridge received the nickname "Bridge to Nowhere" and dubious national attention because its midsection was completed long before the approach ramps were built.

18.8 The western part of Golden Grove, once known as Faubourg Lapin ("Rabbit Suburb") and sold to the New Yorkers, is the location of Colonial Sugars, now the Colonial Sugars Historic District. The sugar-company town was founded in 1896. Its Central Factory processed cane from various plantations in the area. In 1903 the company changed its name to Colonial Sugars. In 1915 it terminated milling operations and concentrated on refining, converting raw sugar to white table sugar. Colonial is the only table-sugar refinery left along the part of the River Road covered by this book. In 1995 its output was almost a billion pounds of processed sugar.

19.2 The general store at the corner of South Millet Street is outside the Colonial Sugars Historic District, which extends only to the downriver side of this street. The historic district can be viewed from South Millet and includes original structures from the 1896–1929 period. Extant within the complex are a row of six grand executive houses, various workers' houses, and a company-built Sacred Heart Church, a rectangular brick structure now relieved of its religious accoutrements and no longer in use. At one time, the industrial town also included a company store and company jail. Two of the factory buildings are original to the complex, although the machinery has been modernized.

19.5 Lutcher corporate limit.

Bonfires on the Levee is an unusual Christmas Eve celebration centered in the Gramercy-Lutcher area. The burning of large bonfires atop the levee is the climax of a month of preparation and an evening of boisterous festivity. Although the best-known explanation of the festival's origin attributes it to Acadians lighting the way for Papa Noël, a more historic version traces similar customs to pagan rituals in pre-Christian Europe and suggests that the early French and German settlers may have brought the practice from their homelands. A more recent possible source was the Marist priests at Jefferson College (now Manresa Retreat House) just upriver. In a New Year's Eve tradition from their native France, the priests lit relatively small bonfires, usually built in a single day, on the batture in front of the college. Historians suggest that the students liked the celebration and introduced it to their families around the parishes, with the event somehow moving to Christmas Eve.

Whatever its origin, the custom was not widely practiced by the 1950s, when civic pride identified it as a potential tourist attraction for Christmas Eve, traditionally a quiet time in Catholic south Louisiana. The revived event has grown to be one of the most bizarre and colorful festivals in the area, premised on torching numerous log pyres that have been painstakingly constructed for many days. More than a hundred pyramidal structures are built with willow logs and other native materials collected during the interval between Thanksgiving and Christmas. Because of contemporary safety and environmental criteria, numerous regulations have been introduced that, to some locals, dampen the festivities considerably: bonfire structures can be no higher than twenty feet; location permits are required; the integrity of the levee cannot be threatened by the building; materials such as old tires are forbidden to be burned. However, cane reeds can still be affixed to the pyres, producing firecrackerlike popping when they burn. Only the local fire department is allowed to build nontraditional structures, which over the years have included a steamboat, streetcar, plantation house, and turn-of-the-century locomotive, among others.

On Christmas Eve at 7 P.M., the fire chief signals the lighting of the bonfires. Along almost ten miles of levee, receding into the distance, yellow-orange flames create a chain of surreal beauty as they dance into a black velvet sky. Thousands of visitors, on foot and in gridlocked cars, wonder at the spectacle.

19.7 The raised Creole plantation home with Classical Revival influences was the home of Etienne Reine, who owned one of the plantations from which the town of Lutcher was developed. The historic house, built *circa* 1800, was later owned by A. H. Mears, who operated a sugar mill and had a steamboat landing and warehouse on his riverfront.

19.8 The St. James Historical Society Museum is housed in a vintage pharmacy building moved here from the College Point area upriver. Exhibits reflect St. James Parish history and culture and include artifacts of local archeological sites, vintage photos, a diorama of the town in its logging heyday, a log from an eight-hundred-year-old cypress tree, a short introductory video of perique tobacco farming, and other historic miscellany. Open to the public.

La. 3193 enters the town of Lutcher. In the late eighteenth century, three plantations covered the area now comprising the town. They were owned, respectively, by Jean Baptiste Ory, Pierre Chenet, and Etienne Reine. The property owned by Chenet (supposedly nicknamed "Perique," for whom the indigenous tobacco may be named) was bought by the Lutcher and Moore Lumber Company for a sawmill town. The company was incorporated in 1891 to log the vast virgin cypress forests that stood in the swamplands back of town; the location was perfect, with transportation available by both rail and water. The railroad had been built in 1882, less than a mile from the river.

The town of Lutcher was named for the company's owner and president. The sawmill was located at Railroad and Cypress Streets, where the *Olive Jeannette,* a cypress patrol boat built for the lumber company in 1926, is now on exhibit (after service along Blind River for Lutcher and Moore, the boat was used by other owners for fur trapping). Perique's Creole house, built between 1797 and 1803, was the residence of the superintendent of the lumber company but is no longer standing. In 1894 the Lutcher and Moore facility was reputedly the second-largest cypress mill in the world. During 1898 and 1899, locals say, it ran day and night. It shut down in 1930 when all the available virgin cypress had been depleted, leaving a community of one hotel, some boardinghouses, a few homes, and a commissary.

The modern St. James Bank stands on the site of a longtime moss gin, which shut down in the 1940s. The United Methodist Church, the first nonblack Protestant church in St. James, St. John the Baptist, and St. Charles Parishes, was built in 1901 on a downriver piece of Longview Plantation property at the instigation of William Curtis, who claimed that lumberjacks working at Lutcher and Moore contributed to a godless community. It is said that tithing to the church was done by payroll deduction.

20.1 Across River Road from the Lutcher–Vacherie ferry ramp (no longer in use) is the site of Jean Baptiste Ory's Longview Plantation,

Longview Plantation house, probably in the mid-1900s.
   Courtesy St. James Historical Society

dating from 1793. An old weathered cistern in an open field marks the spot. The property was called La Longue Vue as early as 1785 for the long, straight stretch of river (this sweep of river is now designated on maps as Grand View Reach). Joseph Gebelin bought the property from a New Orleans bank in 1878. His house reflected a synthesis of French colonial and Classical Revival styles. As originally constructed, it had five rooms and a pair of rear cabinets with an open area between; a widow's walk was added on top. After the 1927 flood, the house was moved back several hundred feet. The stuccoed brick service area was disassembled for the move and rebuilt exactly as before; the second story was renovated. The house burned in the late 1980s.

20.4 The community of Paulina was once called La Longue Vue. According to local story, it was renamed Paulina because a nun by that name lost her prayer book here. The small, faded green warehouse once served the Louisiana Perique Tobacco Company.

21.1 St. Joseph's Catholic Church was originally built as a chapel in 1840 to serve Catholics for whom St. Michael's, upriver in Convent, was too distant. The current church was built in 1921 and the rectory in 1926 after a fire destroyed the previous buildings. The pews in the church and the tall crucifix in the cemetery were hand-carved by Father Chauve, who served the parish until 1955, when he was 107 years old. The cemetery dates from the turn of the century. Just inside the entrance on the right is an Acadian tomb—a small brick tomb with a gable-capped headstone.

21.5 On this site was a perique tobacco warehouse and the last steamboat landing. The warehouse was demolished in the 1960s.

21.6 Kliebert Street is the site of Model Farm Plantation—or Ferme Modèle, as it was called in 1857. The property was originally a Spanish land grant owned by Alphonse Schexnaildre; the grant was confirmed by congressional commission in 1811. Several weathered raised Creole cottages and a large cistern remain.

21.7 Little Texas, also known as the Genre House, is a one-story raised Creole cottage that was remodeled *circa* 1840. It was slightly moved in 1928 but still stands on its original plantation site. Little Texas is among the oldest Creole homes in St. James Parish, built with colombage walls (half timbering with in-fill). The house is an example of a large Creole floor plan, with two full ranges of rooms. The Classical Revival transom and sidelights on a center door show later Anglo-American influence.

22.2 Down Antioch Lane in the wink of a community known as St. Elmo is the Antioch Baptist Church, founded in 1868 by the Reverend A. Glosier. The frame church serves one of the oldest extant black congregations in the parish.

22.8 The chamois-colored Peavey grain elevator is located on the site of St. Elmo Plantation. The plantation was a Spanish land grant to Widow Jean Bourgeois and her two sons.

23.2 On the upriver side of La. 642 is the community of Remy, on the site of Bourbon Plantation, an aggregated tract that claimed sixteen arpents of frontage in 1857, when it was owned by Alexis Ferry. Ferry was married to Josephine Aime, daughter of the legendary sugar planter Valcour Aime, who lived on the west bank. Bourbon was a successful sugar plantation, and Ferry purchased another tract across the river, just upstream from his father-in-law's land, naming the new property Homeplace. Before the Civil War, Ferry was one of the most important landholders in the area. His widow sold Bourbon Plantation in 1870; among its subsequent owners was Pierre Louis Remy, after whom the community of Remy was named.

From Alexis Ferry's journal: Contracts with categories of freedmen labor after the Civil War: Laborers I—monthly sum of $8; Laborers II—$6; Laborers III—$4. They will be fed and cared for in case of illness, [but] the period of illness will be deducted from their monthly wage . . . Workers will be housed without paying rent. Those who put in five full days of work will have the right to take Saturday off. It is understood that they will work on Saturday during grinding season without additional pay.

Side trip: La. 642 to the Belmont Indian mounds and Grand Point, the perique tobacco fields. For a view of the Indian mounds, turn left on La. 3125 for 2.1 miles. The large mound, an independent, tree-covered hillock on the left side of the road in the cane field, is on private property and has been thoroughly excavated by archaeologists. Judging from their geological setting, it is thought that the mounds are more than 2,500 years old and were built before the river took its present course. The large mound may have been a signal elevation or a temple. Another mound about 550 feet away is thought to have been a prehistoric residential site. *Bel mont* translates from the French as "lovely hill." In local legend, the mounds were filled with gold buried by Indians and Civil War planters. Although archaeologists disproved such claims, they could not refute the superstition that Indian treasures are haunted because when the treasure was buried, an Indian (preferably an enemy) was killed and buried with it. The alleged haunting did not, however, stop area residents from flocking to the tall mound for refuge during the floods of 1890 and 1892.

Farther up La. 642 is Grand Point, the only place in the world where perique tobacco is still grown. According to local historians, the name Grand Point was given to the area to designate a land formation created by a flood. When the floodwaters receded, a triangular point of high ground, approximately three miles wide and six miles deep, was left surrounded by swamp. Grand Point was, until recently, a very remote community. It is near Blind River, an important channel in the local network of waterways.

Local lore says that one of Pierre Chenet's Indian guides told him about their unusual tobacco and how it could be cured. Chenet sold his farm in St. John the Baptist Parish, bought land in St. James, and planted seeds he acquired from the Indians. Improving on native curing methods in the 1820s, he became the first to cultivate the tobacco commercially. The pungent, strong-tasting leaf is used in tobacco blends around the world, especially in pipe tobaccos. The painstaking process of growing perique, however, has winnowed out all but a few stalwart, aging farmers, and the plant's future is unknown. Production continues to be by hand in the traditional way. Tiny black perique seed is sown in hotbeds around Christmas and transplanted to the field in March. The plants are topped and pinched for suckers to leave only a few large leaves. Harvest occurs in June or July, and the leaves are cut, bundled, and hung to dry for about three weeks (several weathered drying barns are visible along the road). They are wetted and allowed to soften before the stalks and stems are stripped off, then packed in layers in oak barrels and compressed by hand jack before being stored. After aging for six months, the tobacco is taken to the sole remaining perique manufacturer (just up the river in Convent), where it is pressure-processed three more times. Total curing time for perique tobacco is one year.

St. Philomena Chapel, demolished in 1975, was located at the rear of the settlement, under the present power lines near where the road becomes dirt. It was built in 1911, replacing the St. Vincent de Paul Chapel, which dated to 1874. An old Acadian cottage stands at the rim of the paved road; it belonged to the family of the nun who encouraged the establishment of St. Philomena.

Returning to the River Road:

24.4 The community of Hester grew on the site of Hester Plantation, originally owned by Englishman James Mather, the fourth (and first English-speaking) mayor of New Orleans. The plantation and a gracious mansion were known as Mather or Belle Alliance. James Mather died in 1821. After the property was sold several times, it took the name of Hester. The oak trees at Packing House Road remain from the site of the big house which burned in the 1920s. For many years afterward, the plantation bell could still be seen in the yard, as could two rows of quarters cabins.

25.5 On the property upriver of Kahn Street are several large,

St. Philomena Chapel at Grand Point. In this early view, the little church perches at the edge of a planted field. The crop appears to be cotton.
Courtesy St. James Historical Society

moss-draped oaks—all that is left of Belmont Plantation. The house site is now on the river side of the levee; after the house burned, the chimney was visible on the batture for many years. It is thought that Belmont was named in reference to the Indian mound, which is almost directly behind this location; there are no other hills in the region.

The house, built in the 1850s, was a two-story Italianate Classical Revival mansion surrounded with twenty-eight peripteral columns and enhanced by finely detailed decorative elements—Corinthian capitals, dentil friezework, graceful gallery railings and cupola. Extensive formal gardens were much admired. Edward Everett Hale, the eighteenth-century Unitarian clergyman and writer (famous in his time as author of the story "The Man Without a Country"), visited here, as did Grand Duke Alexis of Russia who arrived wishing to see a sugar plantation.

Perhaps the most auspicious visit occurred, according to local lore, during the Civil War when a Union naval officer came to the door demanding the plantation owner give himself up or the house would be shelled. The plantation mistress responded that she didn't know where he was and the boat would shell only women and children. The officer accused her of lying, and one of the servants, offended by the ungallant behavior, addressed the mother of the mistress of the house—a Mrs. Charles—by name, inveighing her to speak up for her daughter. The officer, hearing the name, was startled to discover that the elder woman was the widow of a man he greatly respected. "I owe everything to that man," the officer exclaimed, "and I shall never forget his kindness to me. Madame, this house shall be protected."

Although the Civil War spared Belmont, and the plantation's production of rice during the postbellum period was a success, the 1888 crevasse damaged the place badly. The break reportedly began with a crawfish hole. The swamp just upriver from Kahn Street and easily seen to the right of the road is an extensive residual slough resulting from the crevasse.

From the memoir of Adele LeBougeois Chapin, who lived at Belmont: "All the drainage on the plantation was destroyed, the garden ploughed up by the water and all the beautiful old trees killed. Willow trees grew all over the place in a year so that it was a dreadful scene of desolation. It seemed

Belmont Plantation house, probably not long before it burned in 1889.
Courtesy St. James Historical Society

*hopeless to attempt to restore the place and it was almost a
relief when the house burnt down [in 1889] for we could not
bear to desert it."*

26.0   A dirt road runs through the site of Welham Plantation on
property belonging to the Marathon Oil Company, which acquired
the plantation in 1975 and demolished the house in 1979. (Seven
of the outbuildings were moved to the Rural Life Museum in Baton
Rouge.) A line of oaks indicates the site of the house. William Welham built his two-story brick Classic Revival home, with a belvedere on top, in 1835. After his death in 1860, his widow purchased
additional properties—augmenting the plantation to 2,300 acres.
The railroad station that served the area was called Oneida, but the
post office was called Hester.

A memoir of Welham recalls that, after the Civil War, a general
store on the property was, like many others in the area, a place
"where field hands exchanged metal tokens for commodities, and
men warmed their backs around a pot belly stove." A section of
the quarters was called Chinese Quarter in 1904 because of the

Welham Plantation house in the 1950s.
  Courtesy St. James Historical Society

immigrant workers recruited to help with sugar production. Early in the twentieth century, a boardinghouse behind the sugar mill housed workers from Paulina, Convent, Lutcher, and Gramercy who came for the whole of grinding season. The property remained in the Welham family until the early 1900s.

27.5 College Point begins here. This bold land formation has been enlarged by river movement, which is why houses are located on both sides of the River Road. This is also the unofficial boundary of the extended community of Convent.

28.0 A creole cottage with plastered front facade.

28.3 The contemporary St. James Courthouse, built in 1981, replaces the old courthouse, built upriver in 1869. This site was formerly occupied by the Zenon Trudeau house, a structure of unusual, almost whimsical, architectural design. Trudeau was a New Orleans lawyer, a brother of Charles Trudeau, the official land surveyor for the Spanish colonial government. The house was built during the early nineteenth century of plastered brick. A broad gal-

The architecturally eccentric Zenon Trudeau House.
Courtesy St. James Historical Society

lery surrounded it. Octagonal garçonnières with pointed roofs were connected at the rear of the house by galleries. A peaky hipped roof with dormers capped the house. In later years, the house was tucked into a tangle of shrubbery and trees. It was demolished after it fell into disrepair. The only reminder of Trudeau's occupancy is the short street going to the levee across the road.

Upriver from the courthouse property are several weathered raised cottages. One is Acadian-style, set back from the road with a center chimney, its side walls covered with tarpaper. Several houses at slight angles to the road suggest that the river and the road have moved.

28.5 A pristine whitewashed brick-and-ironwork fence sets off the grounds of the Manresa Retreat House, run by the Jesuit order. This is the site of the former College of Jefferson, chartered in 1831 to offer a proper education to the sons of area planters so that they would not have to go to the North, to France, or to the College of Orleans down the river. Its founders were leading French Louisianians of the area, including Governor André Roman. Named for Thomas Jefferson and occupying sixty-five acres of the former Vavasseur Plantation, the institution opened its doors in 1834. In 1836 the Classical Revival gatehouses (porters' lodges), Ignatius House (the college president's house, built as a small-scale plantation manor), and the cookhouse were completed. The college also boasted a fine library, a museum of natural history, science laboratories, and numerous decorative paintings.

In 1842 a fire destroyed much of the campus; only the president's house and the porters' lodges escaped (the latter are near the road and easily visible). The main building was rebuilt in Classical Revival style. Supporters helped to reestablish the college, but when the state withdrew financial support in 1845, the school began to founder; it closed in bankruptcy in 1848. It reopened briefly from 1853 to 1856 before closing once more. In 1859 the legendary west-bank planter Valcour Aime purchased the college, reopening it and adding a Gothic Revival chapel in memory of his son, Gabriel. The chapel's exterior is stucco but finished to resemble stone—which, along with the building's buttresses, tower, and pinnacles, gives it a very Continental appearance. Aime donated the building and grounds to a corporation known as Jefferson College, which operated until 1862, when Federal troops occupied the campus. In 1864 Aime donated the school to the Marist Fathers. They renamed it St. Mary's Jefferson College and led the institution until 1927. The grounds and buildings were in the hands of caretakers until 1931, when the Jesuit Fathers of New Orleans, in an inspired act, purchased the beautiful campus and dedicated it as the Manresa House of Retreats, a spiritual sanctuary from the outside world for both Catholic and non-Catholic laymen. Some of the live oaks on the 130-acre property are nearly 150 years old, planted during the time of Vavasseur. The added acreage in the front of the tract resulted from the propitious moving of the levee away from the campus. A gravel road up the levee on the upriver side of Manresa offers pedestrians an excellent river vista.

> *"Two miles below the Convent is Jefferson College. . . . The buildings are roomy, substantial and in thorough repair. . . . There are about 50 students attending. . . . There are six sugar refineries [in the parish], most of them conducted on an extensive scale: those of Valcour Aime, E. J. Forstall, E & LJ Roman, B. Lapice & Bro, Mrs. Winchester and ECE Mire." J. W. Dorr, 1860.*

Just upriver is Poche Perique Tobacco Company, sole remaining dealer and processor of the product.

The community of Convent is the definitive township along this part of the river and stretches from College Point upriver to Romeville, incorporating various older communities. A Houma Indian village may have been at this location prior to European settlement. One of the first settlers, in 1722, was Pierre Baron, and for many years the place was called Baron. In the late eighteenth century it was renamed St. Michel. In gratitude for the Sacred Heart Convent and school opening in 1825, the name was changed to Convent. In 1869, the parish courthouse was relocated from across the river to a site near Jefferson College. It burned in 1904 and was replaced.

Along the River Road in Convent are a number of weathered Creole and Acadian-style cottages.

29.8 Residents grew tired of crossing the river to the town of St. James for church and petitioned the bishop in New Orleans for a priest. The first arrived in 1812, after locals had already begun burying their dead in a cemetery here. The Gothic Revival St. Michael's Church was designed by Florian Dicharry and dedicated in 1833. It was enlarged to the current size in 1870. A bell from Belgium, sent in 1831, is inscribed: "Cast in Louvaine in the name of the Catholics of Belgium for their Catholic brethren in America." The brick cathedral tower assured all viewers that this was a substantial edifice, the church of wealthy landowners, but the steeple atop the tower blew off in Hurricane Betsy in 1965 and has not been replaced.

In front of the church are statues of St. Michael the Archangel and Joan of Arc, suggesting that despite local lore, the church was not named for Michel Cantrelle, son of Jacques Cantrelle, legendary local leader, but for his patron saint. Before the new levee was erected, St. Michael's had a large front yard with cedar trees and a long plank walk with a stairway to the levee to accommodate those who walked to church along the crest. The interior of the church is ornate and colorful and includes a pipe organ, installed in 1856, and a hand-carved altar from the 1889 Paris World's Fair. The replica Our Lady of Lourdes Grotto behind the main altar was added in 1876 and is thought to be the first such creation in the United States. Devised by Christophe Colomb, Jr., and constructed by Dicharry, the grotto is fashioned out of bagasse clinkers—mud-

The Colomb House at its original location.
Courtesy St. James Historical Society

colored, rocklike chunks of charred and dried bagasse—and an in-
verted sugar kettle set with thousands of tiny seashells.

Upriver from the church is the two-story brick rectory. Much of
the cemetery has been claimed by the river, but some old and crumbling tombs remain: that of W. P. Welham of Welham Plantation;
of Samuel Fagot, the owner of Uncle Sam Plantation; and of the
Mather and Malarcher families, among others. Several Gothic-style
tombs with gabled headstones can be found in this burial ground.

30.0 The Judge Poche House, built circa 1866, is a Victorian Renaissance Revival cottage with an unusual front dormer. Felix Pierre
Poche was a leading local figure whose memoir of his Civil War
experience has been published. He was a Democratic Party leader
and a founding member of the American Bar Association. An exterior office and barrel-slat cistern are on the grounds.

Immediately next door, hidden in the overgrowth behind the post
office on the downriver side, is what remains of the quirky Colomb
House, built in 1835 by Christophe Colomb, Jr., a grandson of the
wealthy and well-known local planter Marius Pons Bringier. Colomb was a dentist, inventor, engineer, and amateur architect—the

man who created the bagasse grotto (the first to experiment successfully with bagasse as a construction material, Colomb also used it for the columns of his dental office). The house, originally several miles upriver at Romeville, was moved here in 1982 with plans—still unexecuted—for restoration. It was architecturally unusual, a Classical Revival plantation house in miniature with a room-sized cupola of unique design that was used as a garçonnière (the cupola blew off in Hurricane Andrew in 1992). The story is told that the house's paired columns were rescued from the demolition of the courthouse; they were placed in pairs on Colomb's house because there were too many to fit otherwise. The columns were also too tall, but rather than cutting them, the gallery floor was dropped below the rest of the house to accommodate their noble height. Colomb appears to have been an interesting man.

30.2 The clearing is the site of the old east-bank St. James Parish Courthouse. In the mid-nineteenth century, a hotel stood at this location. The site was sold to the St. James Parish Police Jury in 1869 for construction of a new courthouse, the operational seat of government located across the river, just downriver from the Cantrelle (St. James) Church. The courthouse was wooden and burned in 1904; another was built and used until 1971.

30.4 A single palm, a magnolia, and an oak tree in the cane field mark the site of the old Sacred Heart Convent. The convent was founded in 1825 by French nuns for the education of young women, in association with St. Michael's Church. The plantation tract was bought from Joseph Landry, Jr., who also owned the ferry that provided east-bank residents access to St. James Church across the river. The new convent was erected in 1848, a galleried and graceful French Gothic structure of brick and cream-colored plaster. The central building was three stories in height and had two wings; the chapel, crowned by a cross, was the north wing, and a series of parlors and guest rooms filled the south wing. The building overlooked a lovely garden. Eventually, with free public schools, successive failures of the sugarcane crop, and the rural location, the convent began to falter. A 1926 hurricane caused damage, but the institution survived as a school for Mexican refugees. In 1950, when it was no longer in use, the buildings were demolished except for one small outbuilding that was moved to the grounds of St. Michael's Church.

Sacred Heart Convent, namesake of the town of Convent.
Courtesy St. James Historical Society

> *"The convent of St. Michael, conducted by the Sisters of the Sacred Heart, . . . is situated on the left bank 63 miles above New Orleans . . . a very elegant and extensive building and its handsome front is one of the most prominent land-marks on the river." J. W. Dorr, 1860.*

30.6 Lambremont House is a raised cottage built during the 1860s by either the Vavasseur family or a Dr. Demarest. Several other vintage cottages are in the area, including a shed with a tin roof under which the original cypress shingles show.

31.0 Homesite of local builder Florian Dicharry.

31.6 The IMCC Agrico plant was erected in 1966 on the site of Uncle Sam Plantation. The house had been demolished in 1940 in order to move the levee (the house stood very near the road at the time). It was built in 1841 or 1843 by Samuel Fagot. Until after the Civil War, the property was called Constancia, named for Colonel Joseph Constant, who had acquired several tracts of land after the War of 1812. But it was Samuel Pierre August Fagot, a somewhat

The Uncle Sam main house in deep decline near the end of its existence.
Courtesy St. James Historical Society

mysterious Frenchman, whose identity became imprinted on the site. One story attributes the renaming of the plantation to visits from his nieces and nephews, who arrived by steamboat to visit "Uncle Sam's place." Another story is that Fagot was the first to export sugar with his hogsheads stamped *U.S.* for the country of origin, leading inevitably to identification with the national personification. Fagot died in 1858. The property stayed in the family until 1920, when it was sold at a sheriff's sale. The plantation was inundated by the Nita crevasse in 1890; subsequent levee moves were necessitated until, finally, the house had to be destroyed. At the time of its demolition, Uncle Sam was still one of the most complete plantation communities in the state, although in deteriorating condition. The main house was a square two-story Classical Revival plastered-brick structure surrounded by Doric columns. The lower gallery was brick paved, and the wide second-story gallery encircled the house. On either side of the big house were one-story garçonnières; at the rear were a freestanding Classical Revival kitchen and office buildings, hexagonal pigeonniers with pointed roofs, and a brick barn and stables. In the lobby of Agrico headquarters, an album of photos of the Uncle Sam complex is available for public viewing.

> *As the demolition of Uncle Sam was underway, the Corps of Engineers office in New Orleans received a telegram from the National Park Service: "Have learned of the impending demolition of the Uncle Sam Plantation near Convent, Louisiana. Stop. Can demolition be deferred short time pending investigation by National Park Service to determine possibilities for status as a national monument or historic site?" But it was too late.*

32.1 An old white frame house near Uncle Sam was part of Home Place Plantation, built by the Nicolle family in 1849.

32.8 The Malarcher House, on the upriver side of the intersection of La. 3214, is a raised Creole-style cottage built in 1891 near the site of the mansion of the chevalier Louis Malarcher. The chevalier arrived in 1791 as a political refugee of the French Revolution and became an influential citizen of St. James Parish, one of the leaders who commissioned the building of St. Michael's in Convent. He bought this property in 1811. It became known as St. Michael Plantation; the downriver end was later called Malarcher Plantation. The original mansion was destroyed in 1890 by the levee break that created the nearby Nita crevasse. This house, constructed by Willie Malarcher, a grandson of the chevalier, used materials salvaged from the old house and from quarters buildings on the property. It was abandoned in 1925 and faced a dim future until its purchase and renovation in the 1960s by a local corporation. Malarcher House is now the property of Occidental Chemical Corporation.

33.1 The densely wooded and swampy tract on the right side of the road is a residual effect of the Nita crevasse at the site of Nita Plantation—named, it is said, after a popular song, "Juanita." The break occurred in March 1890, the result of a leaking rice flume, and was discovered by a passing steamboat. The levee—reputedly quite low—could not be repaired until many months later, when the river subsided. The crevasse was very wide, and the properties of many planters were ruined. The Louisiana Lottery Company gave money to the St. James Parish Police Jury to be used for levee protection.

33.7 The settlement of Romeville is named for the Rome family and was once the site of the Webre plantation. Webres intermarried with Romes, who were descended from some of John Law's early colonists—the Rommels—and a large and extended family evolved. Timberton was a settlement behind Romeville, originally built as a sawmill and village nearer the swamp.

34.4 Several oaks are all that remain on the original site of the Christophe Colomb, Jr., house, moved downriver. At one time, descendants of the Randolph family, builders of the grand Nottoway Plantation house across the river in Iberville Parish, lived in the house at this location.

In this area also was St. Rose Plantation; a quarters cabin remains.

34.7 The site of Wilton Plantation is in an area settled in the late eighteenth century by Acadian and German farmers. In 1827 several tracts were consolidated to form one with eight arpents frontage, and the big house was constructed. Persac designates Marson, Seddon, and Wilkins as the partnership property owners. The house was a raised Creole-style plantation with a central stair and central hallway; there were two cabinets on the rear gallery, which later occupants enclosed. Just before the Civil War, Wilton was owned by Oliver J. Morgan. It was an extensive sugar farm worked by 233 slaves on 1,200 improved acres. The plantation grew a large variety of other crops as well—cotton, corn, peas, Irish potatoes, sweet potatoes, hay, rye, tobacco, oats, and orchard fruits; it also produced wool, butter, honey, beeswax, wine, and cheese. Wilton was a large sugar producer until after the Civil War, when it struggled like so many others. In 1908 Louis Hymel bought the property and closed the sugar mill, preferring to consolidate his operation at Helvetia, the plantation he owned just upriver. The big house was demolished in 1972 after the Ethyl Corporation bought the property.

35.0 Several commercial structures remain in the community of Central. The Helvetia Cooperative Sugar Mill can still be seen behind the fields. The area was originally settled by German and Swiss immigrants in the early eighteenth century, but the property was not named Helvetia—the Latin name for Switzerland—until the 1870s. A single large oak tree marks the site of the big house, built between 1835 and 1840 on the downriver part of the property. The

Helvetia not long before its destruction by Hurricane Betsy.
Courtesy St. James Historical Society

raised Creole plantation house was a gracious structure with pairs of identical rooms on either side of a central hallway containing a mahogany staircase. Louis Hymel bought Helvetia in 1908 at the same time he bought Wilton. The properties remained in the family business, Hymel Planting and Manufacturing Company, until 1969, when Ethyl purchased everything but the Hymel store and restaurant on River Road. Hurricane Betsy destroyed the house in 1965—the roof blew into the river; only the steps and foundation remained. The Helvetia Cooperative Sugar Mill was built during the depression with federal aid. A couple of older structures on Helvetia remain.

35.5 The Zen-Noh Grain Elevator is located on the site of Rapidan Plantation. Along this stretch, the river has moved toward the far bank. A settlement of Houma Indians on this site in the early eighteenth century has been documented but was probably only a settlement-in-transit. A mid-eighteenth-century village of the Alibamon Indians was also noted in the area of Central, Helvetia, and White Hall. The Rapidan Plantation house was a modest raised Creole cottage built before 1875.

36.5 White Hall Plantation, also called Maison Blanche, was built in the 1790s as the home of Marius Pons Bringier, patriarch of a large and prosperous River Road family. The house was acknowledged to be the first of the grand River Road plantations, and was also one of the most elaborate and unusual. A French Gothic chateau topped by a balustrade, its exterior was white marble. Marius Bringier was a French émigré who sojourned briefly in the West Indies before arriving in Louisiana in the second half of the eighteenth century. Acquiring five small tracts, he developed them into a plantation on which he grew indigo and cotton. A shrewd businessman who became immensely wealthy, he was also legendary for his hospitality. During the Spanish colonial period, he lavishly entertained the governor and a hundred cavalrymen, refusing compensation. He gave two of his daughters in marriage to intriguing characters: Françoise (Fanny) married Christophe Colomb (Sr.) and Elizabeth (Betsy) married Augustin Tureaud. To each couple Bringier gave a plantation. His son Michel, who lived at the Hermitage, had nine children, of whom one daughter married Duncan Kenner and another married Richard Taylor, son of President Zachary Taylor.

The senior Bringier died in 1820 and left the house to Michel. The younger man found managing both White Hall and the Hermitage too difficult and sold White Hall in 1825 to Wade Hampton. It was bought back in 1847 by Michel's widow, Aglaé, who dedicated the plantation to raising sugarcane. She operated the estate until after the Civil War—although White Hall never recovered from the devastation and grew rice after the surrender. The house itself was shelled during the war and demolished shortly thereafter. A painting of it, made in 1800 by Christophe Colomb, Sr., hung for many years at Tezcuco Plantation. By the 1890s, the property had been subdivided, and the community was called White Hall.

In 1863 Confederate forces set up a battery near here and attacked Union gunboats rounding the point. Taking charge of one of the stricken vessels when the commander was fatally wounded was George Dewey, later to become an admiral and a hero of the Spanish-American War.

36.8 The Union water tower marks the community of Union, immediately upriver from White Hall. The settlement was originally called Pointeville because, according to local residents, a survey of two land grants terminated at a point in the rear. The community was subsequently called Pape Vert and then Ste. Marie du Fleuve (St. Mary of the River, the first name of the present Church of St. Mary). A group of buildings just south of town is one of the best extant collections of Creole cottages; among them are several sugar-mill boilers on short piers.

37.5   Near the large oak was the site of Le Pape Vert, a building that dated from 1849, once owned by a steamboat captain named Jacques Chauvin. Its later incarnations included dance hall, bar, and gambling house. According to local lore, the site was named for a species of bird, the painted bunting, called *pape* in French. The painted buntings indigenous to Louisiana are partly green— *vert*. In antebellum times these little birds were popular as pets, and passengers on the steamboats bought them from locals selling them at the landing. In a burst of marketing genius, someone painted a likeness of a green bunting on a sign at the landing to advertise the sale of the birds, and the place became known as Pape Vert.

The gambling hall closed in 1889 and became a private home; it was then bought by the Thibodeaux family, who ran a store in the front of the building and lived in the back. The building was dismantled in the early 1960s.

> *A 1929 account encourages River Road travelers to visit Union. "Here one finds French spoken almost exclusively. There are quaint shops where sunbonnets are for sale . . . and an interesting plantation house here but it stands surrounded by a mass of cabins and cottages. The river has eaten away the land, the village has been cut in two, but the part which remains is well worth stopping for."*

38.0   St. Mary's Church, in the rural Gothic style, was built in 1875 by the Marist Fathers. It was reestablished from the original Ste. Marie du Fleuve chapel built on White Hall Plantation in 1849. The statuary was transferred from the rectory at Ancient Domain Plantation, which was nearby but has been torn down. In the cemetery are graves from the late nineteenth century.

38.1   On the corner of Legion Lane is a two-story frame store with double galleries.

38.8   The Sunshine Bridge access ramp is built on the former property of Tippecanoe and St. Mary Plantations. Just upriver from the ramp are several quarters cabins of St. Mary, which was owned in 1858 by the Widow H. Boudreau. The house was dismantled in 1974 after being abandoned and derelict.

The Sunshine Bridge opened in 1964, named in honor of Louisiana's "singing governor," Jimmie Davis (1944–1948, 1960–1964), famous for his rendition of "You Are My Sunshine," which he composed. The bridge was yet another Louisiana span known as a "Bridge to Nowhere" because both ramps of the bridge terminated in cane fields for several years before the access roads were added.

39.2 A cement plant occupies the property where Bagatelle Plantation, once owned by the Bringiers, was originally located. A wooded tract behind the road was the site of the house, which has been moved upriver to Plaquemines Point in Iberville Parish. The move was made by river barge, and on moving day, bad weather caused a small outbuilding to topple into the river.

39.3 Star Enterprise is on the site of Union Plantation, built in 1803 as a wedding gift from Marius Bringier to his daughter Elizabeth at her arranged marriage to Augustin Tureaud, a man of the world who enchanted Bringier. After the marriage, Tureaud mended his ways and became a civic leader and respected judge in the parish. The house, attractive and unpretentious, was owned prior to 1877 by E. A. Jacobshagen. It was demolished to make way for the levee in the early 1960s. The small houses constructed with *briqueté entre poteaux* were once guesthouses.

When Union Plantation's post office was moved nearer the church, the downriver village also became known as Union.

39.9 St. James/Ascension Parish line.

A white picket fence and moss-draped oaks announce Tezcuco Plantation, a Classical Revival raised cottage with Italianate influences, built between 1855 and 1861 by Benjamin Trudeau, who married Michel Bringier's daughter Aglaé. The property was a gift from the groom's parents, who lived just next door on Union Plantation. The mysterious name Tezcuco—said to be Aztec for "resting place"—is taken from Lake Tezcuco (or Texcoco) near Mexico City; an island city in the lake was the Aztec capital and the last refuge of Montezuma from Cortez. (Trudeau had fought in the Mexican War.) The house remained in the Bringier family until

1946 and has been privately owned by several different families since then. Gracefully proportioned and relatively small, Tezcuco retains excellent examples of original decorative plaster work, faux bois, and wrought iron. A large, well-preserved cistern stands at the rear of the house.

Outbuildings on the property include the former quarters and overseer's house, along with one quarters cabin from Rapidan Plantation, another from an unidentified property near Darrow, and an 1880 public house from the community of Convent. An eclectic assortment of exhibits includes Civil War artifacts, vintage maps, a stocked commissary, and the River Road African-American Museum and Gallery, focusing on African-American communities in the river parishes. The bearded ghost of a Bringier and an apparition of a woman in a white flowing gown, tentatively identified as Aglaé, have been spotted occasionally, and only in the main house. Open to the public.

40.4 The approximate site of Houmas/Monroe Plantation is marked by a grove of large live oaks within the fence of the DuPont Chemical plant. It was a Bringier family holding until the 1870s. Jacques Amans, a Dutch painter who lived and worked in New Orleans from 1837 to 1856, visited Houmas/Monroe in 1843 to paint the family's portraits. On Persac's map, this important plantation was noteworthy for its two sugarhouses and extensive property.

40.5 DuPont Chemical may be the site of Orange Grove Plantation, a large holding owned by J. D. Igana, according to Persac.

41.0 The Burnside Terminal, a dry bulk storage and loading facility of Ormet, is on property that was part of the Donaldson, Conway, and Clark plantations, owned in the mid-nineteenth century by General Wade Hampton and John Smith Preston, who also owned Houmas House. Historians credit Daniel Clark with being the first to suggest that the United States purchase the Louisiana Territory; on a less positive note, Clark is the man who wounded Governor W. C. C. Claiborne in a duel at Fort Manchac in 1807. The Clark Plantation house burned in 1913, the result of lightning. Revere purchased the property in 1956. The Burnside Terminal is expansive, and its yard is often a rainbow of mounds of minerals in transit.

41.6 Junction La. 942/44 lies in what was the community of Burnside, named for John Burnside, an Irish immigrant and local sugar prince. The town was clustered around this intersection, on a site once occupied by Houma Indians. It had a railroad station and post office and boasted one of the last mule-drawn streetcars in the state; the vehicle transported people to the Burnside–Donaldsonville ferry (the ferry ramp remains on the levee). In approximately 1956, Olin Metals began buying the properties parcel by parcel. Some residents moved with their houses elsewhere, others simply moved. Little remains of the small town that was Burnside. The River Road continues as La. 942.

Side trip: Several "recycled" buildings can be found a mile north on La. 44 at the Cabin Restaurant, which incorporates quarters buildings from Helvetia, Welham, and Monroe Plantations. More salvaged vernacular buildings are at the Ascension Parish Tourist Center and Cajun Village, right on La. 22 to La. 70. The complex includes an early-twentieth-century cypress cabin from Darrow, the Schexnaydre House (*circa* 1840s) from Donaldsonville, a barber shop and mid-nineteenth-century home from Convent, an Acadian-style building from the MBC Plantation (owned by Michel B. Cantrelle) in St. James Parish, a kitchen from an early-nineteenth-century Dutchtown home, and the Acadian-style, bousillage-walled Gaudet House, moved from Lutcher.

42.3 The land on which Houmas House is situated belonged to the Houma Indians, who settled here *circa* 1709–1718. They established a "grand village" that extended from the future community of Burnside to a point just upriver from Houmas House and more than a mile inland from the river. Archaeologists have uncovered Indian and European trade artifacts here. Alexandre Latil and Maurice Conway purchased property from Chief Calabe of the Houmas in 1776, and Latil built a small four-room house that, although modified, still exists. Some Houmas resided in the area until about 1784.

In 1812 General Wade Hampton, the American Revolutionary hero, who owned property across the river at Point Houmas, bought the additional tract from Daniel Clark. Hampton, Virginia born, was a resident of South Carolina and returned there after service in the War of 1812, but he understood the economic value of holding prime sugarcane acreage. When Hampton's son-in-law,

John Smith Preston, came from South Carolina to live and manage the landholdings, he required a more comfortable residence and had the ornate Classical Revival mansion built in 1840. It was Preston who named the place Houmas House.

In 1858 the plantation home and 12,000 acres were sold to John Burnside for $1 million. Burnside vastly expanded the plantation to include four large brick sugarhouses, boiling houses, laboratories, crystallizing sheds, and other outbuildings, as well as an extensive quarters area with gardens. He also acquired Monroe, Orange Grove, Riverton, New Hope, and several other plantations. Before the Civil War, John Burnside was acknowledged as the richest of all planters, and the war seems not to have diminished his standing because, while his southern neighbors were faring badly, he declared his immunity to Federal control under his rights as a British citizen. Houmas House was spared occupation or damage by Union forces. When Burnside died in 1881, his properties were all bequeathed to Oliver Beirne, the son of a former business partner of Burnside's. Beirne, living in South Carolina and uninterested in Louisiana, passed the properties to his nephew, William Porcher Miles, the president of South Carolina College. Miles studied Valcour Aime's diary and learned the economics of sugar planting. He eventually owned not only Houmas House, but also Valcour Aime, New Hope, Armant, and others.

After Miles's death in 1899, most of Burnside's original landholdings were sold. The house fell into disrepair until its purchase in 1940 by Dr. George Crozat. Crozat restored Houmas House to its 1840 grandeur, furnishing the home to reflect that period although adapting it for contemporary comfort. In the gardens are Preston's original garçonnières, but because of levee relocations, Houmas House has lost most of its oak allée and front landscape.

William Howard Russell, an English traveler, visited Houmas House in 1860: "A quarter of an hour brought our skiff from Donaldsonville to the levee on the other side. I ascended the bank and across the road, directly in front, appeared a carriage gateway and wickets of wood, painted white, in a line of park palings of the same material which extended up and down the road far as the eye could see and guarded widespread fields of maize and sugarcane. An avenue lined with trees with branches close set, drooping and overarching a

*walk paved with red brick, led to the house, the porch of
which was visible at the extremity of the lawn with clustering
flowers, rose, jessamine, and creepers clinging to the pillars,
supporting the verandah. The view from the belevedere on the
roof was one of the most striking of its kind in the world."
Visiting for several days, Russell also reveals that one June
morning he was awakened "to a bath of Mississippi water
with huge lumps of ice in it," to which his servant "recommended a mint-julep as an adjunct."*

42.6 River Cement occupies a piece of property reputed to have
an Indian burial ground on it.

43.2 Riverton Plantation was owned in the mid-nineteenth century
by Colonel J. L. Manning, according to Persac. (A relation by marriage of Wade Hampton, John L. Manning had acquired Point
Houmas Plantation, across the river, in 1845.) Riverton was subsequently bought by John Burnside and became one of the holdings
of Oliver Beirne and William Porcher Miles. The big house was
built several hundred yards from the river but was eventually much
closer because of river encroachment and levee work. When the
house was demolished in the 1960s, the owners of L'Hermitage
salvaged much of its millwork, flooring, and bricks.

43.4 Marchand School Road marks the location of the mid-nineteenth-century J. B. Marchand Plantation and of Hillaryville, a
black settlement established on property John Burnside acquired
from Marchand. After emancipation, former slaves of Burnside's,
who had arrived with him from Virginia in 1858, lived here under
the leadership of Hillary Rice, a preacher and politician. The community persisted through the time that the Miles family ran the
former Burnside properties, but after the Houmas Central sugar
factory closed, many residents drifted away.

44.2 Bocage Plantation (the English translation is "Shady Retreat") is a suitably gracious name for a still-elegant setting. It was
built in 1801 as a raised Creole cottage by Marius Bringier, who
gave it as a wedding present to his daughter Françoise, called
Fanny, and her groom, Christophe Colomb. Colomb, an apparently
destitute Parisian who was said to trace his ancestry to Christopher
Columbus, came to Louisiana to escape the French Revolution. Bocage was completely remodeled in 1837, probably by James Dakin,

in the Classical Revival style and is now a square brick-and-wood mansion with a central hallway. At one time a stairway joined the lower and upper galleries, and on close examination the proportion of lower to upper story resembles that of a Creole house—the first floor ceiling was not raised. Colomb was an artist, poet, and socialite; it was Mme Colomb who managed the plantation with the help of her overseer. (It was not uncommon for women along the River Road to own property, build sugar mills, and purchase and sell slaves as early as the French colonial period when official policy allowed this.) A sister of Dr. Crozat, rescuer of Houmas House, restored Bocage.

St. Elmo Road denotes the community of St. Elmo, which was never developed as planned on the property of L'Hermitage. This land formation is Sugar House Point, also called Bringier Point. Early-to-mid-nineteenth century maps indicated a settlement here simply called Bringier, indicating the prominence of that family.

45.1 In 1804, Marius Bringier bought this property as an indigo plantation and made his son Michel—then fifteen years old—its manager. Marius, a clever man, taught the teenager responsibility by charging him with the well-being of land, slaves, and crop and paying him with a percentage of the profit. On the occasion of his marriage in 1812, Michel received the property as a wedding present, and construction of the house began. He later named the mansion L'Hermitage after the Tennessee home of Andrew Jackson, under whom Michel served in the Battle of New Orleans. Jackson, in fact, visited here in 1820 with his wife.

L'Hermitage is considered the oldest extant Classical Revival home in Louisiana, and some experts regard it as a nearly perfect example of the vernacular Louisiana form. The gallery railings are wood, not iron. There is a central hallway and an interior staircase, as well as one on the back gallery. The original portion of the house was built of *briqueté entre poteaux*. The Doric columns were added during an extensive remodeling in 1840.

> *According to an account by her granddaughter, the most festive occasion celebrated in the house was Mme Bringier's feast day, when friends and neighbors would gather in the parlor bearing small gifts of candy and flowers. Two servants waited discreetly upstairs to sprinkle visiting ladies with rose-*

*water to refresh them; the gentlemen gathered in a downstairs
room for stronger libation. In Madame's honor, a roast capon
was always served.*

After the 1870s, the house was poorly maintained by absentee
landlords. In 1911 plans were made to subdivide the property into
a small town called St. Elmo, but no roads were laid and nothing
was built. The mansion was converted to a boardinghouse for people from New Orleans visiting the property. Eventually, however,
neglect reduced the property to such an unfortunate condition that
it was used as a ruin in the movie *The Long, Hot Summer*. Then,
in 1959, L'Hermitage was purchased by new owners. What is now
visible from the road is the result of a long and painstaking restoration. Period buildings have been rescued from other plantations
in the area and moved to the property.

    *The rescue of L'Hermitage as told by its owners (whose
wish for privacy I will honor by not naming them) exemplifies
the preservation story along the River Road: "It hadn't been
lived in well. The plantation was owned by absentee landlords
since the 1870s and uninhabited since the 1940s. When we
first saw it [in 1959], it was surrounded by a fence just beyond
the columns to keep the cows out and within the fence the
weeds and shrubs had grown two stories tall. It was a sad
sight—holes in the roof, a gaping hole through the dining
room wall, missing mantels, rotting wood, gallery railings
snaggle-toothed . . . but it was tempting—a manageable size
and structurally sound and no one told us what an enterprise
it would be."*

    *For thirty years, they worked to restore and preserve the
house. Under cement that had been slabbed on the front gallery, they discovered the original pattern of the brick, facili-
tating restoration. Where elements were missing—shutter
slats, flooring, mantels, bricks—they reclaimed substitutes
from nearby plantations relegated to demolition—Armant,
Helvetia, and Riverton. This approach enabled them to create
a faithful restoration of L'Hermitage, as well as to transplant
something of the spirit of other mansions no longer standing.
And sheer luck enabled the family to acquire an irreplaceable
collection of Bringier papers and records from 1718 to the*

1920s. An alert relative intercepted the documents as they were in the process of being thrown in the garbage and passed them along to the plantation's owners.

Tales are told about the place. In 1920 or so, a large oak on the property was uprooted by a storm, and an elaborately carved chest filled with family jewels and silver was found in the trunk, purportedly hidden during the Civil War by a slave. But the chest mysteriously disappeared and was never recovered. And once, when a pond on the land was drained, on the bottom rested a sword in a rusting sheath with the blade inscribed "Zachary Taylor," perhaps because one of Michel Bringier's daughters married Taylor's son, Richard.

46.0 In this area was property owned by Trasimond Landry and Ben LeBlanc, according to Persac. Landry was a sugar planter who owned several Ascension Parish properties here and across the river from the 1820s until after the Civil War, when he lost most of his holdings. During the war, he served as a state militia officer even though he was in his mid-seventies when the conflict began.

46.7 Junction La. 22. The community of Darrow was first planned by Benejah Gibson and laid out in 1884 as Darrowville, named for a large landholding family. The village included 164 town lots and a steam-ferry landing to connect the settlement with the thriving west-bank town of Donaldsonville. Several blocks of the original town front of Darrow were destroyed when the levee was set back in 1932. The ferry access ramp is at the intersection. The Donaldsonville ferry was moved from Burnside to Darrow. Just across the river is the site of Fort Butler, a Union Army bastion just outside of Donaldsonville.

From the publication L'Ami des Lois, November 3, 1814: "For sale—plantation on the left bank of the Mississippi opposite Donaldson[ville] containing 3 arpents and 6 toises in front, by the usual depth, of the first rate of land. On the premises there is a dwelling house containing 4 apartments, gallery and office; also, a granary, fother-house, stable, kitchen, hen and pigeon houses, well, brick oven, & c. all entirely new and in good repair."

47.9 This is Eighty-One Mile Point, eighty-one miles above the

Canal Street locus once used as the measuring point from which upriver land formations were named in river miles. (In modern river miles, however, Eighty-One Mile Point is 178 AHP.)

According to Persac, Eighty-One Mile Point was divided into many small properties, with only two small plantations, Trasimond Landry's Stensbury Plantation and J. B. Futch's tract, which was located on the tip of the point and included a woodyard. At the turn of the century, this area was a continuous line of small Creole or Acadian cottages on lots one arpent wide and twenty arpents deep.

During the 1927 flood, the levees along this portion of the river were sandbagged and closely guarded by armed men seeking to prevent subversive activity by west-bank citizens, who were suspected of planning to dynamite the east-bank levee in order to protect the Donaldsonville side. Whether the plot was defused or never actually existed is still in question.

50.4 Behind the farthest-downriver house in this cluster of vernacular frame buildings of undistinguished age is a large wood barrel cistern.

> *Cisterns were used for collecting rainwater, a vital function because groundwater in this area was not accessible to wells. The large, barrel-shaped storage units were fashioned from cypress boards, each individually shaped to a special curve. The boards were attached to a round base and held tight by galvanized bands to prevent leakage. The rain that fell onto the roof of the house was diverted through gutters into the cistern. As the cistern filled, the cypress swelled to complete the watertight fit. The top of the cistern was screened to keep mosquitoes from nesting. As a double protection, a rag was often placed in the cistern's faucet to filter foreign objects from the drawn water. In later years, pipes connected the cistern directly to kitchen and bathroom plumbing. Cisterns were often built on tall bases to raise them close to the water coming off the roof of one-and-a-half and two-story houses. Cisterns varied in size, and large plantations had more than one. The capacity of a barrel seven feet in diameter—not the largest—was 2,700 gallons.*
>
> *Even in rainy south Louisiana, however, cistern water was occasionally inadequate. According to the memoir of a local*

woman, during dry spells water was hauled from the river in barrels. "After the mud settled to the bottom . . . then we could use it."

In this area along the inside of the levee is the Marchand Revetment, where in 1983 the last serious revetment failure and levee slide along this portion of the River Road occurred. The river undermined the revetment and gouged a hole into the levee. A portion of the levee was sloughed off, but the damage was discovered and repaired without any flooding.

51.1 On the left side of the road is the Inger Oil site, one of the worst hazardous waste sites in the state. Cleanup is in progress. Along the right side of the road is the Darrow Oil Field.

51.4 This tree-shaded field is the former site of Bowden Plantation, once a significant tract bought in 1858 from H. B. Trist by Duncan Kenner, owner of Ashland Plantation. The property had twenty-four arpents of frontage and adjoined the downriver boundary of Ashland. Bowden was a very productive sugar plantation and one of the first to adopt the Rillieux multiple-effect process for sugar milling.

The community of Belle Helene was the post village for the area. In 1911 the several plantations located here, owned by the Belle Helene Planting and Manufacturing Company, were subdivided into small farms. A large mercantile store here closed in 1915; a brickyard and cotton gin operated here.

The low, swampy area to the right of the road is said to be the result of caving irrigation ditches. Rice was planted at Ashland after the Civil War; irrigation and drainage ditches were fed by steam-powered pumps.

52.1 On the upriver corner of Ashland Road is Ashland/Belle Helene Plantation house, currently the property of Shell Oil and not open to the public. This elegant house, its slave quarters, and its sugar mill were erected between 1838 and 1841 on property that was originally part of Linwood Plantation, just upriver and jointly owned by Theophilus Minor and William Kenner. The epitome of Classical Revival architecture, Ashland was designed by James Gallier or James Dakin for William Kenner's son, Duncan, who named it after Henry Clay's home. Duncan Kenner, elevated socially by his marriage to a Bringier daughter, became one of the wealthiest planters of the antebellum period, and the house ably reflected his stolidity and success. Ashland stands symmetrically columned on four sides, with oak allées at the rear that once led to numerous outbuildings. Formal gardens graced the approach from the river, and a racetrack on the rear grounds provided a site for Duncan Kenner to run his stable of fine horses (he is credited with introducing thoroughbred horse racing to the River Road, and possibly to Louisiana). Kenner was active in regional politics, a state legislator, and a delegate to the provisional Confederate Congress in 1861 in Montgomery. During the Civil War, Federal troops occupied Ashland for four days and took or destroyed almost everything. Jefferson Davis appointed Kenner as a Confederate minister plenipotentiary to Europe in 1865 in a last, desperate hope of winning foreign recognition of the Confederacy. After the war, Kenner's property was confiscated by the United States government, but eventually he was able to reclaim it and regain much of his fortune.

> *From a memoir by Duncan Kenner's daughter, Rosella Kenner Brent: "My father had been riding over the fields with Mr. Graves and a neighbor, Mr. Henry Doyal . . . the three rode towards the river gate [to investigate] a steamboat at the landing. . . . They met a Negro who was coming rapidly towards them and he called out 'Mars Duncan, for God's sake don't go to the river. That boat is full of soldiers and they is all landing.' My father, realizing that it was not only unsafe to proceed further but also to remain on the place, hurriedly gave Mr. Graves a few instructions, to go to my mother and tell her he had gone to Stephen Minor's and then he turned his horse and attempted to ride away [but the horse balked]. Mr. Doyal sprang to the ground saying 'Mr. Kenner, take my horse, he will go and fast.' " Kenner eventually escaped to the still-Confederate interior of the state.*

In 1881, Duncan Kenner and his son-in-law Joseph Brent combined crops; Brent had purchased the property just downriver from Bowden and subsequently took over managing Ashland and Bowden. In 1887 a steam-powered rice mill replaced Ashland's sugar-processing equipment. In 1889 Ashland was purchased by a German immigrant, John Reuss, a sugar planter and large landholder with many properties on the west bank. His Belle Helene Planting

Company was named for his granddaughter, and he renamed the plantation Belle Helene as well. Incorporating both the Ashland and Bowden properties, the tract was subdivided by the early 1920s, and the house has been mostly uninhabited since. Seven movies— among them *Band of Angels, The Beguiled, The Autobiography of Miss Jane Pittman,* a version of *The Long, Hot Summer,* and *Fletch Lives*—have been shot here, as well as several music videos. Prior to its sale to Shell, the home was open for tours as either a work-in-progress or a deconstruction project—there were semifurnished rooms, unfurnished rooms, and a dirt-floored parlor, the original wood floor never having been restored.

A small cypress cabin in a pocket swamp faces the River Road. This structure is thought to be left from the rice irrigation system.

53.0 BASF Corporation is located on three plantation properties, the farthest-downriver of which was Linwood. A grove of large live oaks marks the probable site of the Linwood Plantation house. It was part of the holdings of Duncan Kenner's father, William, after whose death it became the property of Duncan's younger brother, George. The house, a contemporary of Ashland, was set back from the road about half a mile. It was imposing, designed by James Gallier to resemble an Italian villa, with frescoed walls and ceilings reproducing those of the Brenta Villas in Italy and a porte cochère with vaulted ceiling.

> *Author Eliza Ripley, describing a trip to Linwood in 1849, was duly impressed: "The culmination of landscape wall paper must have been reached in the Minor plantation dwelling. . . . The hall was broad and long, adorned with real jungle scenes from India. A great tiger jumped out of dense thickets . . . tall trees reached to the ceiling with gaudy striped boa-constrictors wound around their trunks; hissing snakes peered out of the jungles; birds of gay plumage . . . almost out of sight in the greenery; monkeys swung from limb to limb. To cap the climax, right close to the steps one had to mount to the story above was a lair of ferocious lions."*

During the Civil War, the house was raided by Union soldiers. The property remained in the family for seventy-five years. It was abandoned in 1900. The mansion was considered beyond restora-

Linwood, derelict, in a WPA photograph taken shortly before the house's demolition in 1939.
Courtesy State Library of Louisiana

tion and demolished in 1939 by new owners who turned the property into a stock farm.

53.4 Cottage Farm Drive into the BASF plant is the site of Cottage Farm Plantation. A small cemetery remains on the property. BASF was the first chemical plant to locate in the Geismar area.

54.0 Rubicon, Inc. (Liquid Carbonic) is on the site of Doyal/ Mount Houmas Plantation, originally called Doyal's Plantation and owned by Henry R. Doyal. In 1852 Doyal converted his sugar mill to multiple-effect processing and milled the cane from neighboring properties such as Linwood, Waterloo, and his own Hard Times (Doyal, however, should not be confused with Dr. Henry A. Doyle, who owned Eureka Plantation on the west bank). He established New River Landing and Road to serve his sugar mill and the adjacent properties; the road site has become the approximate route of La. 73. The plantation was sold after the Civil War. By 1896, it was called Mount Houmas and was owned by J. Crosley.

During the war, Doyal was a captain in the Confederate army and was regarded as a guerrilla by the Union army because of his tactics. His plantation was also the scene of a battle—a skirmish, really—fought in August of 1864. Some two hundred members of the 11th New York Cavalry encamped there were surrounded by a Confederate force; somewhat more than half of the northerners fought their way clear, but the rest were captured.

The patch of woods is thought to be the relic site of a crevasse that inundated this area in the 1850s.

54.5 Junction La. 73. The town of Geismar was formerly called New River, named for a distributary of the Mississippi that joined the river here (it was cut off when levees were constructed in the 1820s). Iberville noted a Bayougoula village near New River in 1699; Europeans had settled the area by 1736. A public road ran from New River Landing on the Mississippi to Sorrento inland—the only open road from the interior to the river as late as the 1890s. The road formed the boundary between Henry Doyal's Mount Houmas property and the upriver property of W. J. Minor called Waterloo. In 1879 Louis Geismar established a general store on the levee at New River Landing. After the business prospered and the railroad built a depot at the turn of the century, the station was called Geismar. During the summer of 1893, this area was flooded by the Rescue crevasse on Rescue Plantation, just upriver across the parish line in Iberville Parish. Just off River Road on La. 73 are several vintage buildings, including an old general store and a Creole cottage. The Geismar area is now a petrochemical center.

> *"New River Post office is on the left bank of the river, eight miles above Donaldsonville and 90 miles from New Orleans. At New River, there is a Presbyterian Church. . . . The total population [of Ascension Parish] is between fourteen and fifteen thousand, of whom about seven thousand are slaves."* J. W. Dorr, 1860.

55.5 From the Enron location up to the Iberville Parish line were located several plantation tracts. In Persac's time, they were Waterloo, S. & R. Tillotson (where New River College and the post office were located), and Henry Doyal's Hard Times. By 1879, Waterloo remained, but J. Crosley & Son owned the Tillotson and Hard Times properties, which they renamed, respectively, Riverside and Southwood Plantations.

56.4 Allied Signal purchased part of Southwood Plantation in the early 1960s. Southwood, formerly Hard Times, had consisted of a big house, tenant cabins, barns and outbuildings, a refinery, and a chapel or church, but after a (probably) severe cutbank of the river at the turn of the twentieth century, little remained of the plantation community.

56.9 Ascension/Iberville Parish line and Junction La. 3115. In this area were Arizona Plantation, five and a half arpents of frontage, bought in 1849 by W. R. Boote from Joachim Blanchard, and Maryland Plantation, originally claimed *circa* 1812 by a family named Richard, who later sold it to René Arnous. A large wood-yard is shown on Persac's map. The property was first noted as Maryland Plantation in 1876. Although it had previously been a sugar estate, in the early twentieth century cotton was its crop. By 1933 the tract had been subdivided.

57.5 The Cosmar/FINA plant complex is located on the site of Rescue Plantation. The 1893 crevasse here devastated a large area.

59.2 The Carville Grocery and Post Office is a landmark in the little community of Carville. The town was originally named Island because of the Bayou Goula Towhead, a midriver sandbar-island that could be seen on the Carville–Bayou Goula ferry run. The town was renamed in 1908 for a prominent local family who had been in the area since 1868. The post office once received all mail for Hansen's Disease Center (in those days it was called a "leprosarium") just upriver—although the letters were usually addressed to Point Clair, Louisiana, to hide the identity of their destination.

A right turn follows La. 75, which cuts across the top of Point Clair, one of east Iberville's two prominent river points, and joins the levee farther upriver. After visiting the Gillis Long Hansen's Disease Center, return to this point to continue the mileage-coordinated route, which follows La. 75.

Side trip: La. 141 continues around the tip of Point Clair. The first settlers, arriving in 1774, were Acadians sent by the Spanish to keep an eye on the English upriver. The settlers received homesteads of six arpents frontage. The Carville–White Castle toll ferry runs a limited schedule. A U.S. Department of Justice minimum security facility is just across the road from the ferry landing and next door to the Gillis W. Long Hansen's Disease Center, the world-famous federal institution for research on and treatment of Hansen's disease, formerly called leprosy.

The property is known as Indian Camp Plantation and was an agglomeration of small Acadian homesteads bought by Robert Camp. The name Indian Camp is thought to have double reference: the site once held a Houma village, and the house remained in the Camp family until the latter part of the nineteenth century. (Camp himself, however, called the place "Woodlawn.") Robert Camp had a reputation as a flamboyant businessman and suffered setbacks accordingly, including the sale of this estate, which he later repurchased. In 1859 he hired the famed New Orleans architect Henry Howard to design the raised brick Italianate mansion that is now considered one of Howard's finest efforts. It has been surmised that Camp was impressed with Howard's work on John Randolph's magnificent Nottoway.

Camp lost his property for the final time in 1874, and Woodlawn became a tenant farm under absentee ownership. It was abandoned and in disrepair in the late nineteenth century, when a neighbor informed the board of control for the Louisiana Leper Home in New Orleans that the property could be leased. Leprosy, one of the oldest documented human diseases, was dreaded and much misunderstood. The first patients—five men and two women—were dispatched here from New Orleans in November 1894. Because neither steamboats nor trains would accept them as passengers, they were sent by coal barge at night. They were housed in the former slave cabins, which were, according to contemporary reports, in better condition than the main house. Two rooms in the main house were used for administrative offices.

The Daughters of Charity of St. Vincent de Paul came to provide nursing services in 1896 and have ministered at Carville, as the facility came to be known, ever since. By the turn of the century, a kitchen and dining hall had been added, and in 1905 an innovative system of covered walkways was constructed between buildings. In 1921 the United States Public Health Service assumed control of the center.

Carville was a contained community with its own power plant, fire department, dairy, newspaper, and entertainment for residents. Patients were feared—the disease was thought to be highly contagious (it is not), and the prejudice and social stigma that followed those afflicted was astonishing. Some patients had been abandoned or put out by their families. Except for visits home, patients were not allowed beyond the gates. In 1941, the use of sulfones—the first effective drugs for controlling the disease—was pioneered here, a medical breakthrough that gained universal acclaim through the book and movie *Miracle at Carville*. The drugs stopped the spread of the disease and cleared up the existing cutaneous nodules and blotches. Nevertheless, until a more progressive administrator took charge at the facility in 1956, patients with Hansen's were not allowed to marry and their money and outgoing mail were bathed in alcohol.

In large part because of work done at the Carville facility, it is now known that Hansen's disease, which is caused by a bacterium similar to the one that causes tuberculosis, infects only those who have a genetic susceptibility—less than 10 percent of the population (approximately 2.4 million individuals worldwide carry the bacterium). One unusual feature of research on the disease over the last two decades is the use of armadillos as test animals. They are ideally suited to this purpose not only because the Hansen's bacterium can be grown in them, but also because their offspring are born in identical, same-sex quadruplets.

Today, the main house serves as the administration center for the world's largest hospital and research center for Hansen's disease. The center also is credited with important research on tuberculosis and diabetes. Admission to the hospital is voluntary. Tours offer a glimpse of this facility, which celebrated its centennial in 1994, relishing the changes that one hundred years have brought. Open to the public.

> *From patients:*
> *"When I came [to the hospital] in 1927, I left my family and everything I loved. . . . We changed our name to protect our family—you didn't want to hurt them."*
> *"When I arrived at Carville in 1939, it was not like a hospital—it was more like a prison."*

Upriver from the hospital, a rough, one-lane gravel road circumscribes Point Clair and crosses part of the Hunt Correctional Institute property. This is rangeland, and frequent cattleguards stud the roadway.

A Spanish land grant on Point Clair dates from 1775, when an

Acadian recorded as Francisco Landry settled there with "3 slaves, 12 cattle, 3 horses, 12 hogs, and 20 fowl." Near the tip of Point Clair was Point Clair Plantation. A two-story home, along with cabins and other outbuildings, was purchased in 1878 by a freed slave, Louis Smith, possibly from his former owner, Louis Seginaud. Smith named his place Small Hope. In the late nineteenth century, the Haase family opened a general store on property adjacent to Small Hope. The area became known as Haaseville after the turn of the century when members of the family moved here from Plaquemine, on the west bank. Haase's home still stands. Louis Smith died in 1906. The ruins of a brick chimney and a bell-shaped domed cistern are all that remain of Small Hope.

On the upriver side of the point was Ophelia Plantation, originally a Spanish land grant deeded in 1775 to Joseph Landry. The property had a succession of owners, including René Arnous and Robert Camp, who both owned eighteen arpents' frontage as Sawmill Plantation. In 1877 Miss Ophelia Bruslé purchased the property and it became part of Ophelia Plantation, a productive rice farm. Upriver from Ophelia was Lorrett Plantation, also known as Virginia Plantation, another possession of René Arnous in 1858. Arnous lost Virginia after the Civil War and was succeeded by various owners. The plantation outbuildings are located on what is now the other side of the levee or in the river.

61.0 La. 75 rejoins the levee.

61.9 Ciba Geigy is on the site of Evergreen Plantation, first owned in the late eighteenth century by Oliver Blanchard. A two-story frame Classical Revival mansion with double galleries, a plastered second-floor facade, and a gabled roof supported by fluted Doric columns was built *circa* 1840 by Jeremiah Pritchard. The house was razed in 1955.

Town of St. Gabriel. Indian settlements dating from the late Coles Creek or early Plaquemine period were documented in this area with the discovery of two mounds and a historic cemetery; however, nothing is left of these today. St. Gabriel was settled in 1767 by Acadians. A Spanish fort was established here in 1765 to protect the Isle of Orleans; it existed until 1803.

62.5 St. Gabriel Catholic Church is regarded as the oldest extant church in the Louisiana Purchase territory. Originally called

Church of the Iberville Coast, it was built by the Acadians in 1769 on a Spanish land grant that had first been made in 1733 to the Parish Church of Manchac. The building was moved four times as new levees were constructed—most recently in 1928—and the church lost some of its cemetery to the river. The original construction was in the Creole style; the current Victorian renovation, completed in 1870, reflects a Gothic simplicity with arched windows, door, and transom. The classical influence is more apparent on the interior. Long heart-of-pine posts support the belfry and steeple, and architectural analysis has revealed the original cypress framing in the attic and floor. The graves in the cemetery include a scattering of older ones, many with French inscriptions. Among the tombstones is that of architect Charles Dakin, who with his brother James and partner James Gallier defined Classical Revival architecture in south Louisiana in the mid-nineteenth century. Charles Dakin was in charge of the partnership's office in Mobile, Alabama. It is speculated that he was here to work on the Bringier houses in Ascension Parish, and died of yellow fever. He was twenty-eight.

The rectory steps and a walkway from rectory to the church are paved with unclaimed tombstones from the old cemetery that was abandoned when the levee was moved. The original church bell, donated by the Spanish monarchy, is in the rear of the modern church property.

62.7 On the upriver corner of the La. 74 junction is the St. Gabriel Store. The rambling, two-story, turn-of-the-century frame building once housed a general store; it is now a deli-grocery. The site is thought to be that of St. Gabriel Plantation, first documented in 1777 and created from land granted to the church—a large tract deemed excessive by the parishioners.

62.8 Monticello Street marks the location of Monticello Plantation, now part of the Louisiana State University Agricultural Center's St. Gabriel research station, specializing in sugarcane research. On the downriver corner is Home Place, a raised plantation-style cottage that locals say may have been built in the late 1770s, although documentation is not available. The construction is of *briqueté entre poteaux*. The home was once an elegant local landmark boasting a grand dining room large enough to accommodate two expansive tables. The house has been moved to accommodate the levee. The nineteenth- and early-twentieth-century owners were legendary for their hospitality, utilizing the ground floor for visitors, including visiting clergy who sometimes stayed for months.

63.4 Opposite the LSU research station property is a public access path to the levee, where a cement revetment is visible on the batture side. This general location is the site of Oakley Plantation, established by Tennesseean Edward Moore in 1830 and enlarged by subsequent owners. After the 1927 flood, the levee was moved back and the house, standing on what is now Ag Center Road, was destroyed. The land became part of the St. Gabriel Women's Penitentiary before its current ownership by LSU.

64.0 Willow Glen power station is located on the site of Willow Glen Plantation, listed on the 1883 Dickinson map as the property of Amedée Levert. The heirs of subsequent owners sold the site in 1958 to Gulf States Utilities, which named the power plant for the former sugar plantation.

64.3 Set back from the road are several large tanks and two large oak trees on the site of Avery Plantation, owned in Persac's time by W. H. Avery.

64.6 At Bayou Paul Road is the rustic M. Barthel Store (*circa* 1880), although locals call it the J. A. Barthel Store. The swayback plank porch leads to a dim interior captured for its atmosphere in numerous commercials and films. Although the store no longer stocks general merchandise—buckets, boots, moss, and such—the straightforward display of foodstuffs and sundries on unadorned shelving preserves the flavor of a River Road general store where the proprietor greets everyone by name and business is still done the old-fashioned way.

Next door are several vintage raised cottages; one is the original Barthel home, making the shopkeeper always handy to the shop. Behind the third is a large and well-used cistern.

Nearby stands a raised Creole cottage in the traditional style, its protected front facade painted and the three exposed facades weathering naturally.

65.0 Another local commercial landmark is J. J. Laplace's store and home—a turn-of-the-century country store and River Road cottage.

65.4 Here is the property line of the former Golden Gate Plantation. In the field next door, behind the relic barn, once stood the sugarhouse. Golden Gate syrup, sold in gold cans, was a local favorite. The Golden Gate Plantation property extended across Plaquemine Point.

66.1 The original Lorrett house is a raised Acadian cottage with the attached kitchen still visible on the rear of the house.

66.2 This raised Creole cottage has been renovated and enlarged after being moved from its original site on Golden Gate Plantation.

66.4 La. 327 (Gummers Lane) cuts across Plaquemine Point. In the field on the upriver side of La. 327 is the site of Granada Plantation, the largest single landholding in the area, which extended across Plaquemine Point with frontage on both sides. Ownership of this tract can be traced back to Etienne Comeau, a descendant of the original eighteenth-century Acadian settlers in the area.

A weathered barn and oak trees mark the site where the old Granada Plantation home sat. The house has been moved north of Baton Rouge. On Persac's map, Plaquemine Point was almost bisected by Bayou Paul, which divided properties into small parcels fronting the river along the bottom of the point backing up against small parcels fronting the river along the top of the point.

67.9 Town of Sunshine. Granada Plantation was identified as Forlorn Hope when it was purchased in 1845. The local post office was also called Forlorn Hope. In approximately 1885, the plantation was renamed Granada and the plantation manager applied to change the name of the post office. Congressman Edward Gay had the name changed to the opposite of Forlorn Hope—Sunshine. Thus was the community of Sunshine, strung along this area, named.

68.9 The field with the looming television transmission tower set afar is the site of Lucky Plantation. The mid-nineteenth-century structure is thought to be the Lucky Plantation overseer's house. Note the traditional weathering exterior and painted front facade. The Lucky property also extended across the road. According to local lore, the Lucky big house was blown up by a cannonball during the Civil War.

69.7 Junction La. 991; Sunshine–Plaquemine ferry landing. La. 75 crosses the river on the ferry. La. 991 continues as the River Road.

Manchac Plantation as depicted by Persac from a viewpoint atop the levee.
Courtesy State Library of Louisiana

70.7 This is the approximate tip of Plaquemine Point. A short distance upriver is a shell road marking the old ferry landing. The landing was moved downriver because of bank cave-ins.

73.4 Set far back from the road to ensure privacy is Bagatelle, built in 1841 by Benjamin Tureaud for his daughter. The home, along with two cabins, two small outbuildings, and a cistern, was moved by barge in 1977 from just below Burnside. The Classical Revival cottage is reputed to have had original wall frescoes painted by John James Audubon, who visited there, but they supposedly were destroyed when the house was moved (prior to the 1977 move) to avoid river encroachment. One of the outbuildings can be seen from the road.

75.7 Junction La. 327. Turn left.

76.3 A dark treeline of cypresses and willows at the far end of the open field denotes the upriver line of Manchac Plantation. No original outbuildings remain from the plantation, but the waterway, Bayou Manchac, was a significant artery during the colonial period. Across the field the stacks of Willow Glen—far on the other side of Plaquemine Point—are visible.

76.4 Iberville/East Baton Rouge Parish line. It is difficult to imagine that the barely noticeable Bayou Manchac was once not only an important waterway, but also an international boundary. The bayou was called *ascantia* ("canebrake") by the Bayougoulas, *manchac* ("rear entrance") by the Choctaws, and *rivière Iberville* by the early French. The name Manchac finally won out during the Spanish era. The Bayougoulas introduced Iberville and his party to the stream in 1699 as a shortcut to Lake Maurepas and thence (by way of a channel now known as Pass Manchac) to Lake Pontchartrain and the Gulf of Mexico.

> From Iberville's journal: *"Five leagues and a half from our last stop for the night we came on the right side of the river to a little stream . . . the dividing line between the Ouma's hunting ground and the Bayogoulda's. On the bank are many huts roofed with palmettoes and a maypole with no limbs, painted red, several fish heads and bear bones being tied to it as a sacrifice."*

After Bienville established the New Orleans settlement, Bayou Manchac became part of the northern boundary of the Isle of Orleans (defined by the waters of the Mississippi River on the west, the Gulf of Mexico on the south, and the Lakes Maurepas and Pontchartrain on the east.) When England gained control of West Florida, the British established a small settlement called Manchac on the upriver side of the bayou. Fort Bute, built in 1765, protected the British settlers against Indians and Spaniards and kept the bayou open for trade. Between 1770 and 1776, the settlement of Manchac grew and prospered as a trading and warehouse center for upriver fur trappers and the Mobile and Pensacola buyers who exported the pelts to Britain.

In 1767 the Spanish built a fort on the downriver side of the bayou; the fort was noted the following year by William Bartram, who called it "San Gabriel de Manchac." The Revolutionary War diverted the British from further developing the area, which enticed James Willing, an American, to lead troops against British holdings in 1778. He left a small force at Manchac, and the British fled with the possessions they could carry to the Spanish fort across the bayou (Spain and Britain were at peace at the time, and the refugees were cautiously welcomed). The British then sent reinforcements to recapture Manchac and attempted to rearm Fort Bute, to protect this vital trading artery.

In 1779 Spain declared war on Great Britain and Governor Bernardo de Gálvez quickly moved against British West Florida. He marched north from New Orleans, collecting support along the German and Acadian Coasts. The little army took Manchac without incident because the British troops had been moved to Fort New Richmond (Baton Rouge). After Manchac became part of the Spanish colony, the population swelled to 284 in 1788, but with the river itself under Spanish domination, the settlement ceased to be a significant trading post.

After the Louisiana Purchase, Bayou Manchac was again an international boundary, separating Spanish West Florida from Louisiana until 1810, when Anglo-Americans staged the West Florida Rebellion, establishing an independent republic that was quickly annexed to the United States. The site of the village of Manchac was subsequently swept away by the river.

Bayou Manchac was always a slow-moving stream, although not, according to geographers, a typical distributary of the river. Before the Mississippi was leveed, the bayou flowed in either direction, depending on the level of the river and the amount of water flowing into the bayou from its tributaries. It filled when the Mississippi was high enough to flow through a notch in the natural levee and was dry near the river in low water. Bayou Manchac was also choked with natural debris toward the Amite River, hindering navigation.

In 1814 Andrew Jackson's troops dammed the entrance from the bayou to the river. It was reopened thereafter, but flooding caused landholders to demand its reclosure. A proposal drafted in the 1850s to reopen the bayou as a floodway was never approved.

Manchac Bend is a sharp bend in the river.

76.6 Woodstock Plantation was on the upriver side of Bayou Manchac; part of it was the site of Fort Bute. English land grants ranging from fifty to five thousand acres assured that the properties in the Manchac district would be divided into plantations, as it was by 1766. The E. C. Walker family owned the Woodstock property from 1843 to 1899, during which time it produced prodigious amounts of sugarcane. Documents from 1879 record a big house near the river and workers' quarters, a sugar mill, and the overseer's house toward the back. J. Staring and E. Duplantier bought the property in 1903, reselling in 1920. By the 1970s, all of the original buildings had disappeared.

Joseph Staring was a cotton planter and, in partnership with François Gardere, opened a gin in this area.

77.0 Burtville was settled in the 1880s as a logging camp after the Burton Lumber Company purchased the tract. Kentuckian William I.. Burton and his partner, C. S. Burt, had opened a sawmill in Baton Rouge and opened a second one here that was served by the Yazoo and Mississippi Railroad. The property came to be known as Burtville Plantation. A post office and general store were located at Burtville; local legend claims that Jesse James's brother Frank passed through as a traveling salesman in 1912 and sold shoes to the storekeeper. Burtville Plantation was purchased in 1903 by Sabin Gianelloni, who also owned Longwood.

The Margaret Ebenezer Baptist Church, a white frame country church founded in 1893, is located in what was the riverfront area of Burtville.

78.3 Longwood Plantation house was built *circa* 1785 by Madame Marianne Decoux and enlarged in 1835. Some have ventured that the property was named for the refuge to which Napoleon was exiled. The property was owned by J. M. Rouzan in the mid-nineteenth century and by Lefebre and Gianelloni from the end of the nineteenth century until the 1950s. The Classical Revival big house has been moved and added to; two other old structures remain on the property. The front facade of the home is board-and-batten, although the sides are clapboard.

The levee was set back in this area in 1931, rerouting the road and changing the landscape.

78.6 La. 327 continues as the River Road. La. 327 spur, to the right, follows the same route as a road noted on Persac's map as leading from the river to the Highlands, approximately three miles inland.

Spur 327 is Gardere Lane, the approximate road to the Chatsworth quarters row. It is named for François Gardere, a wealthy New Orleans banker and treasurer of the state, who lived in this area in the 1820s. The Mission Church of the Nativity and cemetery and a schoolhouse were located on land donated to the church by

Chatsworth Planting and Manufacturing Company in 1910. The church was located in what is now a borrow pit on the other side of the levee.

78.8 This property was the site of an Indian village until the 1780s, and then was parceled out to Acadians in the form of land grants. During the 1830s, small tracts in the area were consolidated and acquired by Fergus Duplantier, adopted son of Armand Duplantier, owner of Magnolia Mound. Colonel Anthony Peniston, a Duplantier son-in-law, bought the property in 1853 and named it Chatsworth Plantation. The fifty-room mansion was begun in 1859, planned to be a very grand copy of an English country home, but after the outbreak of the Civil War, it was not completed. The house was Classical Revival with Corinthian columns. A sweeping spiral staircase, arches, finely detailed millwork, and silver hardware graced the interior. Large marble niches for statuary decorated the public rooms. The plantation was purchased by François Gardere in 1865 and continued to operate as a sugar plantation. Chatsworth was the site of lively LSU fraternity parties in the 1920s but lost the ongoing battle with the river in 1930, when it was demolished in order to move the levee back. The site became a borrow pit.

> *A 1929 account of a visit to Chatsworth would not have lamented its subsequent demise: "But for all its grandeur, it is uninteresting. This is due partly to the fact that it was never completed and partly because it was built as a show place rather than as a dwelling. There is a feeling of artificiality about it, as though it were a stage set which had been left out in the rain."*

Between Bayou Manchac and Conrad Point was an Alibamon village noted by William Bartram in 1777: "delightfully situated on several swelling green hills, gradually ascending from the verge of the river: the people are a remnant of the ancient Alabama nation." By the end of the eighteenth century, they had migrated elsewhere.

79.0 The approximate site of Mulberry Grove Plantation in 1897.

80.3 Ben Hur Road signals the former property of Ben Hur Plantation. During most of the nineteenth century, the tract—an amalgamation of several small farms—was owned by the Bird family, Anglo-Americans who arrived in the area about 1810. The property

Chatsworth in its final years.
By Andrew Lytle; courtesy Louisiana and Lower Mississippi Valley Collections, Hill Memorial Library, LSU

had approximately twenty-four arpents of frontage. The name "Hollywood" was bestowed on it in approximately 1855. It was owned for several years in the 1880s by Duncan Kenner and sold in 1888 to James Houston, who consolidated it with downriver Mulberry Grove and renamed it Ben Hur. During its private ownership, cotton, sugar, and rice were grown successively. Ben Hur was sold to LSU in 1936.

84.1 In the trees are the brick and columned remains of the Cottage Plantation house (the name was apparently derived from a summer house that occupied the site before the construction of the mansion). The property originally combined two older tracts: Moore's Point, which New Orleans attorney Abner L. Duncan bought at a sale of Armand Duplantier's property, and the Laiche tract, sold to Duncan by Phillip Hicky. In 1825 Duncan presented the Cottage Plantation and house to his daughter, Frances, and her new husband, Frederick Daniel Conrad. Conrad and his brothers all lived at The Cottage at different times. In 1897 D. Conrad was listed as the property holder for most of what was called Duncan Point. The marquis de Lafayette, Henry Clay, Zachary Taylor, and Judah P.

Benjamin were among the guests who visited the plantation during the Conrads' tenure. A drive edged with yucca plants led to the elegant, modified Creole/Classical Revival mansion with wrap-around galleries and a hipped roof, set in a grove of magnolias and oaks. The Cottage was one of the most successful of the antebellum sugar plantations, although by the 1880s, cotton had become its principal crop.

In 1859, the steamboat *Princess,* heavily loaded with passengers and freight on a voyage to New Orleans for Mardi Gras, exploded in midstream off Conrad's Point. Other steamboats in the area picked up survivors, who were taken to many different towns in the area for medical attention. About seventy are thought to have died as a result of the accident. The lawn of the Cottage was covered with sheets filled with flour in which to roll burned or scalded victims, and planters and slaves alike pitched in to care for the injured.

During the Civil War, cannons blasted the property from the river, ordered—apparently—by Frederick Conrad's nephew, who was commanding a Federal gunboat and wanted to annoy "that old rebel." Later, the house was used as a hospital by Union soldiers, and a small cemetery nearby is filled with graves of northern dead who succumbed to a yellow fever epidemic.

Like many River Road plantation houses, the Cottage had its ghost stories. One was that strange music issued from the upper gallery of the house: the ghosts of slaves, who often entertained the Conrads' guests, had returned to sing their field songs. Another ghost was that of Frederick Conrad's secretary, Angus Holt. Holt was alleged to have mysteriously arrived at sunset one day and asked for a drink, a meal, and a place to spend the night. He stayed on, proving to be experienced in landscape design as well as a classical scholar.

Author Frances Parkinson Keyes wrote her novel *River Road* while staying here from 1943 to 1945. She complimented the singular beauty of the property, including the scents of white wisteria and Cherokee roses beneath the moss-draped oaks.

The Cottage was struck by lightning and burned in 1960; at the time, it was under restoration and open for public tours. Nothing remains of the brick slave cabins, large sugarhouse and cotton gin, overseer's cottage, or other outbuildings.

85.7 Laurel (or Laurel Place) Plantation was a sugarcane planta-

A richly detailed Persac rendering of Hope Estate Plantation.
Courtesy LSU Museum of Art

tion owned by Matthew Ramsey. It consolidated properties of George Mather, who arrived in the Baton Rouge district about 1775 and was a party in the West Florida Rebellion of 1810. The property has been bought and sold several times; a few of the plantation outbuildings, including a late-nineteenth-century Acadian-style overseer's house and tenant shotgun cabins from the early twentieth century, are extant but dilapidated. Two live oaks suggest the possible site of the former big house.

86.6 Hope (Estate) Plantation was on an English land grant made in 1768. The Hicky (or Hickey) family developed Hope Estate, which they owned until the mid-nineteenth century. Daniel Hicky, an Irish immigrant, was the original owner. His son, Philip, a leader in the West Florida Rebellion and subsequently a state senator, succeeded him. Hicky erected the first sugar mill in East Baton Rouge Parish in 1814, having obtained seed cane from Noël Destrehan of St. Charles Parish, who doubted that sugarcane could be grown as far north as Baton Rouge. A Persac painting from the late 1850s shows Hope as a Creole house with numerous outbuildings and a large property. The plantation, which held almost a mile of frontage, grew cotton before the Civil War, then converted to sugarcane. River encroachment eventually destroyed many of the buildings, and that part of Hope Estate that was not consumed by the river or levee setbacks is currently owned by the East Baton Rouge Port Commission.

A 1903 account of driving up the River Road from New Orleans (New Orleans Times-Picayune, *August 26, 1956): "There were immense holes in the [dirt] road made by large drays drawn by four to six mules. . . . When we reached Hope Villa [we] had a long wait as we had to cross the little stream there. There was a small hand-drawn ferry which was a sort of platform pulled back and forth by a rope stretched across the stream."*

86.8 Baton Rouge city limits.

87.4 Brightside Lane is the former site of Arlington Plantation, established in the 1820s. The property boasted about 23.5 arpents of riverfront. Stephen Henderson owned it when it was sold to James McHatton, who married Eliza Chinn in 1852. McHatton died in 1865, and Eliza married Colonel Dwight Ripley in 1873. As Eliza McHatton-Ripley, she wrote several books about south Louisiana life (it was she who described the extraordinary interior at Linwood Plantation in east Ascension.) The house was named Arlington, she explained, for its architectural similarity to Robert E. Lee's Virginia mansion—"so closely following the architectural features of the historic Lee homestead on the Potomac as to give the name of Arlington." The house, the writer recalled, "faced a broad lawn, dotted here and there with live oak and pecan trees . . . and commanded a magnificent view of the Mississippi." She particularly remembered "those grand autumnal days, when smoke rolled from the tall chimney of the sugar-house and the air was redolent with the aroma of building cane-juice."

Plantation guests often arrived with trunks—indicating a long stay. They included a doctor whose lung malady reportedly was cured by sleeping in the sugarhouse and breathing the fumes of boiling cane juice.

After the outbreak of the war and the coming of the Union troops in 1862, the McHatton family fled Arlington. The devastation of the war was compounded by a major crevasse that opened nearby in 1862. After the war, Arlington was sold at sheriff's sale to William Pike.

Arlington grew rice and cotton in the late nineteenth century.

Because of bank erosion and movement of the river, much of its property is now on the batture side of levee.

A small piece of property between Arlington and neighboring Gartness Plantation was owned in the mid-nineteenth century by Frederick Conrad and purchased in the latter part of the century by the Gourrier family, who named the tract Nestle Down Plantation. The property became part of the LSU campus, as did Gartness Plantation.

88.7 Gartness Plantation began with a Spanish land grant to James Hillens in 1786. The property was bought in 1854 by Dr. J. M. Williams, a physician who had moved to the area from Kentucky and become a sugar planter. According to records of sugar planters in 1859 and 1860, it was owned in those years by McHatton and Saunders. From the end of the Civil War until 1918, it apparently was owned by the Williams family, and by 1918 it was called Williams Plantation, or sometimes Williams Grove. It is not clear why it was ever called Gartness. The property—a sugarcane and sweet potato plantation—was bought by a group of Baton Rouge businessmen to hold for Louisiana State University to be used as a demonstration farm for the College of Agriculture. By 1918, LSU had outgrown its campus at the Pentagon Barracks in downtown Baton Rouge and was seeking a property large enough for more buildings and agricultural research. LSU President Thomas Boyd, recognizing the need for a larger campus, held a barbecue for the state legislature at the Indian Mounds—two mounds thought to have been constructed circa 3000 B.C. The party apparently persuaded the lawmakers to allocate the money to buy the property for the new campus. In 1925 the first classes were held in the university's new Italian Renaissance buildings built on the Williams (or Gartness) tract.

Etienne Boré's original sugar kettle is on exhibit outside the Chemical Engineering building on the LSU campus. It is said that the kettle was used during the Civil War to make rum to stabilize the soldiers. After the war, it was sold as junk to a local man who later donated it to the university.

89.5 McKinley Street leads to Nicholson Drive where, a block to the left, is the Magnolia Mound Plantation house. City blocks now consume the original front acreage of this raised Creole plantation home, which remains on its original Spanish land grant, situated on a natural ridge. The property was first recorded in 1786 as belonging to James Hillin, who planted tobacco. When John Joyce purchased the plantation in 1791, he constructed a four-room house and planted indigo. In 1802 Joyce's widow married Armand Duplantier, and the unimposing home was expanded and modernized.

> *Letter from Armand Duplantier to his sister in France, September 1802: "Since the last letter I wrote to you, I have remarried with Madame Joyce, the widow about whom I spoke to you. . . . After studying her character well, I do not believe her capable of putting on a contrefaire [false front] although the father-in-law has a talent for this in general. I always found in her the utmost in sweet disposition and an immeasurable willingness with the children. . . . I speak often to her about you, how you are a good housekeeper. She is very anxious to take some good lessons from you. The Creoles, in general, are not very good at it and the manner of living in Europe and here are so different that a Creole over there would be quite embarrassed."*

Under the Duplantiers' ownership, the house became known as Magnolia Mound and was modified to include a handmade cove ceiling in the parlor, hand-carved moldings, Federal-style mantels, an extension of the front gallery, and additional rooms. The property extended from approximately the site of the LSU football stadium upriver to near the access to the Interstate 10 bridge.

The undocumented, but nevertheless legendary, residence of Prince Murat, son of Caroline Bonaparte, at Magnolia Mound in 1837 led to subsequent references to the property as the Prince Murat House. However, the prince owned a downriver portion of the property, not the part on which the house is located. In 1847 George Hall bought Magnolia Mound. Leaving it under his overseer's watchful eye during the Civil War, Hall returned in 1865 to find that the plantation had been ruined by Federal occupation. In a letter to his wife, he wrote: "Such a state of desolation as the whole country is in, you cannot imagine. It is almost universal and utter ruination to everyone. . . . And the future looks, if possible, still more discouraging." Hall sold Magnolia Mound in 1869 to

Magnolia Mound, an exemplary raised Creole house, has undergone meticulous restoration.
Courtesy State Library of Louisiana

Helen McCullen, whose family retained ownership until 1883. The property was farmed until the beginning of the twentieth century.

In the early 1960s the unoccupied and deteriorating house was sold to a developer who planned to raze the building and erect an apartment complex. A dramatic preservation effort saved the house in 1966 and eventually restored it to the period of the Duplantier residence with sophisticated Creole taste in paint colors, faux finishes, and wallpaper. Also on the property is a reproduction kitchen where open-hearth demonstrations are given, and an exhibit facility explicating Creole life. A pigeonnier, *circa* 1820, was moved from downriver Sunshine, and the Magnolia Mound overseer's house, *circa* 1860, was moved to the grounds from its original location about a block away. Two slave cabins, *circa* 1830s, and the Hart House, built in 1904 as the home of the mayor of Baton Rouge (who at the time owned Magnolia Mound), are part of the complex, as is a kitchen and a garden in which indigo, sugarcane, white and brown cotton, and other Duplantier-era plants are grown. Two of the oaks in the front of the house are thought to have been planted by John Joyce. Open to the public.

Side trip: Baton Rouge along the riverfront. Baton Rouge, the Louisiana state capital, is located on the first highlands above the Gulf of Mexico, along an unusually long, straight reach of river. The area was inhabited by Indians long before Iberville arrived. On the grounds of the present state capitol is an Indian mound that dates to approximately A.D. 1000, and an 1851 account notes two such mounds on the grounds of the military post. A third mound stood at what is now the southeast corner of Lafayette and Convention Streets and was used as a vantage point by Gálvez's troops during the Battle of Baton Rouge in 1779.

Iberville's exploration party saw a tall red pole on a bluff on the east bank of the river. Historians believe that the location was Scott's Bluff—the present day location of Southern University. A sculpture by the late Frank Hayden memorializes the site, standing on the Southern campus at the approximate location of Scott's Bluff and overlooking a spectacular view of the river at Mulatto Bend. Open to the public.

> *From the diary of André Pénicaut, Iberville's ship's carpenter: "Five leagues above Bayou Manchac [we] found very high banks called écorts [bluffs] . . . and in savage called 'Istrouma' which means red stick, as at this place there is a post painted red that the savages have sunk there to mark the land line between the two nations, namely: the land of the Bayagoulas which we were leaving and land of another nation—thirty leagues upstream from the baton rouge, named the Ouma."*

In 1718, Diron Dartaguiette was given a concession at Baton Rouge in the area of Capitol Lake, which was then a creek. Sauvolle, a member of Iberville's expedition, may have noted the site in his journal: "Around three o'clock in the afternoon we put ashore near a small river that looked like a lake and in which the savages gave us to understand that there was plenty of fish; we found several huts covered over with bindings of leather thongs. They had even erected a pole, some thirty feet in height from which hang all sorts of fish bones."

Dartaguiette's concession raised crops and cattle, but when Jesuit Father Charlevoix visited there in 1722, he found it a sad place with little future. By 1727 the site was abandoned, and no further settlement is recorded until the English took over West Florida in 1763. They erected an earthen fort in 1779 near the present corner of Lafayette Street and Spanish Town Road and named it Fort New Richmond. After Gálvez captured the fort in 1779, the Spanish erected a stronger facility, Fort San Carlos, on the same site.

The natural rise of the land along the riverbank at Baton Rouge offered a different setting for a settlement than was available downriver. An American visitor passing through in 1809 noted "sixty cabins crowded together in a narrow street on the river bank, penned in between the Mississippi and a steep hill descending from the plain." Three years later, a small fort and twelve frame houses were mentioned, as well as the small Our Lady of Sorrows Church, founded in the 1790s. This description included Spanish Town, laid out in 1805 by the Spanish governor of West Florida, Carlos de Grand Pré, as a haven for Spanish settlers from Galveztown, on Bayou Manchac; the Louisiana Purchase had marooned some Spanish loyalists on American soil. Spanish Town was laid out east of Fort San Carlos with lots large enough for a house, stable, and garden. The Pino House, at 721 North Street, is on Lot 1 of the original Spanish Town map, although the modified Creole cottage now standing was built in 1823.

Beauregard Town was laid out in 1806 by Elias Beauregard in the European style with a central cathedral square and radiating diagonal streets leading to smaller squares. The project had grand vision, but the cathedral was never built and the ancillary squares never developed. The radiating streets are still in evidence, however. The subdivision's greatest growth came after the Civil War, and especially from 1880 to 1920, when a new flurry of building replaced the structures burned during the war. At the turn of the century, a warehousing district for cotton and lumber was developed in the flat between Beauregard Town and the river. It was called Catfish Town for—according to local lore—the unwanted visitors who swam in the flooded streets when the river was high.

After the annexation of the West Florida Republic, Fort San Carlos was renamed Baton Rouge and, in 1811, became part of newly created East Baton Rouge Parish. Following the War of 1812, the American government decided to make Baton Rouge an important ordnance depot and troop center, which precipitated faster growth. Anglo-Americans moved into the city center. When it was incorporated in 1817, Baton Rouge extended from the riverfront to what is now Twenty-second Street and from Capitol Lake to South Boulevard, with the thickest settlement centered between the river and Fifth Street.

The Baton Rouge riverfront began to bustle after a visit from the steamboat *New Orleans* in 1812. River traffic expanded exponentially as the steamboat era evolved—in 1822, local docking facilities handled more than 400 flatboats, some 150 barges, and 83 steamboats. The riverfront served not only the town, but also the surrounding farming areas.

Baton Rouge was also considered strategic to the military, as Louisiana was the southwestern outpost of the Union from 1812 to 1845, bordering Spanish Mexico, then independent Mexico, and finally the Texas Republic. Therefore the federal government decided to establish a military presence in the town. The Pentagon Barracks were begun in 1819 on a site contiguous to the location of the English and Spanish forts. Four of the original five two-story, galleried buildings still exist. Zachary Taylor was sent to oversee the project and liked the area so much that he made it his official home. His heroic return after the Mexican War and his subsequent departure to be the eighth United States president created an overwhelming sense of local pride.

The military post remained important until after the Mexican War; an arsenal had been added in the 1830s. But with the expansion of American territory westward, the Pentagon Barracks and the post lost their strategic value. In 1886 the barracks and fifty-three surrounding acres became the campus of Louisiana State University.

A small Catholic Church located in the original settlement had been renamed St. Joseph sometime before 1828. In the early 1800s it was used for Protestant services as well as Catholic, because there was no Protestant church. In fact, in 1831, the priest held a service and sermon in English on Sunday afternoons to thank Protestants for their contribution to the church building fund. The Presbyterians built their own church in 1829, the Episcopalians in 1847, the Methodists in 1852, and a Jewish congregation was begun in 1858.

River commerce continued to be a significant factor in the growth of Baton Rouge in the antebellum period, augmented by the Louisiana legislature's decision to make the town the state capital. New Orleans had been the capital, but the state's growing Anglo population believed that the Creole city offered too many tempta-

Baton Rouge in 1855 as seen from across the river by Persac.
Courtesy LSU Museum of Art

tions. Baton Rouge was at the remove, but close enough. And the town's population, which had been 80 percent French and Acadian before 1820, was less than half French by 1850. As befitted an urban settlement, too, most of the male slaves worked at skilled or semiskilled labor in foundries, sawmills, and crafts.

After Baton Rouge was designated the capital in 1846, James Dakin designed a fortresslike neo-Gothic statehouse positioned on a bluff. A disastrous fire that burned a large part of the town in 1849 forced the building's dedication to be canceled, but it opened nevertheless, set in a beautifully landscaped garden with "all the rare and costly trees that one can imagine." A visitor in 1852 noted that "you enter either Chamber . . . they both represent the same follies," although it was never revealed whether his commentary was architectural or political.

Federal forces occupied Baton Rouge in 1862, and an unsuccessful Confederate effort to retake the city resulted in the Battle of Baton Rouge, during which Admiral David Farragut's warships shelled the city, damaging many of the houses and buildings near the river. The State Capitol Building became a casualty of war, gutted by a fire—apparently accidental—that started while Union troops occupied it. The building remained vacant and ruined for nearly twenty years.

From Harper's Weekly, *1866: "From the river, the State House does not look like a ruin at all but near at hand, it is as hollow and empty as the present Legislation of Louisiana . . . nothing is left inside the state house but the bare brick walls. Even the debris seems to have been removed. . . . Near one of the front windows is the mark of a cannon ball."*

The building was renovated and reopened in 1882; architect William Freret re-created the rotunda with a cast-iron framework overhung with stained glass; he also added large cylindrical turrets to the towers. After Freret's renovations, Mark Twain denounced the building in *Life on the Mississippi:* "It is pathetic enough that a whitewashed castle, with turrets and things . . . should ever have been built in this otherwise honorable place; but it is much more pathetic to see this architectural falsehood undergoing restoration . . . when it would have been so easy to let dynamite finish what a charitable fire began." Today the Old State Capitol is open to the public as a museum.

Federal troops remained in Baton Rouge throughout Reconstruction. In 1879 the Pentagon Barracks was released to Louisiana State University for its campus, and the state capital returned to the city after a hiatus in Opelousas, Shreveport, and New Orleans.

The coming of the New Orleans and Mississippi Valley Railway in 1883 brought the first direct rail link between Baton Rouge and New Orleans. (Baton Rouge's only previous rail service had been via ferry link across the river to the Port Allen—Grosse Tete Railroad, which operated from 1857 until the Civil War.) Railways opened Baton Rouge to places that steamboats and the river did not reach and contributed greatly to Standard Oil's selection in 1909 of a site just north of the city to build a refinery. The coming of Standard Oil precipitated a sea-change in the Baton Rouge economy. Governor Huey Long also changed the city's face along the river with construction of the new State Capitol Building in 1929 and the concurrent destruction of older buildings to make way for a large public garden. The site was the former LSU campus, the university having moved to the Gartness tract.

Although the port of Baton Rouge is said to date from 1916, the construction of a municipal dock in 1926 near Catfish Town facilitated offloading cargo from oceangoing ships for transfer to rail or barge. The growth of numerous industries and businesses utilizing the river for transportation catalyzed the expansion of the port of Baton Rouge until, today, it ranks as the nation's fifth largest.

Another significant development was the construction of the Huey P. Long Bridge, opened in 1940—the first bridge across the river between New Orleans and Vicksburg. Local lore said the span was purposely built too low to allow oceangoing vessels passage upriver, forcing them to stop at Baton Rouge (the truth is that the river channel was not dug deep enough farther upriver for large oceangoing craft). The bridge was several miles north of downtown, and because of this relatively inconvenient location, ferries continued to link East and West Baton Rouge Parishes until 1968, when the Interstate 10 bridge opened just below the city's center.

Although riverboat gambling craft add an ornamental, pseudo-steamboat flavor, the river at Baton Rouge is now primarily a bustling center of maritime enterprises and businesses related to the commercial shipping industry and the River Road is a byway among bustling city streets.

DOWNRIVER ALONG
THE WEST BANK

~~~~~~~~~~~~~~~~

Note: This linear route along the River Road, with occasional side trips, extends from West Baton Rouge Parish downriver to the St. Charles/Jefferson Parish boundary, offering a traveler a pleasurable outing into the area's history, culture, and lore. Numbers indicate mileage as measured beginning at point 0.0—the junction of La. 988 and the River Road (this point can be reached by heading south on La. 1; La. 988 intersects La. 1 beyond the Intracoastal Canal). A new set of mileage numbers begins after Donaldsonville. Mileages given for side trips are independent.

Side trip: The River Road from the old Mississippi River Bridge to Port Allen. To follow this section, take La. 1 north (upriver) to La. 987-1, turn right to the River Road—La. 986—and turn right again.

0.0 At the intersection of La. 987-1 and La. 986. This, the older of two Mississippi River bridges in Baton Rouge, is often referred to as the Huey P. Long Bridge, as it was planned during Long's administration. At its completion in 1940, it was designated a memorial to the late Louisiana governor and United States senator. Just above the bridge is Wilkerson Point, as it is noted on current Corps of Engineers maps (the name may be a misinterpretation of Wilkinson, a longtime local landowner). The point juts out into the dramatic river formation known as Mulatto Bend, a nearly ninety-degree elbow.

    At this approximate point in the river lie the remains of the *Arkansas,* a Confederate ironclad that sank in August 1862. The *Arkansas* had suffered damage while engaging the Union fleet at Vicksburg but was ordered to Baton Rouge to battle Federal gunboats while Confederate ground forces attempted to recapture the city. As the *Arkansas* approached the area, its engines broke down, and to prevent the helpless craft from falling into enemy hands, the captain ordered it fired. The burning ironclad drifted downstream, exploded, and sank near the present site of the bridge.

.25 The property was originally an indigo plantation owned by Pierre Favrot, who served as commandant at Baton Rouge (Fort San Carlos) and at Mobile during the governorship of Bernardo de Gálvez. Favrot was also the judge in the 1779 trial of Mary Glass for what was described as the most heinous crime of the colonial period, the brutal torture and murder of a fifteen-year-old orphan girl. Glass was convicted, taken to New Orleans, and hanged. Pierre Favrot died at Monte Vista in 1824. His grandson Louis built this somewhat understated Classical Revival home *circa* 1857. Much of the building material was delivered to the site by the steamboat *Capital.*

Monte Vista's unusual location—between the road and the levee—evokes part of the plantation's colorful history. Originally the house was eight hundred feet behind the levee, with a long driveway lined by a double row of live oaks and gardens. But over the decades all the oaks were consumed as the river lapped nearer. The story goes that when the levee was to be moved after the 1927 flood, the Corps of Engineers determined that Monte Vista and Poplar Grove, just downriver, would both have to be sacrificed. The owner of Poplar Grove invited the engineers to his house for a splendid south Louisiana repast—including an ample supply of liquid refreshment. His guests were greatly admiring the house and grounds when the owner pointed to the surveyors' stakes. The engineers agreed to reroute the road.

> *From the diary of Henry Favrot, son of the builder, April 27, 1859: "The river is very high and rising. The levee is worked on and bagasse put upon it."*

Across the road from Monte Vista is the main house of Barozza Plantation, built *circa* 1850–1855, moved here from the plantation site upriver. The house was reconstructed from original materials after a tornado demolished it.

.9 Poplar Grove Plantation. When French explorers first arrived in the area, this tract was part of a Houma Indian settlement. It is believed the property once belonged to Bienville, then to Armand

Duplantier (owner of Magnolia Mound in East Baton Rouge), and was purchased in the 1820s by James McCalop. The name derives from a grove of poplars that stood between the house and the river. Horace Wilkinson came to manage the plantation in 1886 and subsequently became its owner. The main house was built by Louisiana architect Thomas Sully not as a plantation home but as the Bankers' Pavilion at the 1884 Cotton Exposition in New Orleans. Poplar Grove's owner bought the unusual late-Victorian building at a sheriff's sale in 1886 and shipped it upriver to the site. After the flood of 1927, the levee was set back to within thirty feet of the house and the River Road was moved as well. The 1950 crevasse at Mulatto Bend upriver covered the plantation with water.

1.2 Poplar Grove was an operational sugar plantation until the 1970s. Down Scale House Road, the remains of the complex are easily visible—1850s quarters, laborers' houses from a later period, a blacksmith shop, and a church. A Creole-style overseer's house, built sometime between 1840 and 1860, was moved from St. Delphine Plantation and restored. The relic mill, used until 1973, was unfortunately demolished in 1995.

The first steamboat disaster on the lower Mississippi River occurred in this area in July 1814. Because of bad weather, the captain of the *New Orleans* tied up on the west bank overnight. In the morning, when the crew fired up the engines, the boat merely spun around; the river had fallen during the night, settling the boat on a large stump. The crew threw fuel overboard and worked the boat off the snag, but the hull immediately began to leak. The *New Orleans* sank so quickly, reports say, that it was a challenge to rescue all the passengers.

1.5 On the levee embankment at the site of what was once Anchorage Plantation are the remains of a railroad incline/overpass. The overgrown, half-destroyed timber support structure was part of the access to a ferry that ran between Anchorage and Baton Rouge until the railroad bridge was completed upriver. The ferry was the eastern terminus of the Baton Rouge, Grosse Tete and Opelousas Railroad, connecting West Baton Rouge with Livonia. A steam ferry, the *Sunny South,* made three trips daily to transport people and goods from trains across the river. The railroad, abandoned during the Civil War, reopened thereafter but was short-lived. In the 1870s the Southern Pacific Railroad bought the line.

From 1909 until 1947, when the railroad bridge was completed, a train ferry operated here, carrying from three to five rail cars at a time. Uncoupled from an engine on one bank, they were recoupled to another on the opposite shore.

2.0 Faye Lane was once part of the community of Sunrise, originally on the property of J. P. Allain. Alex Banes, a former slave who worked at Homestead Plantation, just downriver, purchased the tract in 1874 with the help of Homestead's owner, John Hill. The growth of the railroad in the 1880s helped develop the settlement—the station was just a few miles northwest of Banes's farm. Placid Refining Company bought out the community, and only a couple of houses remain.

2.5 Chaudoir House is a Classical Revival cottage moved here from Homestead Plantation. Built *circa* 1850 for a maiden aunt of the Hill family, Chaudoir was joined by a covered walkway to the Homestead main house.

2.7 The present house called Homestead Plantation was built in 1915 by George Hill, John's son, for his bride. Its Classical Revival styling emulates the grand houses of the antebellum era. The levee and road have been moved west, cutting off part of the front yard of Homestead, and the present house sits farther back on the property than the original plantation house did.

2.8 Hill Place retains part of the original Homestead Plantation house. The two-story Creole raised cottage was built sometime between 1800 and 1820 on a Spanish land grant made to Alexander Barrow. It seems to have remained in the Barrow family until John Hill bought the property at a sheriff's sale in 1866. Originally, cotton was grown at Homestead, but the plantation converted to sugarcane before 1849. In 1917 the house had to be moved; its brick first story was demolished, and only the upper story survives as the current house.

John Hill was a Scots-born entrepreneur who settled in Baton Rouge and operated a foundry there—manufacturing, among other things, the iron fence surrounding the Old State Capitol. During the Civil War shelling of Baton Rouge, Hill's town house was badly damaged. He obtained permission from Union admiral David Farragut to move to Port Allen, where he decided to try his luck with sugar. Homestead Plantation boasted a Classical Revival-style sugarhouse, complete with columns and front gallery; its operation was discontinued in 1921. The house is once again a private residence after having been owned by a school and a church, and then being divided into apartments.

2.9 Rosedale Road into Port Allen. The custard-colored Acadian-style frame cottage at this corner was built after the Civil War as the Homestead Plantation overseer's house. Just a bit up the road is a school building built in the 1930s in a very mannered Art Deco style similar to that of the new State Capitol.

Port Allen town tour: The River Road continues south (one way) as Third Street (First and Second Streets are now in the river). Michel Mahier, a French doctor living in Baton Rouge and employed by the Spanish crown, acquired land in 1809 and laid out a town with streets, lots, and a public square. He called it St. Michel, for his patron saint. At that time, this side of the river was United States territory as part of the Louisiana Purchase, while Baton Rouge on the opposite bank was still part of Spanish West Florida. The first West Baton Rouge Parish Courthouse was in St. Michel, but the river began to claim the settlement, and by the 1830s, the community was only two blocks long. By the late 1850s, it had all but disappeared.

> *"I write from the site of the ancient city of San Michel [over which the Mississippi now rolls]; there is nary a street left and but half a dozen buildings . . . the last grab the river made at it being in 1858 when it nipped off a large slice of land and among others ejected Judge Hyams from office and dwelling and drove him into his spacious and airy quarters in the old court-house. The new courthouse, a handsome and well adapted building, is some quarter of a mile distant from the ferry. . . . A good steam ferryboat plies across the river between Baton Rouge, the West Baton Rouge landing, and the Grosse Tete depot, a few hundred yards above. . . . There is no post office at the parish seat of West Baton Rouge, mail [being deliverable] at Baton Rouge, across the river. There is a post office at Bruslé Landing, six miles below [West] Baton Rouge and here is about the largest settlement in the parish . . . [and] the principal Catholic church." J. W. Dorr, 1860.*

In 1852 Henry W. Allen, a Virginian who became a prominent

Henry W. Allen, Civil War veteran, governor of Confederate Louisiana, and namesake of Port Allen.

Courtesy State Library of Louisiana

local citizen and, in 1864, Confederate governor of the state, bought land nearby. He laid out the town of West Baton Rouge to the west of San Michel in 1854. It was renamed Port Allen in 1878 in his honor. When the levee was set back in 1931, many local landmarks, including the courthouse, were lost.

The first ferry in the area operated between San Michel and Baton Rouge in 1820, and ferries connected the two banks until the Interstate 10 bridge was completed in 1968.

The West Baton Rouge Museum, 845 North Jefferson Avenue, is housed in the former records vault of the third West Baton Rouge Court House, built in 1882. The Classical Revival facade was added. Among the museum's eclectic collection are a working model of a 1904 sugar mill; sugar plantation artifacts; an 1850s Allendale Plantation quarters cabin, furnished to provide an interpretative exhibit, including open-hearth cooking demonstrations; and Aillet (pronounced eye-yay) House, a good example of a Creole cottage. Aillet House was built *circa* 1830 by Jean Landry and passed into the Aillet family in 1880; Dow Chemical bought the land and moved the cottage from its original location near Sandbar Plantation, downriver from Port Allen. Significant elements of the one-and-a-half-story house include bousillage in-fill, exposed beaded ceiling beams, French doors, and wraparound mantels. Open to the public.

Directly across the street from the museum is a galleried two-story antebellum commercial building—first a bank, then a Masonic lodge, with various subsequent uses. On the corner of Jefferson Avenue and Court Street is a vintage drugstore building, formerly the mercantile establishment at Cinclare Plantation; it was moved to this location in the 1920s due to river encroachment.

The Mississippi River overlook at the old ferry landing, at the intersection of Court Street and the levee, offers a view of the busy Port of Greater Baton Rouge. The deepwater port was enhanced in 1953 with dedication of the grain facility—elevator, docks, and conveyors.

Downriver from the Interstate 10 interchange is the Port Allen Lock, completed in 1961. It can be reached by a roadway to the port off La. 1 under I-10. The lock and canal replaced an older lock at Plaquemine (downriver) and connect the Mississippi River with the Intracoastal Canal, cutting the waterway distance to the Gulf of Mexico by 160 miles. The locks, 84 feet wide and 1,180 feet long, are very busy, but the operators welcome visitors to the lock-house to watch the swap of water levels—as much as 49 feet—between the river and the Intracoastal Canal. The locks can also be used for flood control.

Return to La. 1, cross the Intracoastal Canal, and turn left at La. 988 (Beaulieu Lane) to reach the River Road.

0.0 Junction La. 988 and River Road.

0.5 Sandbar Plantation, at 4234 South River Road in Brusly, was originally a Spanish land grant to Joseph Landry, an Acadian whose daughter married Dr. Thomas Vaughan (sometimes spelled Vaughn). Vaughan came to Louisiana in 1834 on what was to be a farewell voyage—he was suffering from a malady unanimously considered by his Virginia doctors to be terminal. He completed the Classical Revival cottage in 1852 and lived there happily, dying at the age of ninety-four. The property was acquired in 1880 by Emile Gassie, who christened it New Prosperity. It was later renamed Sandbar for a small sand embankment, visible only during low water, that locals traditionally used for recreation. During and after Reconstruction, local and state politicians used the plantation house's front porch to address their constituents. The house fell into disrepair during the first quarter of the twentieth century but was bought and restored by Charles Dameron, recognized as a leader in levee engineering; as an experiment, he purchased the first steam shovel used in Louisiana for levee building. Next door is a Classical Revival cottage built by the owners of Sandbar *circa* 1890.

1.0 Antonio Road is named for Antonio Plantation. The Levert House, *circa* 1820s, is a raised plantation house with red-brick front stairs added.

1.2 Facing the road are two weathered quarters cabins moved from their original location on Antonio Plantation.

1.6 Terrill Road is the entrance to the Cinclare Plantation complex, which is situated between River Road and Highway 1. Cinclare is the only sugar mill still operating along this part of the River Road; it is believed that a sugar factory has operated here since 1804. The property was sold and named Marengo Plantation in 1856, then resold in 1873 to a partnership in which L. Cinclare Keever was a member, at which time the name again changed. In 1903 the old sugar factory was replaced with a new Cinclare Central Factory, subsequently modernized. A line of trim white frame houses on either side of the River Road entrance to Cinclare hints of a mill town. Marengo House is thought to have been constructed *circa* 1850 and moved to its present location in 1906. The present Cinclare Plantation house was built in 1906 in the preferred style of its Cincinnati, Ohio, architect—not well suited to the south Louisiana climate. The 1903 headquarters building is the administration center of the operation. A weathered, retired sugar mill and an aged green mulebarn with a cupola add a decadent grace to the property. A restored "dummy" (a small steam engine that pulled cane trains in from the field) and a handcar are displayed near the La. 1 entrance. Cinclare's holdings now include a number of area plantation properties, among them St. Delphine, Stonewall, Antonio, Denby, Bains, Australia, and St. Mary (also known as "Chenango," Senecan for "large bull thistle").

2.0 The Brusly Middle School was built as the community schoolhouse in the late 1930s by the WPA.

The Creole-style cottage at 227 North Kirkland is thought to date from the first half of the nineteenth century.

2.3 Town front of Brusly. It has been said that the name of this small town (pronounced BREW-lee) is derived from the burning of brush to clear the land; the French for "burned" is *brulé,* and this and other forms of the word were often given as names to new settlements on land cleared by fire. However, it is also possible that Brusly was named for Henry Brusly, a steamboat captain who often stopped in this area during the 1830s. The community is the oldest in West Baton Rouge Parish. Among the earliest settlers were Acadian farmers named Hébert, who arrived in 1785. In antebellum times the settlement was called Brusly Landing, and its dock was used by plantation owners who lacked river frontage. A number of these planters grew cotton until the mid-nineteenth century. The River Road in Brusly is called Kirkland Street, after a late-eighteenth-century plantation owner. The levee and the River Road were several blocks east before they were set back in 1929; the houses and commercial buildings at the town front were either moved or lost to the river.

Mutt's Bar opened at the turn of the twentieth century as the Brusly Saloon and has been a local landmark ever since. The ramp to the old landing is across the River Road.

Side trip: Up Main Street (La. 989-2) are several interesting structures. The Hébert House, 915 East Main Street, built *circa* 1835, is a raised Creole cottage with Classical Revival influences. Its original location, on the River Road in front of St. John the Baptist Church, is now on the other side of the present levee; the house was moved in the early 1930s. Redman Hall, 833 East Main, is a turn-of-the-century brotherhood hall moved to this site from the River Road and raised. Now a private home, it still has a large cistern to the rear. The Vaughan-Bres House, 114 East Main, is located on property acquired by Daniel Benoit in a land grant from the United States government in 1803. At least part of the tract was in the Bird family for many years. According to local legend, Thompson Bird buried his fortune here before going off to serve in the Confederate Army; shortly after his return, he suffered a stroke and was unable to convey to his wife where the money was buried. Mrs. Bird subsequently was forced to mortgage the property. When later owners suddenly seemed to have a great deal of money, the rumor circulated that they had found Bird's buried gold. The original house was demolished in the 1930s.

Henry Vaughan, a Confederate ship's captain and the son of Dr. and Mrs. Thomas Vaughan of Sandbar, bought the property and built the country Creole-style house in 1878. The house and a large tract of land were purchased in 1918 by Joseph Hughes Bres, and it remains in this family. Alterations to the house have been made, but it still faces the river, as it has since it was built.

To the right on the La. 1 service road (called Vaughn Drive), at 230 North Vaughn, is the Lockmaster's House, a raised Creole plantation-style home constructed *circa* 1900. The building served as the private residence of the lockmaster of the Plaquemine locks until the 1950s, when the locks were closed. The house was moved to the current location (previously occupied by the Red Hat Saloon) in a difficult process that took four months.

A block downriver from Main Street, at the corner of Lejeune and Gwin Streets, is the Union Baptist Church, a black congregation organized in 1883. The current church building was remodeled in 1962.

The Eastlake-style cottage at 427 North Kirkland was built *circa* 1900.

Resuming River Road mileage at River Road and Main Street:

2.5 St. John the Baptist Church and Cemetery. The congregation began in approximately 1792, when a priest was assigned to serve it. The first chapel was erected before 1800, with the priest commuting from Baton Rouge by skiff. The church parish was not chartered until 1835. The original church and cemetery, located just downriver from the present site, were consumed by the river; a subsequent church burned in 1907 and was replaced by this white frame Gothic-style structure. The contemporary bell tower was erected in 1985 to commemorate St. John's sesquicentennial. A small meeting hall on the upriver side of the church was moved here in 1931 from the Sardine Point settlement, downriver on Australia Point, where it was the St. Francis of Assisi Chapel, dedicated in 1888. It was moved to Brusly in 1931 because of levee construction. St. John the Baptist and its cemetery are on land deeded to the church by Jean Baptiste Hébert, who died in 1838 and is buried here. The cemetery was relocated before the Civil War because of river encroachment. A sprinkling of mid-nineteenth-century tombs remains.

Down Bourgeois Street is the Babin House, also sometimes known as Cazenave. The front portion of the raised Classical Revival-style structure is thought to have been built *circa* 1838, but the rear of the home was once part of a general store that was moved to save it from the river.

2.6 At 610 Kirkland, corner of St. Francis Street, is the small Creole-style Kirkland cottage, *circa* 1850. The Creole cottage at 723 East St. Francis, built *circa* 1830 and moved from the River Road to this location in the 1930s, has been greatly altered.

3.0 Billups Road marks Lukeville community, a two-street black community founded by Luke Billups (or Billoups) in 1866 and named for him. A classical Acadian-style cottage with a chimney built flush on the end wall stands at the corner. Billups purchased 100 acres of land and built a church, then sold homesites to church members so they could live nearby. The church, rebuilt in 1958, is a block up Billups Road.

3.2 The post office for the settlement of Mark was located here. Mark was named for Dr. Mark Levert, whose father owned St. Delphine Plantation. From 1898 to 1904, the post office also served the community of Addis, just downriver.

The trees on the levee side of the River Road in this area remain from before the levee and road setbacks in the 1930s.

3.4 Morrisonville Acres is a resettlement community to which residents of Morrisonville, downriver, were moved by the Dow Chemical Company.

3.9 Creole cottage, thought to date to *circa* 1830. Three gnarled and aged mulberry trees stand in front of the house.

4.1 Trees on the levee indicate that the road was moved.

4.6 Junction La. 990 (Addis Lane). The town of Addis is centered off the river. The community developed because of the arrival of the Texas & Pacific railroad in 1882. The original name, Baton Rouge Junction, was changed in about 1910 to honor J. W. Addis, superintendent of motive power and rolling stock for the T & P. [*Side trip:* Approximately a mile west on La. 990, across La. 1, is the town center. Numerous homes built for the late-nineteenth-century railroad workers survive in Addis. The original La. 1 is First Street. Just beyond is the large railroad yard; the old roundhouse no longer exists, but the red-brick, porticoed bank building, *circa* 1880, remains facing the railroad.]

The cane fields on the downriver side of La. 990 were once part of St. Delphine Plantation.

5.2 To the rear is the Oxychem (Occidental Chemical) Plant, built in 1979 on the site of St. Delphine Plantation. Originally a Spanish land grant, St. Delphine was acquired by Isadore Daigle in 1831. Construction began in 1857 on the square Classical Revival mansion, an imposing two-story structure completely encircled by a gallery decorated with ornate ironwork railings between large columns. The house was named for Daigle's wife. In 1871 the plantation was sold to Auguste Levert. The belvedere was blown off in 1906 by a tornado that wrecked the upper story and the roof. The house was repaired, and a gabled roof with dormers was added for a third floor, but it was all torn down in 1932 to make way for the levee. The land remaining after the levee setback became part of Cinclare Plantation.

In 1866 the steamboat *Keokuk* pulled up at the St. Delphine landing during a terrible storm, and the passengers spent the night in the mansion; the next morning, they discovered that the boat had sunk.

5.7 Copolymer property. This is Missouri Bend, a curved reach around the east-bank Duncan or Conrad Point. The Missouri Bend area was settled in the late eighteenth century by Acadians. Here were St. Mary's Plantation (or Chenango), which became part of St. Delphine in the early twentieth century, and New Hope Plantation.

5.9 On the Dow Chemical property was the late-nineteenth-century Eliza Plantation and a related settlement, Eliza.

6.9 Manchac, or Australia, Point, also formerly known as Sardine Point, straddles Bayou Bourbeaux. The River Road cuts across the base of this point for approximately a mile, not far from a late-nineteenth-century road. Manchac Point has historically been susceptible to flooding, and the Atchafalaya Basin Levee District, in conjunction with the Corps of Engineers, determined in 1932 to construct the present levee. Landowners were forced to vacate, and the point is now considered batture.

The first settlers along this point were small farmers, but by the Civil War, many tracts had been consolidated into small plantations. On the upriver side of the point was the Sardine Point settlement and Sardine Point Plantation and sugar mill. A church at Sardine Point remained in use long after the levee was built. The end of Manchac Point was the property of Sosthène Allain, according to Persac, and sold to Lewis Woods in the late 1870s. It was Woods who named the property Australia Plantation. New Hope and Eliza plantations were also along the upriver coast. Along the downriver side of the point were Resterege, Clara Belle, Medora, Cutoff, and Mayflower Plantations. Clara Belle, originally known as Rheamsland Plantation, had a mere seven and three-quarters arpents of frontage; it was renamed Clara Belle by new owners who acquired it in 1867. Medora Plantation was originally owned by Baltazar Dupuy, a descendant of the eighteenth-century Acadians. The name Medora was given the plantation by new owners in 1867.

The Medora archaeological site, discovered on Medora Plantation property, was one of Louisiana's most significant Indian mound sites. Archaeological evidence suggested the existence of a large community occupied by Indians of the Plaquemine culture from approximately A.D. 1300 to the late seventeenth century, just prior to French exploration of the area. Two temple mounds separated by a 400-foot-long plaza were located near Bayou Bourbeaux. Pottery shards, stone tools, and other artifacts indicated that the residents hunted, fished, and tended gardens of corn, squash, pumpkins, and beans. It is not known why these people left or where they went.

7.6 West Baton Rouge/Iberville Parish line.

At the boundary of West Baton Rouge and Iberville Parishes is the site of the settlement of Morrisonville. When the Corps of Engineers mandated removal of Australia Point's residents in 1932 to construct the levee, some Point dwellers reestablished themselves here. In 1989, however, Dow Chemical purchased all the property from the curve of Missouri Bend to the company's Plaquemine plant as a "green," or safe, zone. Dow helped the residents move elsewhere and demolished the remaining structures. The area is now virtually uninhabited.

8.1 The levee rejoins the River Road.

Dow is the most extensive petrochemical complex in Louisiana, and its property encompasses parts of what were Union, Reliance, New Hope, Mayflower, and Homestead Plantations. The streets within the Dow complex are all named either for the plantations that comprise the plant site or for chemicals manufactured here.

8.9 Off the road, hidden in the trees, is Dow House, built in 1910 by Andrew Gay as the main house of Union Plantation. It is in grand bungalow style and was remodeled in 1923. The house was situated in a vintage 1905 grove of oaks, cedars, and pecan trees planted in the shape of a Maltese cross. Union was purchased by the Gay family during the Civil War and sold in 1928. Dow bought the property in 1956. Open to the public.

9.4 Town of Plaquemine corporate limit.

9.5 Homestead Avenue marks the site of Homestead Plantation, established on what is now called Bayou Jacob, just above Plaquemine, by Jacob Schlatre, a German who migrated to Louisiana from Pennsylvania about 1774. The Schlatre family was the first to grow sugarcane on the highlands in this area. A massive-columned, two-and-a-half-story brick mansion was built by Jacob Schlatre's grandson in 1861. Schlatre's Landing on the Mississippi River served the several Schlatre plantations along Bayou Jacob. During the Civil War, the plantation was used for recruiting and training Confederate soldiers and was called Camp Schlatre. Andrew Gay later bought Homestead and joined it with Ridgefield Plantation, next door upriver. The Ridgefield house was built as a two-story Creole-style home with a bricked first story and frame upper story connected by an under-gallery stairway. In 1879 or 1880 the levee caved in, and the new levee was constructed at the front door of Ridgefield. Eventually, both Ridgefield and Homestead had to be torn down. The replacement Homestead house is a block off River Road down Homestead Street. Local lore says that Dow House and Homestead were constructed to identical floor plans for Gay's daughters.

9.9 At Jacob Street, the broad green swale is the former location of Bayou Jacob, which once joined the Mississippi River, although Persac shows it cut off in 1858. It has been filled in. Bayou Jacob is the upriver boundary of Turnerville.

10.0 Follow La. 988 as it turns right to La. 1.

Side trip: Ahead is the Old Turnerville District. Turnerville is a late-Victorian community established during the height of the cypress-lumbering era. The land had been Jacques Devillier's Island Plantation in the early nineteenth century. A racetrack was the attraction of note here between 1870 and 1883, but caving along the banks of Bayou Plaquemine caused the course to close. The village is made up of mixed residences, almost all constructed of local cypress. Some houses have been lost to the river; of the remaining cottages, two are open to the public.

10.2 At the junction of La. 1, turn left into the town of Plaquemine.

10.3 Bayou Plaquemine. The town of Plaquemine, incorporated in 1838, takes its name from the bayou, which once flowed from the Mississippi River. Legend says that early explorers shared food with the Indians made from the plentiful local persimmon, which in the Natchez Indian language was called *piakemine* or *pliakemine*. Settlement began when the entrepreneurial Thomas Pipkin observed that travelers using the bayou on their way to the Attakapas region (present-day Lafayette) would need services. He bought land, which he subdivided in 1819 as the "Town of Iberville," located on a tract between Bayous Jacob and Plaquemine, and ran a ferry and a tavern. A yellow fever epidemic killed most of the settlers. The town of Iberville became the town of Plaquemine in 1838. Because of its location on an acute bend, much of the early settlement, including Pipkin's town, was destroyed by the river. Nevertheless, the intersection of Bayou Plaquemine and the Mississippi was a strategic one, and the town became an important steamboat landing. Before the Civil War, it was a regular stop for packet boats. In 1880 much of the riverfront portion of the town again fell into the river when the bank eroded. During the latter part of the nineteenth century, Plaquemine bustled with activity from the lumber industry. Many plantation tracts in the area were sold to lumber companies, and related businesses—some still surviving—developed. The lumber business is considered by many as the backbone of Plaquemine's growth.

Bayou Plaquemine was noted in Iberville's journals. During high water, Mississippi River boat traffic could use this meandering waterway to reach the Atchafalaya. In his travels through Louisiana between 1796 and 1802, James Pitot—soon to be New Orleans' first mayor—noted that the bayou would be an important artery if it could be kept cleared. But in 1866 the Iberville Parish authorities determined to build a levee to counteract continual flooding. The levee cut off access to the bayou, so Congress was petitioned to fund a lock system. The Plaquemine Lock was begun in 1895 and completed in 1909; at the time, it produced the highest freshwater lift of any lock in the world. The designer of the lock was George Goethals, who went on to become chief engineer and builder of the Panama Canal. In May of 1927, during the Great Flood, the gauge at the Plaquemine Lock rose to forty-three feet. The lock was used until it was decommissioned in 1961, when the Port Allen Lock replaced it. The site has been transformed into a historical park; the original pumphouse is a tourist information center. Behind the building is a river overlook. Open to the public.

Side trip: Within the town of Plaquemine.

"The town of Plaquemine . . . is situated at the junction of Bayou Plaquemine . . . with the river. It is a well built, thriving and bustling town doing a great business with a populous back country. There are a number of fine brick stores here . . . [McWilliams, Deblieux & Co, Ross & Gallagher, Haase & Bro., Kahn, etc.]. There are two hotels . . . the Iberville Hotel near the steamboat landing and the Tuttle House, a very handsome building and elegant and luxurious house of entertainment . . . There is a good working lodge of Masons in Plaquemine.

*"The Mississippi . . . is continually biting mouthfuls of
[Plaquemine's] river border and compelling people to look
well to their levees. Bayou Plaquemine is a troublesome neighbor also with its powerful current for it is gnawing away at
its banks continually. Four new levees have had to be built on
its banks within the town in four years past. [Citizens] are
very desirous that it should be closed." J. W. Dorr, 1860.*

Across the street from the Lock is the Old Plaquemine City Hall,
formerly the Iberville Parish Courthouse, erected in 1849. Plaquemine became the Iberville Parish seat in 1835, after the government
had moved twice, the first time from Galveztown on the east bank
to west-bank Point Pleasant in 1810. Initially, the courthouse was
in a hotel, but the river forced abandonment of the site in 1848,
prompting the construction of this traditional Classical Revival
structure, which served until 1906. The tourist information center
and chamber of commerce are located here.

The Old Plaquemine Main Street District features both commercial and residential buildings and offers a glimpse into a small Mississippi River town of the late nineteenth century. Eden and Church
Streets (one-way streets that form La. 1 within the town) are the
main arteries. The main commercial area includes the Bruslé Building, Eden near Main Street, built in 1889 as the Bank of Plaquemine; the old Post Office Building, People's Bank Building, Barker's
Pharmacy, and Roth Building all date to the same period. Along
Church Street are the Joseph Wilbert House, Church at Meriam,
built in 1906; the Frederick Wilbert House, just off Church at 207
Court Street—the surviving Queen Anne cottage in town, a sand-
and-turquoise Victorian confection of gables and turrets and enhanced balustrades; the Kaufman House, built in 1829 as a town
house; and the Bickham House, an Acadian cottage at 410 Church
Street, built as a town house in 1898. St. Basil's, at Church and
Court Streets, was built in 1850 as the home of Dr. Edward Scratch-
ely on what was then an outside corner of the four-block township.
In 1859 the house was sold to the Catholic church and developed
as St. Basil's Catholic girls' academy. Union troops occupied the
building in 1862, but it was returned to the church after the Civil
War. When the church built a new school in 1975, the property
became a restaurant; it has subsequently been restored as a private
home.

The imposing St. John the Evangelist Catholic Church, at Main Street near Church, was built in 1927 in Italianate basilica style, replacing the original 1850 edifice. Designed by Albert Bendernagal, St. John exemplifies the eclectic styling that characterized church architecture in the early twentieth century. In the St. John Cemetery are the tombs of Joseph Schlatre (son of Jacob) and other local luminaries.

The Middleton Home, at the corner of Eden and Plaquemine Streets, was built *circa* 1845 by a relative of Jacob Schlatre on property that had been a Spanish land grant. The white, raised, modified Creole plantation house is typical of Plaquemine's antebellum homes. It was shelled by Federal gunboats during the Civil War. On the river side of Eden between Court and Meriam are two row houses, surviving examples of the cottages built in the early 1900s for lumber-mill workers.

At Eden and LaBauve is the Spedale House, built of cypress from local mills and (in its original, smaller form) taken by barge to the 1904 St. Louis World's Fair to advertise the beauty of cypress construction. It was returned to Plaquemine and reestablished on site after the exhibit.

Side trip: Along Bayou Plaquemine. Court Street south joins La. 3066 for a colorful meander along broad Bayou Plaquemine to Variety Plantation, approximately three miles. This raised Classical Revival cottage, built in 1850 on Homestead Plantation, was moved here and renovated in 1973 after the original Variety Plantation home burned. The land has been in the family of German settler Anton Wilbert since approximately 1850. Wilbert was a cabinet-maker who expanded to the manufacture of coffins and in 1868 began operating a sawmill, which prospered during the great lumbering boom. The complex features two important plantation dependency buildings—a doctor's office and a kitchen.

11.3 To rejoin the River Road by the levee, turn left off Eden Street at La. 75.

11.5 The landing for the Plaquemine–Sunshine toll ferry is at La. 75 and River Road.

11.9 Reveilletown is a resettlement development for former residents of Reveille, a black community established after the Civil War. Georgia Gulf, just downriver, created Reveilletown when the company purchased and cleared the Reveille property as part of its green zone.

Morrisonville Estates, next door, is the resettlement site for residents moved from Morrisonville, at Manchac Point, when Dow established a green zone.

12.1 True Hope Lane is the approximate site of True Hope Plantation, originally a Spanish land grant. The house was built *circa* 1852, a Creole plantation "high enough to walk under and where our dairy was located," according to the granddaughter of former owner Edward Gay. The large front gallery was shaded by a rose vine, and in the front pasture was a small building once used as a country store, then as a schoolhouse. The sugar mill ceased grinding in 1924. True Hope adjoined St. Louis Plantation and became part of it after the Civil War. The house burned in 1962.

12.5 St. Louis Plantation. Captain Joseph Erwin established Home Plantation in 1807 on a Spanish land grant. Erwin was a successful cotton and sugar planter and became the largest landholder in Iberville Parish, but flooding of his property in 1817 destroyed him financially. He is said to have drowned himself in a vat (possibly a cistern) of river water that was to be used by the household. His responsibilities were assumed by his son-in-law Andrew Hynes. (Another Erwin son-in-law, Charles Dickinson, was killed in a duel with future president Andrew Jackson in 1806; Dickinson reportedly had made insulting remarks about Jackson's wife.) The original house was swept away by the river in the 1850s. The present grand home was built across the road from the original homesite in 1857 by Edward Gay, Hynes's son-in-law and a onetime U.S. congressman. Gay named the house St. Louis, for his hometown. It is galleried with Ionic and Corinthian columns and decorated with ornamental ironwork and a belvedere or captain's walk. The design is a sophisticated version of American Classical Revival somewhat akin to that of many houses in the New Orleans Garden District. St. Louis was built with a cellar, very unusual in this area. In a rear wing is an old kitchen, original to the house. The formal gardens of St. Louis were famous for green roses. According to Mr. Gay's granddaughter, her grandmother invited female passengers from the steamboats that stopped at St. Louis landing to come for a walk in her gardens, perhaps a forerunner of the formal garden tour. Along the side street is a former overseer's house.

13.3 Old Evergreen Road and (**13.9**) Evergreen Road are evidence of Evergreen Plantation, owned by Nicholas Wilson in the early nineteenth century, and then by Dr. John Stone, according to Persac. A Classical Revival mansion was built *circa* 1840. One of Stone's daughters married John Andrews, the scion of Belle Grove, just downriver. The Evergreen house was used as a school before it was abandoned in the 1940s.

14.0 Approximate site of the Reveille community.

14.1 Rebecca Road is on the site of Rebecca Plantation, named for Mrs. Nathaniel Cropper, who owned it in 1858. The plantation was bought by the Croppers in the early nineteenth century and was passed to Nathaniel's nephew, Norbert.

14.5 These old moss-draped oaks with sprawling limbs are thought to be the Rebecca homesite.

14.8 Ashland Chemical is on the site of Allemania Plantation, known as Hard Times Plantation until 1883, when it was purchased and renamed by John Reuss, an Ascension Parish planter who kept it until 1907. Allemania was not a large sugar plantation—only 1,800 acres—and the home was appropriately modest—a one-story house with galleries on three sides. It burned in the early 1930s. An additional home on the property was erected in 1908 by Alphonse Koch, then a partner in the Allemania Planting Company. Koch dismantled his family home in Waterloo, Louisiana, barged it down the river, and reassembled it at Allemania.

In the cane fields may be the site of Retreat Plantation, located just downriver from Allemania in the mid-nineteenth century. According to the memoir of a former owner, Retreat was named during the Civil War when her grandfather moved the family to the safety of the plantation as Federal troops threatened the citizenry of Plaquemine. The writer described the plantation in the prewar era: "Our house was about half a mile back from the river. . . . A whitewashed picket fence enclosed the big front yard. . . . In the rear was an extensive vegetable garden and an orchard of fruit trees." The plantation was largely self-supporting: "Very little food was bought on the outside except coffee, tea, ice and a few other table delicacies."

16.5 Somewhere amid these pasturelands and small farms once stood the little settlement of Soulouque, named for the plantation belonging to Théophile Allain, mulatto son of white planter Sosthène Allain and a slave woman. (Faustin Soulouque was a Haitian who proclaimed himself emperor in 1849 and was overthrown in 1858.) The younger Allain was well educated and a successful businessman who served in Louisiana state government from 1872 to 1890 and was instrumental in the founding of Southern University, the first Louisiana institution of higher education for blacks, opening in 1880. A post office established in Soulouque in 1876 was on the perimeter of Allemania Plantation; Théophile Allain served as postmaster. No structures from the settlement or plantation of Soulouque survive.

17.7 The cane fields are the site of Golden Ridge Plantation. An old barn and a quarters cabin survive down the gravel road.

18.2 The community of Point Pleasant was the oldest of three Louisiana towns so named. In 1810 the little community was selected as the second seat of government of Iberville Parish, replacing Galveztown, but the government offices did not move here until 1824, when a school building was pressed into service as a courthouse. After 1843, when the parish seat was shifted to Plaquemine, the building was used as St. Raphael's Chapel; it was demolished in 1936. The post office was closed in 1883. At the turn of the century, Point Pleasant was home to a large Italian community.

18.7 The small, rural St. Raphael's Cemetery contains the wrought-iron enclosed tomb of Paul O. Hébert, twelfth governor of Louisiana, whose plantation was a short distance upriver. Hébert was married to a daughter of John Andrews of Belle Grove Plantation. This grave and others were moved from the cemetery at Bayou Goula. The marble tomb isolated at the right front corner of the cemetery is the Ricard tomb, dating from 1860. Ricard was a descendant of Pierre Belly, a local Frenchman of substance who died in 1814. Belly's wife was Jamaican; his descendants were free blacks and people of means, although they were socially ostracized—even after death, as reflected in this tomb's placement. Some believe Belly's remains and those of his wife were moved here from the cemetery at St. Gabriel.

19.1 The Point Pleasant Baptist Church recalls that the river formation is still called Point Pleasant even if the town itself has dis-

Paul Octave Hébert, planter, army officer, state engineer, and governor of Louisiana (1853–1856).
Courtesy State Library of Louisiana

appeared. A large church bell, or old plantation bell, is in front of the church.

19.3 The oaks on the left side of the River Road suggest a former homesite, probably from before construction of the modern levee and road.

20.1 The overgrown, faded green cinderblock building is the Old

Salvato Store, one of the landmark businesses of the Italian community. The remains of a factory where tomato products and syrup were canned are located to the rear.

20.4 Chapel of the Madonna. The story most accepted for the founding of this tiny church involves one Anthony Gullo, a member of the Italian community who settled in Iberville in the latter part of the nineteenth century. When Gullo's daughter fell critically ill in 1901, he pledged to build a church if his prayers were answered and she recovered. She did, and he built the Chapel of the Madonna—an eight-foot octagon—just large enough for a priest and two altar boys. When the levee was moved in 1928 and the chapel was replaced, it was enlarged to nine feet square. Services are held on August 15, the Feast of the Assumption of the Blessed Virgin Mary. Outside the chapel is the requisite church bell.

20.5 Over the next quarter mile appear several remnant buildings thought to be from Palo Alto Plantation, which belonged to Pierre Ayraud. Jacob Lemann bought the property in 1867, one of several plantations that the Lemanns of Donaldsonville bought from financially troubled landowners in this area during the postwar period.

20.9 The approximate site of Elizabeth Plantation, a sugarcane and cotton plantation. A new Southern Colonial house was built on the property in 1961 using cypress from the slave quarters at Glenmore and bricks from the St. Elizabeth sugar mill and Belle Grove plantation. Old bells found beneath the house date to the early nineteenth century. St. Elizabeth remains a working plantation.

Two weathered cabins on the property may be quarters.

21.0 Troxclair Drive is the site of Dunboyne Plantation, named for family property in Ireland. A Creole-cum-Classical Revival home was built in 1832 by Colonel Edward Butler, whose wife was a grandniece of George Washington. Edward Gay bought the property in 1874. The house was in grave disrepair when it was demolished in 1967. The land is now owned by Union Carbide.

22.5 This field is the approximate site of an archeological investigation of Indian mounds dating from the Plaquemine culture. Nothing remains; the mounds were plowed under after the archaeologists completed their study.

Dunboyne Plantation house in decay, probably *circa* 1960.
Courtesy O. J. Dupuy Collection

Iberville's journal describes an Indian village—the main village of the Bayougoulas—"about 65 leagues from the mouth" of the river, approximately where the town of Bayou Goula is located today. The village contained about 100 huts—"windowless and covered with split canes"—and a temple "made of staves, thirty feet across and round, built with wood to the height of a man within a 10 ft. wall of cane." The hospitable Indians fed the Frenchmen sagamite (made by boiling cornmeal and wood-ash lye), beans, and corn cooked in bear grease.

In 1700 the Jesuit missionary Paul du Ru erected a small church with mud and moss walls and a thatched palmetto roof. He traded an ax and knife to an Indian named Longamougoulache for a field in which he raised a cross and attempted—unsuccessfully—to convert the Bayougoulas. The church was destroyed shortly thereafter.

From du Ru's diary: "This evening I went to the village which is more than 600 years old. There is a huge plaza in the midst of it and at the end of this two temples of about equal size. The one belongs to the Mougoulachas, the other to the

*Bayogoulas, for the village is composed of these two tribes.
These temples are made of thatch and are covered with cane
mats. Their shape is quite like the dome of the portal of the
College du Plessis. . . . One of these temples has two little
points like steeples on which there is a figure of a rooster facing the east. . . . I entered [both temples] and saw the lamp of
eternal fire which is maintained because there is no other light
when the door is closed. I saw there many rows of packages
piled one on the other. These are the bones of the dead chiefs
which are carefully wrapped in palm mats. Their cabins are
large, especially those of the chiefs where nearly 300 persons
can be assembled . . . of the same materials as the temples."*

Later in that same year of 1700, the Bayougoulas turned on their
neighbors in a surprise attack that all but exterminated the Mugulashas.

22.8 Town of Bayou Goula. It is thought that the name derives
from the Choctaw *bayuk* and *okla* meaning "bayou or river people." The Bayougoulas had a settlement at the head of the Bayou
Goula waterway; archaeologists believe that the original site of the
main village was perhaps three miles away from the river, which
has subsequently meandered. Soon after the arrival of the French,
the tribe provided refuge to the Taensa Indians, who had been
driven from their traditional lands to the north. In 1706, in a bloody
reprise of what the Bayougoulas had done to the Mugulashas, the
Taensa turned on their hosts, virtually wiping out the Bayougoulas.
The Taensa remained in the area until 1718 or so. The few surviving
Bayougoulas fled—in 1707 they were living downriver from the
future site of New Orleans. In 1725 the group moved just upriver
from New Orleans. By 1739, the remnants of the tribe were living
among the Houma and Acolapissa, with little cultural distinction.

No European settlement existed in this area until after the Taensas' departure, when the Duverney concession was established,
growing indigo and tobacco. French and Acadian settlers arrived
in the late eighteenth century, and over the next century Bayou
Goula grew to be a major service and supply center for the area.
By the 1840s, it was an important port and steamboat landing.
When native son Paul O. Hébert ran for governor of the state in
1852, a large rally was staged at Bayou Goula Landing.

"I made my way along the levee road . . . to the village of Bayou Goula . . . a pleasant looking but very loosely settled place. It looks as if it had been fired off at random and scattered along the coast. There are . . . two hotels of considerable dimensions named, respectively, the Bayou Goula Hotel and the Buena Vista Hotel. . . . The dancing hall and the dining hall at [the Buena Vista] are painted in a highly elaborate and ornamental manner." J. W. Dorr, 1860.

Several Civil War skirmishes occurred in the area. After the war, Bayou Goula continued to grow through 1910 despite levee setbacks that forced the abandonment of much of the original settlement. Some of the buildings were relocated, but many were destroyed. After the turn of the century, the White Castle Shingle and Lumber Company downriver drew population away with new job opportunities, and Bayou Goula began to wither.

A local legend growing out of Creole voodoo is that *loups-garous* (werewolves) held their annual Louisiana ball on the banks of Bayou Goula until the 1940s. Visitors were warned that watching this festivity was dangerous, even when armed with the requisite antidotes of a bag of salt or live frogs. Believers reported such transmogrifications as the local who turned himself into a mule in order to plow his fields.

Voodoo, or voudou, is a religion that originated in Africa and was widely practiced by the blacks of Haiti; it was brought to Louisiana by slaves both directly from Africa and from Haiti. Voodoo is based on principles of animism and ancestor worship, and uses trances and sacrificial rites in its practice.

23.0 At Herman Brown Street (Parish Road 2) is St. Luke's Methodist Church, built in 1868 and remodeled in 1901 to serve a black congregation. Church scenes in the film *The Autobiography of Miss Jane Pittman* were shot at St. Luke's. Behind the overgrown cottage next door is a large barrel cistern.

23.1 St. Paul's Catholic Church, built in 1871, is located near the spot where Father Paul du Ru built his rudimentary church—the first French mission church in Louisiana—in 1700. (The actual site is now on the other side of the levee.) A white frame country Gothic church with a graceful octagonal steeple, St. Paul's stands on property donated by Paul Hébert. The wooden interior is decorated with an Italian influence—brightly painted altars and frames of the Stations of the Cross, reflecting the influence of a sizable Italian population. During the 1927 flood, the riverbank caved in at Bayou Goula. When the levee was set back, the church was moved, as was the cemetery, which had been behind the church; many of the tombs were relocated to St. Raphael's Cemetery in Point Pleasant.

Next door to the church is a raised yellow Victorian cottage once used by the manager of the adjacent mercantile establishment. This brick store was built by Jeremiah Supple after the Civil War. Supple lived downriver in Donaldsonville, and his store and home there were destroyed by Federal troops. He moved to Bayou Goula, but finding no available plantations nearby, bought Kinsale Plantation downriver, where he and his family stayed, thus necessitating a manager for the store. The store closed in the 1960s.

Next to Supple's Store is a second commercial building, a frame structure with a shedded gallery—Engolio's Store. The uneven roofline denotes that this building had two separate functions: the downriver end was a grocery; the upriver end was a saloon dating back to the early 1800s.

Bayou Goula Landing was across the road from these stores.

23.2 Just downriver from Engolio's is the unimposing but historic Richard House. This antebellum home in booming downtown Bayou Goula was shelled during the Civil War. Local lore says that a wedding was taking place at the time, and the owners sent a servant to the landing to flag the gunship and ask its officers and crew to quit shooting and come to the celebration. According to the tale, the Federals camped at the house thereafter, and the locals cooked for them—thus assuring themselves of a continuing supply of food. In the early twentieth century, the upstairs was used as a school.

Several maritime catastrophes have occurred on the river at Bayou Goula, including the 1851 collision of two steamboats, the *Autocrat* and the *Magnolia*. The *Autocrat* sank; thirty years later, it was joined on the bottom by the *Laura Lee* after a similar collision. In 1908 the sternwheel packet *H. M. Carter* exploded and sank at Bayou Goula Bend.

Bayou Goula Towhead is a midstream island in the river, one of the few islands along this part of the Mississippi. The towhead was created by the lateral erosion against the outside of the bend.

Side trip: Just past the Richard House, unmarked La. 69 (gravel) to La. 1. Turn right at La. 1 and left at Augusta Road, across the highway from the Bayou Goula Landing historical marker. In this area were several sugar plantations, including Forest Home, where John Hampden Randolph lived before building the lavish, riverfront Nottoway. Along Augusta Road can be seen a graveyard, on the site where the Blythewood house once stood, and The Oaks, a small Classical Revival cottage, *circa* 1840, with several outbuildings. Farther along the road is Forest Home, located five and a half miles from the Mississippi River but fronting on Bayou Goula. Dr. Henry A. Doyle purchased the property from the federal government and Gideon Pearce in the 1830s and built the house. John Randolph purchased it from Doyle in 1841. After the war, Randolph returned his former slaves to Forest Home as freedmen. The house is modest and architecturally simple; a kitchen extension and one wing have been removed. Although Randolph wrote that he preferred the backwoods location of Forest Home, his success and the superior location along the Mississippi dictated his move to Nottoway.

23.4 A stand of trees just downriver from the corner of Murrell Street is the site of Tally Ho Plantation house. Parish records indicate that the property was obtained by Jean Fleming, a free man of color, sometime before 1835. Several owners succeeded Fleming, including John D. Murrell of Virginia, who bought the plantation in 1848; it has remained in the family ever since, although the house is said to have been moved back from the river twice. The name Tally Ho is presumed to reflect John Murrell's Virginia fox-hunting background.

After the Civil War, the Murrell family managed to retain their property by diversifying sugar production with cotton and moss ginning. The current home is an Acadian raised cottage with Classical Revival influence and was at one time the overseer's house, but became used as the main house after a fire on the property in 1945. Except for the removal of corner stairways, the main facade is original. An earthen loading dock at Tally Ho was the site of showboat performances; the *New Sensation,* the first of the Mississippi troubadours (1878), stopped here to perform vaudeville-type shows. The Tally Ho property was enlarged through purchase of The Oaks, Blythewood, Augusta, St. Mary, Glenmore, and Forest Home.

The Tally Ho barn and office are down a side road. Just past them is a quarters cabin.

23.8 A sign on the levee honors the *White Alder,* a Coast Guard ship that sank here in the 1960s after a wreck with a freighter. All on board the *White Alder* perished.

24.0 In the cane fields is Eureka Road, site of Eureka Plantation, owned by Dr. Henry A. Doyle, according to Persac, and comprising approximately 1,200 acres. The Eureka Overseer's House, a raised Acadian cottage built *circa* 1830, was moved next door to Nottoway Plantation. Eureka's main house is now in the river. It is said that a three-story building housing racehorses on the first floor and jockeys and racing fans above was a local landmark at Eureka. Locals believe that a Confederate cemetery exists somewhere along the property between Tally Ho and Eureka.

24.7 John Hampden Randolph completed Nottoway Plantation House in 1859, one of the last grand antebellum mansions built before the Civil War devastated the countryside and the economy. The name is said to be from the Algonquin *nodowa,* "rattlesnake"; the Algonquins were a tribe in Virginia, and Randolph was born on the Nottoway River in that state. He bought the Nottoway property in 1855, while he was living at Forest Home.

Architect Henry Howard was contracted to design the impressive neo-classical and Italianate mansion, literally an American castle, to serve as home to Randolph's family of eleven children. Primarily constructed of native cypress, the home featured cutting-edge amenities such as (primitive) indoor plumbing, gas lighting, and coal fireplaces. The house has sixty-four rooms and 53,000 square feet under roof, including a large white ballroom with hand-carved columns, archways, lacy friezework and medallions, original crystal chandeliers, and white marble mantels. The friezes were the handiwork of Jeremiah Supple, the Donaldsonville store owner, who worked for Howard on this project.

During the Civil War, Randolph and a son took the family's slaves and movable property to Texas while Mrs. Randolph stayed at Nottoway. The house survived the war because, according to an often-told tale, a northern gunboat officer had previously been a guest there and ordered it to be spared; a small cannonball, however, is still lodged in a wall near the upstairs gallery, and Union soldiers did steal the plantation's livestock—although they returned it the next day. A painting in the Nottoway collection shows the house's setting when the Randolphs lived here; an additional seven acres separated the house from the river, but the migration of the channel necessitated a levee setback in the 1950s that captured most of Nottoway's gracious park. Randolph also owned and ran Blythewood, Augusta, and Forest Home Plantations.

Nottoway remained in the Randolph family until 1889 and was subsequently sold four times. The house has never been vacant and was restored in 1980 to reflect the grandeur of the Randolphs' residency. Because the house is tall, the river view from the upstairs front windows is especially dramatic, a vista including Bayou Goula Towhead. Open to the public.

From the memoir of M. R. Ailenroc, the pen name of John Randolph's daughter, Cornelia Randolph Murrell, is a description of the grounds of Nottoway as it looked in her youth: "Across the public road from the foot of the levee, a stately gate with a small one on either side for pedestrians, guarded the carriage approach which wound at leisure over the front pasture through groups of catalpa, magnolia grandiflora and other trees, until it reached a green iron carriage gate dividing a low hawthorn hedge, beyond which it continued its way through a long avenue of Normandy poplars, where at intervals stood mythological characters in marble. When the drive left the poplars it turned around a circle leading to the mansion and through which a narrow walk rambled. . . . The terrace was formed by what was said to have once been an Indian mound. . . . There was a narrow walk on the highest part, running east and west, bordered by oleander trees. . . . Beneath it was a grotto facing the walk in the circle. . . . On the right of the avenue was the greenhouse and near the turn of the circle was a fancy shed used as a shelter for waiting vehicles and saddle-horses. Flower beds sprawled around here wherever it was suitable to have them. In the distance from here was a vista of majestic live oaks and a fence screening the negro quarters. . . . [Left of the avenue] was an orchard*

of several acres, filled with semi-tropic fruits and nut trees and
stretching on in ample proportions, a garden for the planta-
tion family of several hundreds.

"To the rear . . . a row of althea trees and a tall cistern
obscured the back yard where were pigeon houses, a terrapin
pond . . . the gas house, other outhouses, and a commodious
stable, rabbit hutches and hunting dogs' kennels. Opening
into this on the south was a generous fowl yard, a space within
inclosed by long split cypress palings which the negroes called
a fort, to keep young turkeys and their mothers from going
astray."

25.3 D'Orcy Road and LaCroix Road are the streets of Dorseyville
(sometimes written as Dorcyville), named for the Reverend Basile
Dorsey, a black minister and landowner who lived here in the late
nineteenth century. The settlement was created when freed slaves
from nearby plantations bought land and built homes around the
St. John Baptist Church. The church, located on LaCroix Road,
was established by the Reverend Dorsey in 1868 and is still in use.
The cemetery behind the church dates from the same period. Local
lore says that construction of the church was underwritten by dues
and tithes signed with Xs, as none of the parishioners knew how
to write. Before the baptismal pool was built in the 1920s, baptisms
were conducted in the river. The school building, originally an elongated Creole-style cottage, today much altered, is just across La-
Croix Road. It was erected in 1891 and is now used as a church
facility. The community had a post office from 1881 to 1918.

25.5 According to Persac, the property just downriver of Randolph's plantation was owned by Durand and Dubuclet. Antoine
Dubuclet was born a free black and became the wealthiest African
American along the River Road prior to the Civil War. He owned
more than 100 slaves. He served as the highly respected state treasurer during Radical Reconstruction (1869 to 1877).

Catherine Road: Catherine/Kinsale Plantation may be located
on part of Dubuclet's property. The plantation was developed by
Jeremiah Supple, who emigrated from Kinsale, Ireland, as a child.
In 1852 he married Catherine McGillick, another Irish immigrant,
and settled in Donaldsonville. As noted, he worked with architect
Henry Howard and created the friezework for Nottoway. After
Supple's home and business were burned during the Civil War, he

moved to Bayou Goula and opened another store; it seems to have been run by his wife while he continued to create ornate plaster friezework for Howard's spectacular houses. Supple apparently did well with his enterprises; he was able to buy nearby Teresa sugar plantation and factory, which he renamed Kinsale, and other plantations. In 1906 the Kinsale sugar factory burned and a new mill was erected at Catherine, on the far side of La. 1 off Catherine Road. Near it is the present Catherine Plantation home, built 1939–1940 in the same style as the original, as well as a nineteenth-century overseer/manager's home.

25.8 Down Richland Road, just across La. 1, is the house—much altered enlarged—alleged to have been Pierre Belly's original home on Cedar Grove Plantation, although it may actually date from subsequent owners in the late nineteenth century. Belly, a Frenchman, received a Spanish land grant and settled in Iberville Parish in 1774 (he is said to have fought under Gálvez in 1779). The property was called Bayley's Estate on a map drafted in 1814, the year Belly died. His wife—a former slave—and six daughters inherited a quarter of Cedar Grove, including a three-by-eighty-arpent tract that became the property of Belly's daughter Eloise and her husband, George Deslondes. Deslondes was a wealthy free person of color who himself owned slaves. The Deslondes' son Pierre inherited the property and became Louisiana's secretary of state from 1873 to 1877. Part of Belly's family is buried in the Point Pleasant Cemetery. The plantation was sold at sheriff's sale in 1867 and purchased first by Antoine Dubuclet and subsequently by others, including August Lasseigne, a large landholder from east-bank St. John the Baptist Parish.

A portion of the property became known as the Zacharie Plantation in the 1830s, and later as White Castle Plantation. In 1875 it was bought by Leonce Soniat, who modernized the sugarhouse and improved production. In 1939 the sugarhouse was replaced with a new structure, the stack of which is still visible on the far side of La. 1. The big house, probably surviving from Soniat, was in bungalow style. Crape myrtles, oaks, and willows may indicate its former site.

26.0 A large oak tree may be the site of the White Castle Plantation house, built in the early nineteenth century for Thomas Vaughan and owned by Mrs. H. L. Vaughan in Persac's time. Legend attributes the naming of the house to future governor Paul Hébert's bride, née Vaughan, who arrived there after her wedding trip in 1842 and exclaimed, "It looks like a white castle." The house was two and a half stories, gabled, columned, and galleried, at the end of a quarter-mile drive overhung with weeping willows. A beautiful garden with marble statues was well known. The house was moved four times to escape the river, and it lost sections with each move. What eventually remained is said to have been divided into two cottages now in the town of White Castle.

26.2 The town of White Castle was not named for Nottoway, as is often presumed, but for White Castle Plantation. A portion of the plantation property was subdivided in 1884 by its part-owners to develop a company town for the local White Castle Lumber and Shingle Company. Along Bowie Street (La. 69) in White Castle are some of the homes constructed for lumber-company personnel. An old bank building has been preserved for commercial use. A passenger ferry operated from White Castle to the Hansen's Disease Center until the 1950s.

26.4 Junction La. 69; the River Road follows the levee as Highway 405.

26.7 A decorative yard sign proclaims Texas Plantation, part of the aggregated property that became the Cora Texas Manufacturing Company in 1928. Houses facing at a slant to the road indicate that the levee and road were moved. Texas Plantation was a holding of Norbert Cropper, who died in 1856.

26.8 Up Texas Road is a large sugar mill between the River Road and La. 1, the largest in this area. Cora Plantation was established in the late 1800s and is credited with being the first to introduce (in 1892) the sophisticated nine-roll sugar mill, which extracted a much higher percentage of juice than previous mills. The sugar mill burned in 1920; the plantation railroad was then extended three miles across Cedar Grove Plantation to Catherine so that Cora's cane could be processed at the Catherine refinery.

27.3 Cora Road.

27.4 The approximate site of Alhambra Plantation, part of a Spanish land grant to Pierre Sigur. *Alhambra* is a Spanish derivation from the Arabic *al-hamrā,* "red house." The plantation house was an impressive mansion built *circa* 1855 by Kentuckian Christopher Adams and was, indeed, painted red with a tile roof, a hard-to-miss landmark for passing steamboats. The house was torn down in 1917.

27.6 Laurel Ridge Road denotes the site of Laurel Ridge Plantation. This small piece of a larger holding was willed to the "faithful servants" of Julie Marionneaux, widow of Thomas Cropper. Cropper arrived in the area just prior to 1800. The house, Italianate Classical Revival in design, is thought to have been constructed in 1874. It received little attention, however, because of its location between the eye-catching Alhambra and the extraordinary Belle Grove.

28.0 White Castle–Carville toll ferry landing.

28.1 Stone and Ware Streets are named for the last owner, Stone Ware, of the spectacular Belle Grove Plantation, which was on this site. One of the grandest plantations in the Mississippi River Valley, Belle Grove was designed by James Gallier for John Andrews. A sampling of the group of beautiful oaks for which it was named form a line parallel to the River Road. The grand mansion was begun in 1857, while John Randolph's Nottoway was under construction, and it has been claimed that Andrews was trying to outdo his neighbor. The house was a tall, rose-pink, two-story structure with basement and seventy-five rooms. Corinthian columns, Roman arched windows, pilasters, friezework, and iron-railed balconies were a few of its grand elements, complemented by features such as twelve onyx marble mantels and silver doorknobs and keyhole covers. It is said that the first bathtub in the South was installed at Belle Grove. Twenty-eight acres of gardens surrounded the house, which boasted three-quarters of a mile of river frontage.

Henry Ware purchased Belle Grove in 1867. Mary Eliza Stone Ware, married to Henry's son, furnished the home lavishly. Two racetracks were added to the grounds over several decades by Mary Eliza's husband and their son. Descendant Stone Ware was forced to auction his furnishings and abandon Belle Grove when his sugarcane crop failed in 1924. The house, fallen to ruin, burned in 1952.

29.0 In this approximate area is the location of Celeste, a sugar plantation established *circa* 1807 by Edward Lauve, a Frenchman from New Orleans, and named for his wife. The Lauves had nine-

Belle Grove, once the grandest of Mississippi Valley plantation houses, was abandoned and deteriorating in this 1930s photograph.
Courtesy Louisiana and Lower Mississippi Valley Collections, Hill Memorial Library, LSU

teen children. When Edward died in 1843, he was buried in a sepulcher in front of his sugarhouse. His wife then ran the 3,000-acre property until her death at age eighty-one in 1869. The house and the burial tomb were swept away by the river. During the latter part of the nineteenth century, the plantation changed hands several times until James Ware incorporated it into Belle Grove holdings in 1896.

29.2 Cannonburg Road denotes the site of Cannonburg Plantation and store, named for Captain John Cannon. A post office was established at the Cannon Store in 1879 but closed in 1895. A church—Brazil Church and cemetery are nearby—and a public hall were also near the landing. The settlement was called Mt. Salem in the 1880s.

31.1 The approximate site of Claiborne Plantation and Claiborne Landing, owned by William C. C. Claiborne. A commissioner to receive the Louisiana Purchase territory, Claiborne was made governor of the Orleans Territory in 1803. As an American, he met considerable resentment from the Creole population, but his good character eventually won them over and smoothed the way for the institution of representative government in Louisiana (it did not hurt that, after his first wife died of yellow fever, he married a woman from a good Louisiana family, and that after she, too, died, he married a woman of Spanish and New Orleans Creole background). In 1811 Claiborne wrote to Julien Poydras that he had bought a plantation and would become "a plain, simple planter"; soon thereafter he was elected as first governor of the new state of Louisiana. In 1817 he was elected to the United States Senate, but he died before taking office; he was forty-two years old. He left his papers to Henry Johnson, a local luminary and friend who served as governor of Louisiana from 1824 to 1828. A post office existed at Claiborne Plantation in 1833 and, later, a store and steamboat landing. Claiborne Island, situated just beyond the levee, continues the name.

31.4 A sprinkling of Creole-style cottages comes into view near the parish line. The vista from atop the levee is of Claiborne Island.

From History of Louisiana, *by François Xavier Martin, 1827: "Between Bayou Lafourche and Bayou Plaquemine, the banks of the Mississippi are thickly settled, but the sugar plantations are few and the planters not so wealthy as below Donaldsonville."*

31.8 Iberville/Ascension Parish line.

32.0 A grove of live oaks in a pasture marks the site of Chatham Plantation, established as a sugar plantation by future Louisiana governor Henry Johnson *circa* 1820. The property was originally several small cotton farms. It is said that many important personages visited at Chatham Plantation, among them Henry Clay, whose sojourn was marked by champagne flowing "deep enough to float a battleship." According to Persac, J. R. Thompson owned both Chatham and Claiborne Plantations in 1858. The Chatham property was owned after the Civil War by John Reuss. The home burned *circa* 1930, but a few of the magnificent live oaks that surrounded the house survive, as does an old cistern. The downriver end of Claiborne Island runs in front of the Chatham homesite and downriver to Hohen Solms.

32.2 The lowland on the left side of the road is thought to be a relic of a crevasse site.

32.8 A raised Creole-style cottage and old store.

33.1 Hohen Solms was a small agricultural community established in the mid-nineteenth century in the center of a group of sugarcane plantations by German immigrant Johann (John) Reuss (pronounced locally as "Rice"). The settlement's name was derived, according to locals, from Reuss's home, the principality of Hohenzollern. Son George B. Reuss later purchased Ashland Plantation, across the river, and renamed it Belle Helene for his daughter.

In this area was Dominique's store, where a Civil War skirmish took place in 1865.

33.3 Germania Plantation house and (**33.5**) Germania Plantation store. The house—overgrown and sadly deteriorated—is a Victorian bungalow with Eastlake influences, including a cast-iron balustrade. John Reuss purchased the property in 1867 and built this house *circa* 1885, although it is believed that the rear of the home is antebellum, predating Reuss's additions. Numerous outbuildings remain, including a church and barns. Germania was created when Reuss combined several plantations.

33.7 The Mulberry Grove Plantation complex was built in 1836 for Virginia native Dr. Edward Duffel, his Acadian bride, and their first child (Mrs. Duffel was a descendant of Joseph Landry, a planter and high governmental official in the Ascension and St. James area). After the Civil War, the property was acquired by John Reuss, who made Mulberry Grove part of Germania. The current Mulberry Grove house was once the overseer's home. Fallen into disrepair, it was rediscovered in 1951 being used as a hay barn and was graciously restored as a Classical Revival mansion with some Virginia influences and Creole elements. The two-story home, galleried with squared columns, shares the property with a weathered red barn and four small tenant quarters, *circa* 1890, strung downriver along River Road.

34.4 The red-brick, faintly neo-Gothic Elsie school, tucked in a stand of trees, is thought to have been built *circa* 1900 for classes through the eighth grade. It is on the property formerly known as Elsie Plantation, another Reuss family holding and named for one of his children. The school was in operation until approximately 1926. It was later converted to a private home.

34.8 In these cane fields was the approximate site of Cuba Plantation, another of Reuss's late-nineteenth-century holdings. By the

1920s, part of the downriver arpentage of Cuba was Africa Plantation, owned by a prominent black physician. He employed black workers in a sugarcane cooperative.

35.2 Here is the approximate beginning of the community of Modeste, thought to have been named in 1908 after a local Italian priest named Modestinus.

Along this stretch of Philadelphia Point was the property of W. C. S. Ventress. It was later called Home Plantation and owned by Colonel Louis Landry before its sale in 1882 to the partnership of Seymour and Yale. Next downriver was Woodstock Plantation, owned for most of the second half of the nineteenth century by Edward Duffel of Mulberry Grove. Woodstock is said to have had the first rice field in this area.

Modeste is on the upriver side of Philadelphia Point, also called Glinnar Point on Persac's map. Modeste was the locus of operations for merchant and leading citizen Henry Bruyere, who opened a store at his residence here and started a woodyard, also noted on Persac.

35.6 Julien Street celebrates local musician and inventor Leonard Julien, who in the 1960s created the first mechanical cane harvester. He field tested the machine in 1964 before three hundred onlookers to prove his claim that he could plant twelve acres of cane in one day with five men, three small wagons, and two tractors, rather than the conventional team of sixteen men, eight wagons, and four tractors. Despite obtaining a patent for his design, Julien—who was black—never realized great profit from his invention; it is said that someone else bought a machine, slightly altered the design, and went on to market it with great success. Nevertheless, Julien was recognized by state and local officials in 1974 and lived with his accolades until his death in 1994.

35.9 Ruins of a Creole cottage with a rear under-roof shed addition.

In this area was Pellico, or Pelico, Plantation, owned by Edmond Bujol, according to Persac, and owned in 1882 by the partnership of Bujol and Emile St. Martin, son and son-in-law of Edmond. Just downriver was the Melancon tract, marked for more than fifty years by damage from the crevasse of 1828.

36.5 Mt. Calvary Baptist Church was founded in 1895. Just past the church, the River Road takes a dramatic right turn, indicating a levee setback. On the inside of the levee along this area of Philadelphia Point, the batture is in some places almost a half mile wide. It is thought that the flood of 1882—the great flood of that period— tore through the levee, which would have been located on the outside of the current levee. Since 1882 the river has migrated east and created the large batture.

37.2 This postbellum cottage is on property that was part of a Spanish land grant.

37.7 Caballero Road is the site of Ascension Plantation, owned in 1846 by Captain Narcisse Landry, a veteran of the War of 1812. His raised plantation house had Classical Revival renovations, including a central front stairway and an enclosed, plastered lower story. After the Civil War, John Burnside bought the property. During Oliver Beirne's administration after Burnside's death, the New Hope sugar refinery was built on the boundary between Ascension and New Hope Plantations. The mill could process more than two million pounds of sugar annually.

The levee here seems lower than elsewhere, but that is because the road is slightly elevated relative to the fields.

38.9 New Hope Road is the site of New Hope Plantation, first owned by Trasimond Landry in 1817 as a family partnership. The raised plantation house was built *circa* the 1840s; the front gallery has been partially screened. Trasimond Landry's father, Joseph, was one of the first Acadian exiles to settle in this area. He became district commandant during the Spanish colonial period and a member of the legislature following statehood. At the time of his death in 1814, he was a prosperous man and his family owned holdings on both sides of the river. New Hope remained in the Landry family until its sale to John Burnside after the Civil War.

39.7 The property in this area has been in the Evan Jones–McCall family since the late eighteenth century. The upriver portion, once owned by a Joseph Blanchard, became part of the McManor plantation of Richard McCall, a son of Henry McCall and himself the father of thirteen children. Henry McCall came to Louisiana in the early nineteenth century and married Celeste, daughter of Evan Jones. When Celeste died a year later, he married her younger sister and continued his relationship with the Jones estate.

The Evan Hall Sugar Mill in operation in the late nineteenth century.
Courtesy Louisiana and Lower Mississippi Valley Collections, Hill Memorial Library, LSU

39.9 Here the River Road veers away from the river. To the left, in antebellum days, stood Evan Hall Plantation house, built by Henry McCall near the original Creole house of Evan Jones. The magnificent house, in modified Classical Revival style and raised several feet, was torn down when the levee was moved. The plantation was one of the grandest and most extensive in the area.

Evan Jones was an "American immigrant" to Louisiana who purchased Spanish land grant property from the heirs of Desiderato LeBlanc in 1778. Jones had traded in the West Indies and spoke fluent French and Spanish. He received a Spanish land grant for additional acreage in 1787 and served as commandant for several years. His first crops here were indigo and cotton, but the plantation was converted to sugarcane in 1807. After Jones's death, Henry McCall operated the plantation. His sugar mill ran on horse power until 1830, when McCall erected a steam mill. The partnership of Evan Hall–McCall–McManor was one of the most important nineteenth-century sugar producers. The plantation was given the name Evan Hall in 1860 to honor Jones's memory. After the Civil War, the family managed the property on an absentee basis. A plantation store was built *circa* 1870 and a school for the plantation children—

black and white—*circa* 1890. The property was still owned by the heirs of Henry McCall at the turn of the twentieth century, but the mill closed in 1901. The property was lost to a New Orleans bank creditor in 1916. Evan Hall mill reopened in 1936 as a cooperative among a group of local sugar farmers.

40.5 Extant from the plantation community are two brick structures thought to have been quarters—one has been renovated, one is in ruins—dating from approximately 1850. Brick quarters cabins were rare along the River Road.

At La. 1 is the Evan Hall Sugar Cooperative Mill, a working mill. (Turn left on La. 1.)

41.4 On the right is the site of Souvenir Plantation—once the property of Valéry Landry, who was killed in the Civil War. The property was sold, then reclaimed by an heir, Prosper Landry, who named it Souvenir. By 1882, it had been acquired by Leon Godchaux, whose sugar empire was based across the river in Reserve, in east-bank St. John the Baptist Parish. A double row of oak trees is visible. On the left is a house—thought to be the overseer's home—from Souvenir Plantation; it has clearly been moved from another site and positioned to face the road.

42.0 The settlement of Smoke Bend was known in the mid-nineteenth century as Faubourg la Boucane—"neighborhood of the smoke." Legend attributes the name to the sight that early river travelers had when they rounded the large bend just above here and saw towers of smoke rising into the air from Indian campfires. The settlement was once a separate community, boasting its own post office until 1953. The levee was moved after the 1927 flood, and some of the small community was lost.

42.8 Donaldsonville corporate limits, now including Smoke Bend and Port Barrow.

42.9 The St. Francis of Assisi Chapel was begun in 1884—"the largest building in Smoke Bend settlement," according to contemporary documents. It was destroyed by the hurricane of 1909 but rebuilt in 1910; that building in turn was replaced in the 1970s with the current structure. All were at the same location.

43.8 Bayou Lafourche and La. 18. The settlement of Port Barrow was on the upriver side of Bayou Lafourche at the Mississippi River.

The only permanent bridge from Port Barrow to Donaldsonville was located to the left of La. 1. Bayou Lafourche, often called "the longest street in the world" because of the side-by-side settlement along it, extends from here to the Gulf of Mexico. The bayou was long considered a mixed blessing—a vital transportation artery but an ever-present threat to flood area plantations when the Mississippi was high. Closing the bayou's mouth at the river was debated as early as 1855, when the first bridge was erected for crossing from Port Barrow and points north. In 1903 locals built a dam and blocked the channel; the dam was deemed official in 1935. In recent years debate has arisen regarding the controlled reopening of the channel at the river, the primary purpose of which is freshwater diversion to the coastal marshes.

> *"This is about sixty miles above New Orleans; the inhabitants along here are called Arcadians [sic], . . . The old people all speak good English (moved from Cape Britton) but the young ones who have been born and raised here French. Many of them [are] wealthy and make a large quantity of cotton, but their part of the country is not so highly cultivated as the Dutch [German] Coast joining below or the French still lower toward Orleans." Dr. John Sibley, 1802.*

Left on La. 18: Port Barrow was incorporated in 1862 and known as a hotbed of Confederate guerrillas, according to Union general Benjamin Butler. In 1863 Federal troops constructed a star-shaped log-and-earth fort, Fort Butler, at Port Barrow. The fort guarded the strategic confluence of Bayou Lafourche and the Mississippi. In 1863 a Confederate force attacked and briefly entered the fort but, with the arrival of Union gunboats, was driven out with heavy losses. Part of the fort's moat wall is still visible. An Acadian-style cottage near the levee is thought to have been within the fort walls. Downriver from the fort site is a rolling greensward, Bayou Lafourche's source, now filled in. Port Barrow became part of Donaldsonville in 1930.

> *Tolls for the bridge crossing Bayou Lafourche, 1855: Passengers, 5 cents; gig or buggy, 25 cents; four-wheeled carriage, 40 cents; empty cart or wagon, 15 cents; loaded plantation cart, 20 cents; peddler's cart, $1.*

Side trip: La. 18 south (to the right) meanders along the west

Fort Butler, 1863.
Courtesy State Library of Louisiana

side of Bayou Lafourche to several lovely and well-preserved plantation homes. A steamboat landing once operated where Opelousas Street intersects the bayou. Approximately three miles down the bayou is Palo Alto, a large Creole house completed *circa* 1850 and one of the few homes remaining that are documented by Adrien Persac paintings. (It is said that Persac augmented his paintings of houses and landscapes by cutting human figures out of *Collier's* magazine and pasting them on his work.) Many large oaks shade the grounds, which include a garçonnière and outbuildings. An old cypress picket fence, exemplary of the once-prevalent fences along the River Road, encircles the rear of the house. Behind the main house is a smaller raised Creole cottage. A sugarhouse, one of the finest in the area, was razed in 1916.

A short distance farther is St. Emma, originally called Kock's (sometimes written as Koch's or Cox) Plantation. This Classical Revival home, built *circa* 1850, was owned from 1854 to 1869 by Charles A. Kock, one of the largest sugar-plantation owners and slaveholders in the area. A large Civil War skirmish took place at St. Emma and Palo Alto in 1863 when Union forces on a foraging mission from Donaldsonville unexpectedly ran into a contingent of Texas troops and were routed, suffering 56 men killed, 217 wounded, and 186 captured. St. Emma provided quarters for the Confederates.

Across the bayou from St. Emma is Belle Alliance, which also belonged to Kock. The Classical Revival home, whose name means "beautiful union" or "beautiful marriage," was built in 1846 by Henry McCall and sold to Kock in 1859; it remained in the Kock family until 1915. The Belle Alliance property had been the site of an Isleño (Canary Islander) settlement during the Spanish colonial period.

Side trip: Continue on La. 18 to the left to tour the town of Donaldsonville. Located on the downriver side of the confluence of Bayou Lafourche and the Mississippi River, the town was founded at the approximate site where Iberville encountered a Chitimacha Indian village during his explorations along the river in 1699. The French called the bayou La Fourche des Chetimaches—"the Fork of the Chitimachas." After a group of Chitimachas killed Father St. Cosmé near here in 1707—allegedly, the missionary was murdered for his luggage—Bienville banished the tribe and opened their territory for colonial settlement. The tribe moved west to the Atchafalaya River Basin but, after peace was made with the French in 1718, reestablished itself along the river between Bayous Lafourche and Plaquemine. With colonial settlement, however, their lands were soon occupied and the Chitimachas pushed out. The tribe, federally recognized, now resides in Charenton, on the west side of the Atchafalaya Basin.

Acadians arrived in the Donaldsonville area in 1765 and 1766, and their settlements became known as the Second Acadian Coast. The newcomers farmed on a smaller scale than the large indigo planters downriver. The Spanish established a church parish for the area in 1772, and the settlement around it was called L'Ascension.

The town of Donaldson (*ville de Donaldson*) was founded in 1806 when William Donaldson bought property from the widow of Acadian Pierre Landry. Donaldson also owned east-bank property that became part of the large Houmas House Plantation. He is said to have built the first steam-powered lumber mill in the United States in 1807. The tract he purchased from Widow Landry had a river frontage of seven arpents one toise and a depth of several blocks, with Bayou Lafourche its western boundary. Donaldson laid out a plan of his town as the seat of both parish and state government and named a street or square for each county in the Territory of Orleans—Orleans, German Coast, Acadia, Lafourche, Iberville, Pointe Coupée, Attakapas, Opelousas, Natchitoches, Rapides, and Ouachita (some of these street names have since been

This building was Louisiana's seat of government during the brief reign of
Donaldsonville as state capital.
Courtesy State Library of Louisiana

changed). According to an account written in 1816—it might easily
have been penned by Donaldson himself—the new settlement was
"the first village on the river above New Orleans worth noting."
The town was renamed Donaldsonville in 1822 and selected to be
the state capital in 1825. Because of politics, however, New Orleans
remained the capital until 1829, when the legislature removed to
Donaldsonville only long enough for the 1829–1830 session. Supposedly the town's muddy streets and a strong lobbying effort by
Baton Rouge newspapers negated any chance of Donaldsonville's
retaining its political distinction.

> *"I have made my grand entrée into the first town which
> graces its banks above Jefferson City—Donaldsonville being
> a town proper, for it is incorporated. It is the parish seat of
> Ascension, one corner of which juts across to the right bank
> of the river. [The confluence of Bayou Lafourche and the Mis-
> sissippi] is crossed here by a well-constructed drawbridge
> which lets the steamers out and in and the road travelers over.*
> *"Donaldsonville . . . is laid out with right-angular regular-
> ity and the streets are very pleasant, handsome residences
> being not unfrequent upon them, and handsome trees every-*

where. . . . The population of Donaldsonville is almost exclusively Creole. . . . Donaldsonville has a finely and substantially constructed wharf, the first this side of New Orleans on the right bank, and boasts two hotels—Jarry's House . . . and the Planter's Hotel, a roaring concern if there ever was one with a popular five cent bar, a popular cock-pit in the yard, and a popular rush of all sorts of populace playing kino all day Sunday in the barroom, a cockfight coming off in the pit at stated intervals of one hour from morn till night." J. W. Dorr, 1860.

Donaldsonville was oriented toward the river until after the arrival of the railroad in 1871, when the centers of population and commerce moved closer to the depot. Crescent Place, on the downriver side of Bayou Lafourche and looping off Mississippi Street, faced the river and was a commercial hub. Two blocks behind it was the town square, now called Louisiana Square. It was bounded by Cabahanossee (now called Railroad Avenue), Claiborne, Chetimaches, and Attakapas (now Nicholls) Streets. The state capitol was built on the south side of the square. After its abandonment as a statehouse, there was talk of converting it to an educational institution, but that never happened. The capitol building was partially demolished in 1848, and over time the bricks and debris were thrown into the head of Bayou Lafourche to help dam it. The courthouse and jail were built on the west side of the square in 1810. In 1815 Brigadier General Stephen A. Hopkins, a former speaker of the Louisiana House of Representatives and a hero of the Battle of New Orleans, was assassinated at the courthouse after he had successfully prosecuted a case. His killer was angry because Hopkins refused to argue the outcome with him. The original courthouse burned in 1846. A new courthouse and jail were destroyed during the Civil War shelling of Donaldsonville. In August 1862, Union gunboats bombarded the town as a haven of Confederate snipers and guerrillas; the Federals then came ashore and burned much of what had survived the barrage. The section near the Catholic Church was spared, but only seven buildings remained intact after the war.

From Admiral's Farragut's report, August 18, 1862: "At the town of Donaldsonville they have pursued a uniform prac-

tice of firing upon our steamers. . . . [I] ordered them to send their women and children out of town as I certainly intended to destroy it on my way down the river, and fulfilled my promise to a certain extent. I burnt down the hotels and the wharf buildings; also the dwelling house and other buildings of a Mr. Philip Sandy who is said to be a captain of guerrillas. . . . General Butler personally expressed to the Sisters of Charity . . . his sorrow at the damage inflicted upon that institution during the bombing."

Federal occupation lasted only a month, and the Confederates returned to construct a small earthwork fort for defense at Port Barrow. The following winter, Union forces took over the location and built Fort Butler. Skirmishes between North and South continued in this area throughout the remainder of the war.

The present courthouse was built in 1889 and is considered an interesting example of the Romanesque Revival style, although subsequent expansion has somewhat altered its appearance. The jail, built in 1867 just behind the courthouse site, is a geometric building of whitewashed brick with bars visible on the windows of the upper story.

Several blocks downriver from Crescent Place is the Church of the Ascension of Our Lord Jesus Christ, originally established on this site in 1772 as a small wooden chapel. The church owned a long but narrow property on which was built the first brick church in 1819; the building was replaced in 1840 with a grander one. The current Romanesque Revival edifice was begun in 1876 but not dedicated until 1896 because of various internal difficulties in the Catholic hierarchy. A noticeable variation in the brick facade is the result of interrupted construction. The original steeple was removed in 1936 after storm damage.

A block behind the church on its property is St. Vincent's Institute, founded by the Sisters of Charity in 1843 as a school and hospital.

> *Dr. François Prévost, a native of France, settled in Donaldsonville in 1799 and practiced medicine for fifty years. In the early 1820s he became only the second physician in the United States to perform a successful Cesarean section. At the time, the procedure was seldom used because it was almost always fatal to the mother. Prévost saved seven of the eight women*

*on whom he did Cesarean surgeries in his long career. Two
of them were slave women who were freed on their recovery.
How Prévost achieved his remarkable rate of success is unknown.*

The St. Vincent's building was an orphanage as well as a convent
from 1845 to 1977. Currently it houses a Catholic primary school.
The exterior still bears scars of cannonballs fired by the Union navy
during the Civil War. According to the diary of Sister Mary Gon-
zaga, who lived at the convent, a Sergeant Scott was ordered to
burn St. Vincent's; after a nun persuaded him to spare the building,
he was executed for disobeying orders. The diarist tells another tale
of divine intervention: as the nuns were praying before a statue of
the Blessed Virgin during an attack, a cannonball came through the
ceiling and struck several fingers of the statue, then fell to the floor
without exploding.

Several blocks behind St. Vincent's is the church cemetery, dating
to the late eighteenth century. It contains the gravesites of the Bringier, Colomb, Kenner, and other prominent River Road families,
as well as of Confederate and Union soldiers. The Landry tomb is
thought to have been designed by architect James Dakin. In 1856
the church was authorized to sell certain small tracts for two burial
grounds—one for Jews and one for Protestants. The Jewish cemetery was used for the burial of prominent Jewish residents of New
Orleans who had died in a yellow fever epidemic but could not be
buried in the city's Jewish cemetery because it had run out of space.
The congregation of the Old Episcopal Church, at 520 Nicholls
Street, was founded in 1844; the eclectic Gothic building dates from
1872. The Gothic Revival First Methodist Church, 401 Railroad
Avenue, was completed *circa* 1844 and has been discreetly modified.

The Donaldsonville Historic District includes a number of other
buildings. B. Lemann and Brothers Store, at Mississippi and Nicholls Streets, was founded about 1840 by Jacob Lemann. The Italianate commercial structure, replete with ornamentation and a cast-
iron gallery, was built in 1876 and was, for many years, the oldest
still-used department store building in Louisiana. The Bel House, a
Creole-style town house at the corner of Chetimaches and Mississippi, was built in 1873 and is perhaps the only town house of this
style between New Orleans and Baton Rouge. The white frame St.

Peter's Methodist Church, Houmas at Claiborne Streets, was established shortly after the Civil War and has continuously served its black congregation. The Rodrigue Home, 222 Lessard, built *circa* 1900, is an especially well-preserved Victorian cottage thought to have been a Sears catalog model home. The Guinchard House, at 212 Lessard, was originally owned by Jean Baptiste Lessard in 1797. An Acadian cottage with bousillage construction, it was moved to this spot; the present house, modified Classical Revival in style, was built around it. Vega House, 202 Lessard, built in 1868, is a Classical Revival–style cottage.

The gray frame house on the corner of Railroad and Claiborne was headquarters for Union cavalry during the Civil War, while the Union infantry took charge of the house at 212 Railroad Avenue. A contemporary storefront facade obscures the original entrance, but from a distance the gabled roof of the house is still visible.

Donaldsonville was the birthplace of Louisiana governor and state supreme court justice Francis T. Nicholls in 1834, but his house, at the (present) corner of Nicholls and Houmas, has been torn down.

> In 1839, A. Lussan published a dramatic tragedy in five acts in Donaldsonville entitled Les Martyrs de la Louisiane. The characters were the heroes of the revolt of 1768, defying Spanish governor O'Reilly.

The River Road route resumes on La. 18 at the Church of the Ascension of Our Lord Jesus Christ with mileage 0.0.

0.3 Peytavin Plantation House, a Creole raised plantation house, differs from its original appearance due to the bricked first story. Peytavin and the downriver properties to Point Houmas were operated in the 1880s by the Donaldsonville company of Bernard Lemann and Brothers.

0.5 The raised Thibaut home was built *circa* 1920 by Duborg Thibaut, a sugar planter and entrepreneur. This was the approximate site of Conrad's Plantation, which was sold by the Lemanns to the Jacob brothers from New York, who changed the name to Stella Plantation.

1.7 Triad Chemical's office is the former Riverside Plantation house, built in 1899. The white frame Victorian cottage replaced an earlier home on the site and is dwarfed on all sides by the looming geometry of the chemical plant, making the house look even more elegant and demure than it would in a pastoral setting. The property was originally Mollere Plantation and had a sawmill in the 1850s. It was renamed Riverside after a sale to James Teller in 1868, when it was greatly enlarged and included the former Atkinson and LeBlanc properties.

2.0 La. 3120. On the upriver side was the Dugas Plantation. Charles Dugas, one of the first Acadians to arrive in the area, received a Spanish land grant of five arpents on which he probably farmed and raised hogs.

On the downriver side of La. 3120 is the site of Viala Plantation. Viala was also sold by the Lemanns to the Jacob brothers, who named it Raccorci. The Viala Plantation house, a raised Acadian cottage, was built in 1797. The legendary pirate Jean Lafitte is said to have visited at Viala Plantation, and some say that Lafitte's son Jean Pierre married Marie Emma Viala in a wedding held in this house. Local lore says that Viala made a small hidden channel off the Mississippi River for Lafitte to dock his boat and store his contraband. The house fell into disrepair in the 1950s but was restored in the 1960s, then moved downriver in 1974 and converted to a restaurant.

2.3 Musco Road and Abend Road comprise most of the settlement of Abend. This community, located at a bend in the river across from east-bank Bringier Point, was developed after the Civil War by former slaves from nearby plantations and, according to local lore, called A Bend Settlement. Later, the area became the locus of Italian truck farmers.

A block off the River Road on St. Amico Road is the St. Amico Chapel, established in 1912 by a local Italian farmer whose son was struck with a life-threatening fever. A mysterious stranger appeared, rubbed the boy with herbs and oil, then disappeared. When the child's fever broke soon after, he pointed to a faded picture of Saint Amico hanging on the wall and identified him as his savior. The grateful father erected the shrine. The Sunday following Easter is the observance of St. Amico. A traditional barefoot procession is held on that day to the Donaldsonville Ascension Church.

2.5 On the left is Mt. Bethel Baptist Church and cemetery, a black congregation serving this area since 1868.

2.9   Point Houmas is a sharply articulated formation, easy to see across the vista of sugarcane fields. The point is named for the Houma Indians, who moved from the east bank, routed by the Tunicas. The Houmas developed a reputation among the Europeans for courage and kindness. General Wade Hampton, a hero of the American Revolution, acquired the point in the early nineteenth century, although he was largely an absentee owner, living in South Carolina; Hampton died in 1835. Cofield Settlement was a small community named for wealthy planter J. C. Cofield, who acquired Point Houmas in 1873. In the 1920s Cofield Point was a "bathing resort" where locals came to swim between the old and new levees. The federal government rented land on Point Houmas Plantation in the late 1930s for construction of a military airport, which was only lightly used and closed after World War II.

4.3   Point Houmas Plantation house was noted in the *Louisiana Gazette,* March 31, 1812: "Point Houmas Estate will be sold Thursday, the 30th April next . . . late the residence of the honorable Edward D. Turner. This estate is so well known and so completely established in the sugar business that a particular description would be useless." The man who purchased Point Houmas that year was Wade Hampton, although he was to be largely an absentee owner, directing its management from his South Carolina residence. After his death in 1835, the property was divided among his heirs. Colonel John L. Manning of South Carolina, the brother-in-law of Hampton's son-in-law, John Smith Preston, acquired Point Houmas Plantation in 1845. (In Persac's time, Manning owned Riverton Plantation, across the river.) John Cofield bought the property in 1873, and it subsequently changed hands several times. The house is a raised cottage that has undergone both modernizations and neglect.

4.6   It is said that this is the area where the missionary St. Cosmé was killed by Chitimachas. The tale is told that only one of St. Cosmé's guides survived—a young Indian boy who made his way to Fort St. Philip below New Orleans. The French recruited their Indian allies from the Mobile area for a retaliatory expedition. The Indians voyaged to the Lafourche area in longboats, found the Chitimachas inland on Bayou Lafourche, and killed many in the village. The Chitimacha brave identified as having slain the "black robe" was taken to Mobile and decapitated.

5.5 The wooded stand surrounded by cane fields is thought to be the site of a plantation house, possibly Mandesir or Pedesclaux.

6.2 Lemannville Cutoff Road is the principal street for the community of Lemannville. The property was bought by Pierre Pedesclaux in 1829. Pedesclaux Plantation was owned and run by his widow until after the Civil War. She lived on the property with her son and daughter-in-law, a granddaughter, an overseer, and a gardener. Jacob Lemann bought the property in 1871, and the settlement is named for him.

6.6 Although no sign denotes the boundary between Ascension and St. James Parishes, Buena Vista Road is in St. James Parish.

7.2 The Sunshine Bridge is built partially on what was once Salsburg Plantation. Where the bridge touches down is St. James Parish; however, just past the toll booth, La. 3089 enters Ascension Parish, a boundary change effected with, some say, political motivations, when the bridge was completed in 1964. The blue frame cottage on the downriver service road is the relocated Viala Plantation house.

7.5 Salsburg Lane is the site of Salsburg Plantation, originally part of a Spanish land grant from 1766. The property was owned by C. P. Melancon in the mid-nineteenth century, according to Persac. A three-story house built *circa* 1877 by Jacob Lebermuth stood on a landscaped terrace. Materials from the house were moved to Baton Rouge in the 1960s. The small white frame house along the lane was just across the road from the big house. It is thought that Lebermuth named the property Salsburg.

7.6 The large oak tree remains from the site of the Salsburg Plantation house.

8.0 The Agrico–Faustina plant is on the site of St. Joseph Plantation, which belonged to Joseph Gautreau. St. Joseph was in the family for 115 years; the family tomb is in St. James Cemetery just downriver. In 1881 the property—with six arpents, thirty toises of frontage, was sold to Mary Ann Robertson. She renamed it for a daughter, Marie Faustine, who had died at the age of eight. The Spanish-style plantation house was destroyed by a nighttime fire *circa* 1895. The property at one time included several family homes, thirty quarters cabins, a commissary, stables, cornhouses, and barns. For many years, stray animals that damaged crops were rounded up and brought to be held at a pound on Faustina Plantation; the owners had to pay a fine to reclaim them. A ferry crossed from the Faustina landing to the town of Union on the east bank.

8.3 The Chevron plant is on the site of Lauderdale Plantation. The Lauderdale store was in the curve just downriver from Faustina.

8.6 LaPice Road is on the site of Elina Plantation, as it was known in the mid-nineteenth century. It was subsequently known as the Bertaud tract and in 1877 belonged to someone named DeVerges. In 1884 Elina suffered from a fifteen-foot-wide crevasse caused by a rice flume. LaPice was a property behind Elina. On the downriver side are two weathered Creole cottages; the one farthest downriver was moved here from Faustina.

8.9 The large old cedar tree marks the homesite of the Mire property, as it was called by Persac. It was later known as Acadia Plantation, which in the latter part of the nineteenth century was somehow altered to Arcadia Plantation.

Also in this area is Buena Vista Plantation, the property just downriver from Mire. Buena Vista had twelve arpents of frontage and was bought by Maryland-born Judge Benjamin Winchester in the 1820s. He married a French Ascension Parish girl in 1820, and she may well have been the Widow B. Winchester who owned Buena Vista in Persac's time. The plantation was sold in 1868 to William Aymar and became known as Aymar. The Winchesters' house was destroyed by fire at the turn of the twentieth century. The American Red Cross acquired the tract in 1943.

9.8 The relic chimney marks the site of Minnie Plantation. Called St. Victoire by Persac, the property was owned by the Gaudet family until 1877. Clerville Himel bought the property and changed the name to his wife Lavenia's nickname. Three rebuilt quarters cabins are still on the property.

10.1 The Welcome water tower is at the approximate former location of St. Alice Plantation.

10.5 Site of St. Louis Plantation and the old St. Louis schoolhouse.

10.6 Mt. Calvary Baptist Church, founded 1907, is a rural black congregation.

10.8 Site of New Hope Plantation.
At Jones Street is a Creole cottage with additions and screened front gallery. This settlement is called Jonestown.

11.2 White Cloud is an Acadian-style cottage built *circa* 1850 for Irma Arceneaux and her husband, Professor Henri Chevet. A detached kitchen from the next property was brought to White Cloud and added to the back of the house. The two pairs of French doors open onto equal front rooms sharing a center fireplace.

11.5 Welcome Farm is the approximate site of Welcome Plantation and part of the community of Welcome, which extends to the upriver end of Brilliant Point. Richard Esterbrook, a famous English architect believed to have designed the St. James Church built in 1840, lived with his wife and a large library in Welcome.

11.9 Brilliant Point, also called Point Brilliant, is a gently curved landform, in contrast to the many sharply defined points on this part of the river. Brilliant Point was purportedly named for the sparkle of the setting sun on the water. In 1769 a Taensa Indian village was in this area.

12.6 A stately oak tree denotes the site of St. Claire Plantation, dating from an 1812 land claim. The area is locally known as Hymel; the Hymel Post Office opened in 1921 and closed in 1958. Another area, downriver, is also known as Hymel; it is where the St. James Sugar Co-op is located, although Corps of Engineers maps call that site St. Amelia. Post offices in this area of the Acadian Coast have been at Cantrelle in 1855, which changed its name to St. James in 1872, to St. Amelia in 1902, and to Hymel in 1921.
Several Creole cottages are part of the community of Hymel, which was established in 1915.
Freetown Lane marks the settlement of Freetown, founded by emancipated slaves. Today this small cluster of homes is part of the extended Hymel community.

14.3 Chatman Street indicates Chatman Town, a typical small River Road settlement of parallel streets. This area is the downriver reach of Brilliant Point.

15.1 Burton Lane denotes an area called Burton, where William L. Burton, a lumber magnate from East Baton Rouge Parish, settled and built a mansion *circa* 1890. Burtville, just downriver from Baton Rouge on the east bank, was a small lumbering community that Burton and his partner, C. S. Burt, established.

15.3 To the left of the River Road is the above-ground mechanical apparatus of Capline, one of the largest oil pipelines in the world. Opened in 1969 by Shell Oil, it stretches 632 miles from St. James to Patoka, Illinois. The old River Road remains by the levee, but the new road was built to swerve around Capline property. In 1824 Judge Joseph Fabré built a large Creole cottage called La Banque on part of this property. The brothers LaPice bought the property in 1836, and it was known as St. James Sugar Refinery. It is said the LaPices produced the first white sugar in Louisiana, doing so before the introduction of centrifuge machinery.

15.5 Large oaks on both sides of the road indicate the site of Jacques Cantrelle's Cabahanoce Plantation. The Capuchin Fathers conducted missionary work in the area in 1722. The first Acadians came in 1765. Cantrelle, a Frenchman, arrived in Louisiana in 1720 and settled first at the so-called Arkansas Post far upriver, then at Fort Rosalie (present-day Natchez), where his wife was killed in the great uprising of the Natchez Indians in 1729. He then lived in New Orleans until the Spanish authorities dispatched him to serve as commandant of the Acadians. It is thought that St. James was named for Cantrelle's patron saint.

Cantrelle established an indigo plantation called Cabahannoc; his return address was Cabahannocee, placed under his name on his stationery with a small oval occupied by a duck over a field of marsh grass. When he died in 1778, his son Michel succeeded him as commandant and was subsequently appointed by Governor Claiborne as a member of the convention that drafted the state's first constitution in 1811.

C. C. Robin, traveling in 1803–1805: *"Twenty leagues above New Orleans the Acadian coast begins and runs about another twenty. Like the Germans, they work their own farms; farms are subdivided in strips of two or three arpents of frontage. Each plot is forty arpents deep but only half is cultivated—the rest is inundated and covered with cypress and swamp vegetation. Rice, corn, several kinds of beans, melons (in season), pumpkin, salted pork and beef make up their principal diet. They love to dance . . . more than any other people in the colony. Everyone dances, even grandmere and grand-*

pere. There may be only a couple of fiddles to play, only four candles for light, nothing but long wooden benches to sit on and only a few bottles of tafia diluted with water for refreshment. No matter. Everyone dances."

Once past the Acadian Coast, the houses become more widely separated.

15.7 The Church of St. James was called St. Jacques de Cabahanoce when it was built in 1770 on land donated by Jacques Cantrelle. That site is now in the river. When it was replaced in 1841 with a fancy new church—a Romanesque structure constructed of hand-made brick with three steeples and large rafters carved from swamp cypress—the church bell was given to the Chapel of St. Joseph at Paulina on the east bank. Valcour Aime presented the new church with statuary, magnificent silver candlesticks, and a set of Italian oil paintings of the Stations of the Cross. St. James Church functioned as the religious center of a large parish until the construction of St. Michael's, across the river in Convent, in 1809. During 1918 and 1919, the levee was moved so close to the church that the front steps landed on the road. When a new levee was built in 1929, the old church could not be moved, so the present building was erected. The church rectory was demolished in 1968.

A picturesque and somewhat crumbling cemetery across the River Road dates from the founding of the original church. Always threatened by flooding, the cemetery has lost many tomb sites to the river. The remains of Valcour Aime and his wife were moved in 1929 to St. Louis Cemetery in New Orleans, although the original gravesite is still here, surrounded by the altar railing from the old church. Other significant local tombs include those of the Armant, Roman, and Gautreau families and a "Protestant Row" where non-Catholics were buried.

The tract just downriver from the cemetery, acquired from Jacques Cantrelle's grant, was a civic center. The Acadian-style St. James Courthouse and jail were built *circa* 1845. After the parish seat was moved to Convent in 1869, the courthouse building became a store and residence until it was overwhelmed by the river in 1904. A post office called Cantrelle operated at this location from 1855 to 1872, when its name was changed to St. James. A ferry also operated here from the colonial period to 1961, linking St. James on the west bank with Convent on the east bank.

*"Cantrelle is the name of the post office at the parish seat
of St. James and here are clustered a few houses. The courthouse building is an unpretending but properly adapted erec-
tion. Cantrelle is on the right bank, 65 miles above New Orleans. The Vacherie Road, 55 miles, is the other post office on
the right bank, and on the left are Grand Point, 55 miles,
Convent, 63 miles, and Touro's, 73 miles, above New Orleans." J. W. Dorr, 1860.*

15.8 The Strategic Petroleum Reserve is an enormous oil tank farm
begun in 1978. It is connected to two large river docks by pipeline.
This property was originally part of Jacques Cantrelle's land grant.
In 1845 Edward Forstall acquired it and called it St. James Estate,
building a lovely plantation home that was remembered long after
it succumbed to the river at the turn of the century.

A cistern visible on the property marks the approximate location
of the Amelia, or St. Amelia, Plantation house. Records show that
the title dates to a Spanish land grant of 1769 to Judge Poyfarré,
son-in-law of Jacques Cantrelle. The property was sold in 1855 by
J. B. and Eugene Ory to their brother Ludger, who entered partnership with Pierre Webre. Webre built a raised cottage on the
property *circa* 1867. In 1870 the partnership became Webre and
LeBoeuf, and the plantation became known as St. Amelia. It was
sold to Leon Godchaux. Godchaux resold it to Antonio Sobral,
who had also bought Oak Alley.

16.5 Several Creole cottages occupy the site of MBC Plantation,
so called for the initials of its owner, Michel Bernard Cantrelle, son
of Jacques. Michel was commandant and judge of the First Acadian
Coast and moved here *circa* 1782. This plantation, with ten arpents
of frontage, was part of his father's original land grant and remained in the family until 1872. The main house—reputedly large
and elegant—fell prey to the river in the early twentieth century. A
garçonnière from the plantation was moved to the Ascension Parish
(east bank) tourism center.

16.7 Hymel Road.

16.9 St. Paul Baptist Church is an antebellum congregation begun
as a church for the slaves on land belonging to Bon Secours Plantation. The plantation property, now called Graugnard Farms, lies
behind the church. Bon Secours—"Good Help"—was built *circa*

1790–1820. The large, one-story Creole cottage has been moved three times—the last during the 1880s—but has remained on the same property. The house was originally a raised Creole plantation house with frame upper floor and a brick basement story. Other rooms were added. The walls are bousillage. The home's large floor plan is unusual. Fortune Graugnard, the original Graugnard here, immigrated to the United States in 1877 and worked as a bonded servant in his uncle J. B. C. Caire's store, near Edgard downriver. It is said that as late as 1910 about six Houmas palmetto huts in the rear of this plantation sheltered a few remaining members of the tribe.

17.1 The St. James Co-op sugar mill was organized in 1945 and began processing in 1947, milling cane from a number of growers in the area.

17.4 Sidney Street marks Sidney Plantation, on a Spanish land grant. Early owners included Jacques Cantrelle Jr. and George Webre, who is thought to have built the home. The property was acquired by Fortune Graugnard *circa* 1890. The F. A. Graugnard and Son General Store served Bon Secours and other local residents.

17.5 The Graugnard House, a large Creole cottage with Classical Revival renovations, is thought to have been built by George Webre *circa* 1820, perhaps as the Sidney Plantation house.

17.6 St. Emma Street is the site of St. Emma Plantation, part of a 1765 Spanish land grant made to Nicolas Verrett Sr. in 1765. Verrett was the husband of Marie Cantrelle, daughter of Jacques Cantrelle Sr. Joseph Villavaso acquired the property from Verrett, but St. Emma returned to the original family in 1816 when Michel Cantrelle bought the tract and gave it to his son. It remained in the family until near the end of the nineteenth century.

18.1 At the junction of La. 912 is the St. James community post office, near where the old post office and courthouse stood until they were demolished in 1929 to make way for the levee. A historic marker notes the location of Cabahanoce Plantation, part of Nicolas Verrett Sr.'s land-grant property. Through separate grants in 1762 and 1765, Verrett acquired a very large tract, thought to have extended from Bon Secours through Richbend with thirty arpents of frontage and a depth to the swamps and waterways. His home and plantation were located on part of the second land grant. Verrett served as commandant and judge of the First Acadian Coast. He died in 1775. Michel Cantrelle lived here for a time before moving upriver. The property was sold to the Roman family, and future governor André Roman acquired title in 1816. Roman was the first Louisiana governor to serve two terms (1831–1835 and 1839–1843). He introduced parklike grounds and an oak allée to the plantation, and apparently anglicized the name to Cabanocey. The house was destroyed by the river.

18.8 The settlement of Richbend owes its name to a riverboat captain. The long, deep, crescent bend of the river as it curves around College Point on the east bank gave its name to the land on the west bank and to a small sugar plantation there. Richbend Plantation was the property of Valcour Aime's daughter Edwige and her husband, Florent Fortier, who was her first cousin (the couple were the parents of the noted Louisiana historian Alcée Fortier). Florent's brother Septime married Edwige's sister Félicité. The Fortier brothers operated Richbend until Florent gave the property to his daughter in 1857 as a wedding gift. The young couple lived there until at least 1874.

19.1 Junction La. 3219. On the upriver side was Moonshine Plantation, and a community called Moonshine once existed in this area.

19.2 St. Luke Baptist Church is on the left side of the road, built in 1900 to replace the original 1874 building. Next to the church is the Chenier House, which continues to face the river, reflecting the old location of the River Road before both road and levee were set back.

The community of Lagan received its first post office in 1894, named in honor of a New Orleans congressman who had helped the area achieve postal status. The extended community included settlement between Richbend and Bay Tree Plantations.

19.7 Down Pikes Peak Street, which indicates the site of Pikes Peak Plantation, is a line of tenant cabins and several other outbuildings. Pikes Peak was owned by the Roman family until the late 1880s.

20.2 Chopin Street designates the site of Choppin/Home Place Plantation. The property, with twelve arpents of frontage, was

André Roman, scion of a wealthy River Road family, served two terms as governor of Louisiana.
Courtesy State Library of Louisiana

bought by Valerian Choppin for his wife Eugénie during the second half of the nineteenth century. Behind the contemporary house facing the road is a tiny gray house with the inscription "Lagan P.O. LA"—the original post office building for the community of Lagan.

21.0 Bessie K. Street recalls the site of Bessie K. Plantation. Originally a Spanish land grant issued to Manuel Landry, the property was sold in 1808 to Pierre Delogny and stayed in the family until

1894, when it was sold to John Henderson. Henderson renamed it Bessie K., honoring his wife, Bessie Katherine. The sharp bend in the road follows a levee setback, approximately at the site of Laurel Ridge Plantation, which became part of Bessie K. in 1906.

21.6 Bay Tree Road was the site of a 1908 meeting hall and school in the community of Bay Tree.

22.0 Bay Tree Plantation Cottage—called Deloney (Delogny?) Plantation in the early nineteenth century and referenced on the Persac map—belonged to members of the Roman family who owned Oak Alley next door. This one-story frame Creole cottage built *circa* 1850 is thought to have been the overseer's house; it was renovated with Classical Revival influences in 1880. Two outbuildings have been moved to the grounds.

22.1 The sweeping landscape of Oak Alley Plantation—twenty-five lush acres—gives a very real sense of the spacious grounds and splendor of an antebellum plantation. The property was first documented as a Spanish land grant and became part of the consolidated holdings of Valcour Aime in 1820. The Classical Revival house was built (1837–1839) for Jacques Telesphore Roman, Aime's brother-in-law. Aime had bought the property, which adjoined his mother-in-law's land downriver, while Jacques bought the Roman homestead. The two brothers-in-law then transacted to exchange properties. The spectacular quarter-mile-long avenue of live oaks is thought to date to the early eighteenth century when a now-unknown French colonial settler planted them and located a modest dwelling at the end of the allée. The oaks number twenty-eight, identical to the number of columns surrounding the house. Riverboat captains considered the home a landmark and referred to it as Oak Alley.

Roman's wife, Célina, named the plantation Bon Séjour ("Pleasant Sojourn"), although she much preferred life in the city (New Orleans) and is remembered as hating to come out to "the river." When Jacques died in 1848, Célina took little interest in the plantation and ran up such bills that she created friction with her brother-in-law, André Roman, who was in charge of the estate. During the Civil War, son Henri took charge, but to no avail; the family was forced to auction the property after the war. Jacques' daughter, Octavia, and her husband, Philip Buchanan, were asked to stay on as administrators.

In 1881 Oak Alley was purchased by Antonio Sobral, a thirty-seven-year-old Portuguese immigrant and Confederate army veteran living in Donaldsonville. He restored the sugar crop and reaped great success on Oak Alley before selling it in 1905 to the Hardin family, who are credited with taking uncommon care of the eponymous oaks; among other things, they successfully battled the Corps of Engineers when several of the oaks were threatened by levee setbacks. The Stewart family bought Oak Alley in 1925, after the Hardins had relinquished the property. The Stewarts are responsible for the adaptive restoration of the house and furnishings, and the construction of new buildings and land use changes on the grounds. When Mrs. Stewart died in 1972, Oak Alley became the property of the Oak Alley Plantation Foundation. Today the old overseer's house is the home of the foundation's director; a garçonnière serves as a ticket booth for visitors, and behind it the foundation's offices occupy what was once the jail. Oak Alley has been used in numerous movies and television productions, including a 1985 version of *The Long, Hot Summer* and the 1994 film *Interview with the Vampire.* Open to the public.

Oak Alley has a special place in the annals of horticulture thanks to Antoine, a slave gardener of Jacques Roman's, who successfully grafted pecan trees in 1847 and created the first named variety—Paper Shell—which led to commercial production. Antoine's achievement was recognized at the St. Louis Louisiana Purchase Exposition. None of his original pecan trees are thought to survive.

"I noticed particularly [the plantations] of Valcour Aime and . . . Henry J. Roman [Oak Alley?], which is one of the handsomest, most costly and tasteful on the coast. . . . The avenue of ancient live oak on this plantation is one of the most magnificent on the coast and the grounds are a paradise of rare and beautiful plants, trees, and shrubs." J. W. Dorr, 1860.

Just downriver from Oak Alley was the birthplace of Henry Hobson Richardson, famed American architect. He was the great-grandson of Joseph Priestley, who discovered oxygen. Richardson was born in 1839 at his grandfather's plantation, designated on Persac as "Widow Priestly and heirs." Richardson specialized in Romanesque Revival designs; the Confederate Museum in New Orleans is the closest example of his work.

22.6 St. Joseph Plantation House. Built in 1820 by Dr. Cazamie Mericq, the house was purchased from his widow in 1847 and remodeled in 1858 by Alexis Ferry and his wife, Josephine, a daughter of Valcour Aime. They called it Home Place or Josephine House and lived in the traditional raised Creole cottage while operating Ferry's large landholding, Bourbon Plantation, on the east bank. Ferry enclosed the first floor, added two rooms on each end, and remodeled in the Classical Revival style. A storm devastated the property in 1866. Ferry's widow sold to Edward Gay, who resold it to Joseph Waguespack. Numerous outbuildings surround the house.

22.8 The St. Joseph Plantation store was part of the plantation. Two Creole cottages facing the road stand just downriver.

23.0 The Classical Revival Felicity Plantation home was built *circa* 1850 by Septime Fortier, married to cousin Félicité Aime. The mansion combines French colonial and Anglo-American elements behind a crape myrtle allée. The house has a wide central hall and red Italian marble mantels with a carved cypress balustrade in a wheatsheave pattern similar to that at Oak Alley. Original quarters houses and barn remain on the property.

23.7 On the upriver side of Valcour Aime Street, in the midst of a cane field, is a large, thick stand of trees, all that remains of the remarkable Valcour Aime Plantation. François Gabriel Aime, called Valcour by a nurse and forever known by that name, married Josephine Roman in 1819. The young couple moved into his mother-in-law's house to help her manage her property as her husband, Jacques Roman, had died. In an exchange of properties with his brother-in-law, Valcour became the owner of the Roman property and incorporated the Roman house into a new Classical Revival mansion that he built in the 1830s. Valcour was highly educated, cultured, and had a reputation as a bon vivant. His extensive additions to the mansion's interior included marble mantels, crystal chandeliers, and similar extravagances. Valcour was respected for his business acumen and plantation management—the St. James Sugar Refinery was on his property—and civic actions, such as his rescue of Jefferson College. But his legendary reputation was established by his lavish lifestyle. He was enormously rich and spent his money openly on such whims as a private steamboat that ferried him and his friends to New Orleans for good times. It is said that he once collected on a $10,000 bet that he could entertain his guests at the most elegant dinner with everything—from wine to cigars—the product of his plantation. Also part of Aime's engaging legend is the story that he owned a gold table service, which, when Federal troops approached during the Civil War, he dumped in the river rather than have it captured.

Valcour Aime's gardens were a flamboyant part of his personal expression—and the overriding reason that the plantation became known as "Le Petit Versailles." He hired a French landscape gardener to transform the swampy area in front of the house into a masterpiece ultimately considered one of the finest and most complete American botanical gardens of its time. Rare plants were imported from around the globe; tropical fruits were grown in hothouses, and exotic fish swam in artificial ponds and streams. A private zoo and songbirds from all over the world added interest; game birds were imported for more exotic hunting pleasure. A ten-foot hill was constructed into which was carved a grotto; on its summit stood a Chinese pagoda. An artificial river, fort, and Roman bridges added to the spectacular ambiance. The gardener remained to provide ongoing care of the gardens—an unheard of extravagance—until Aime's world fell apart. With the death of his son in 1854 and of his wife and a daughter not long after, Aime turned the management of his property over to his son-in-law. Valcour died in 1867. John Burnside bought the property from Aime's family in 1867, but subsequent owners left the house empty for many years. It burned in 1920. Vestiges of the garden follies were last seen decades ago, before the gardens reverted to the almost natural state.

24.8 Toth Lane is part of the Armant Plantation property. To the rear stands a tall, dilapidated two-story building—the Armant sugar mill, which closed in 1978.

A historic marker about Colonel Leopold Armant stands amid huge moss-draped oaks at the site of Armant Plantation. The land, once part of the second village of the Bayougoula Indians, was acquired by Joseph Blanpain in 1740 for a *vacherie*—cattle ranch. Jean Baptiste Armant purchased the property before 1800. A raised Creole cottage built by Armant *circa* 1800 was one story with the upper floor added later. A smaller house next door was Mme Ar-

Valcour Aime, legendary for his wealth and hospitality.
    Courtesy State Library of Louisiana

mant's after her son, Jean Baptiste, married. In 1845 J. B. Armant introduced on his plantation the largest Rillieux sugar-processing equipment that had yet been made.

The younger Jean Baptiste died in 1854 and is buried in St. James Cemetery. John Burnside owned Armant before and after the Civil War, bequeathing it in 1881 to Oliver Beirne, from whom William

Valcour Aime's luxurious mansion was abandoned and approaching ruin when this photograph was taken in the early 1900s.
Courtesy St. James Historical Society

Miles acquired it. The big house was razed in 1969 after being vacant for more than ten years. The land currently is owned by Southdown Sugar. Records suggest that it has been continuously devoted to sugar operations since 1796.

25.2 La. 20, town of Vacherie. Local Indians referred to the area as Tabiscania. Several land grants were bestowed in this area in 1755, including one to Louis Ranson explicitly for the establishment of a *vacherie* (cattle ranch); the beef raised on the ranch was to feed the military and the New Orleans market. The grant was on or near the tract held by Joseph Blanpain as a *vacherie*. Blanpain was arrested in 1755 by the Spanish in what is now northwest Louisiana/northeast Texas; he was caught trading with the Indians—a crime for a Frenchman in Spanish territory. He was jailed at Los Adaes, where he died.

Settlers moved up to this area from the German Coast and were followed by Acadians, the first small group in 1764 and a second group of two hundred who arrived in 1765 from Saint Domingue. The town was called St. Patrick from 1872 to 1924, the name taken from a chapel located at the present-day junction of La. 20 and the River Road. It regained its designation as Vacherie in 1924.

Side trip: La. 20 to La. 644, South Vacherie, formerly known as Back Vacherie (along the River Road, the word *back* was often used to designate the part of a settlement that was away from the river). Two large, moss-draped oaks signal the location of Désiré Plantation, also known as Alcidésiré, its main house a raised Creole cottage built *circa* 1835 with bousillage walls and exposed beams; Gothic jigsaw cutouts along the dormer were added in the 1850s. The plantation grew perique tobacco and in the 1890s featured a perique cigar factory, known as Cigar Factory No. 79, in one of the back rooms of the main house. A store connected to the home, D. LeBlanc General Merchandise, existed from the 1880s until about 1920. Today the cottage is very weathered, with a plastered facade and low front stairway, but despite more recent additions, many elements of the original house remain.

Farther along La. 644 is Notre Dame de la Paix, Our Lady of Peace Church, a Norman Revival–style brick monolith completed in 1895 that dominates the cane fields and exurbs near it. The parish began in the early nineteenth century, and the first chapel was built in 1854 on land acquired by the Diocese of New Orleans. The current building was designed to emulate rural French architecture.

Several blocks past the church on Lily Road are the remains of Shell Hill, an Indian midden attributed to the Taensas, Houmas, or Bayougoulas. The mound was originally thirty feet high and five hundred feet wide at its base, but it has been almost destroyed by use of the shells for the foundations of Notre Dame de la Paix Church and for fill by road construction crews. (Shell Hill is almost on a direct line from the Belmont Indian mounds across the river, leading to speculation that a geological fault that cuts through this area may have created a reach of high ground that the Indians utilized.)

The Mad Stone of Vacherie is a small black stone allegedly possessed of magical curative powers. As the story goes, a Chickasaw Indian came to trade with German settler Joseph Webre. During his visit, a neighbor, Mrs. Gravois, went to her garden to cut a cabbage for dinner and was bitten on the finger by a rattlesnake. The Indian took a small, flat, black-brown stone from his pirogue and applied it to the wound. The woman miraculously recovered. A year later the Indian came again to trade and became ill. Mr. and Mrs. Gravois nursed him back to health, and in gratitude, the Indian gave them the magic stone—about three inches long and as big as a man's thumb. He told them to keep it and never sell it; it would always work for their family. The stone, said to be from the heart of a white deer, was kept in the Gravois family for a century and a half, reportedly curing more than four thousand infections, bites, etc. of area residents. Applied to the afflicted area, it stuck until all the poison was gone and then automatically fell off. In cases that required several days for a cure, the Gravois family offered the patient overnight accommodations. The stone diminished slightly with each use. Today it is reputed to be in two pieces, each too small to be of further value. "There is something mysterious in the stone," Mrs. Gravois was quoted as saying several years ago. "I do not blame those who cannot believe."

Returning to the River Road:

25.3 Near the corner was the Hubbell and Waguespack Store, a local landmark opened in 1904. It burned in 1975. In the center of the property stands the Waguespack House, also called the Bourg House for onetime owner Thomas Bourg; built *circa* 1786, it is thought to be among the oldest Acadian houses on the River Road. Though remodeled and painted white, the original building is evident from the location of the center chimney and the double pitched roof.

25.4 Laura, also known as Waguespack, Plantation is the oldest surviving plantation complex in St. James Parish. It stands on the site of the Indian village and ceremonial center Tabiscania. Native huts were on the property in 1805, and Indians resided on Laura property until 1915.

The house was built in 1805 by Guillaume DuParc, commandant of Pointe Coupée. It was called Duparc and Locoul, according to Persac, and was only named Laura in 1891, when great-granddaughter Laura Locoul sold a portion of her acreage to Florian Waguespack and stipulated that the house and grounds retain her name. The Creole plantation house has been remodeled or renovated three times—in 1822, 1905, and 1922. Among the changes are the addition of a central front door and enclosed side galleries. The largest of the outbuildings is the Maison de Reprise (House of

Respite), built in 1829 for the matriarch of the family, who—as custom demanded—moved into her own quarters when she retired from running the plantation; it is believed to have been used as a hospital during the Civil War. Also on the grounds are barns, a carriage house, and six quarters cabins.

Laura Plantation is also thought to be part of the cradle of the Br'er Rabbit tales, which derive from Creole folklore—Senegalese stories recorded in the 1870s by Alcée Fortier, grandson of Valcour Aime, who told them in a French patois as he had learned them from the slaves on the plantation. Fortier's book *Folk Tales of Louisiana,* published a decade before Joel Chandler Harris made Br'er Rabbit a household name, included tales of Compère Lapin and Compère Bouki—Brother (Br'er) Rabbit and Brother Bouki (*bouki* is a West African word for "hyena," although in Louisiana folk tales Bouki is generally a goat).

The Laura complex focuses on presenting the story of its colorful Creole culture. Open to the public.

> *The irony of a natural disaster: In January 1943, a measurable earthquake occurred in St. James Parish, west along Laura Plantation property. A fissure five feet wide resulted, but with time the event was forgotten. In 1981 politically connected businessmen bought the plantation site with the intention of selling it to the state as the access point to the planned new bridge. They would, of course, demolish the standing structures. But geologists discovered the fault, and the bridge was constructed two miles downriver, thus saving the historic plantation complex from destruction.*

25.8 Local pride named this S-curve in the River Road after a resident who fought construction of a new segment of road that would have straightened out the curves and partitioned his property.

25.9 Magnolia Park is named for Magnolia Plantation, the earliest documented land settlement in St. James Parish, dating from 1755. The land was claimed by the Frederic family in 1807. Sosthène and Zenon Roman bought the property and added others to it between 1812 and 1827 to amass a sugar plantation. The house was a raised Creole cottage with some Classical Revival influence, built *circa* 1850, with square Doric columns and pilasters on the dormers. After the Civil War, the Romans faced financial difficulties and turned 'to raising rice. The tract was subdivided into nine small parcels in 1881. The house was eventually demolished. The property is now part of residential Vacherie and follows narrow streets that probably trace the old eighty-arpent depth lines.

26.3 The Old Vacherie Road, called the *Chemin militaire* in the French colonial period, is the dividing line between the German and Acadian Coasts and served as the main road to Thibodaux and Bayou Lafourche as early as the late eighteenth century. It roughly follows the high ground of an old Indian trail through swampland from Bayou Lafourche to the Mississippi River and was used by troops of both sides during the Civil War.

27.2 The schoolhouse on Waguespack/Home Place Plantation, built in the latter part of the nineteenth century, is now a residence. The land was bought by the Waguespack family in 1781, and a home built prior to 1809 stood until 1964.

Next door was Crescent Plantation, also known as Hymel, which was owned by Eugene Champagne in 1815 and operated as a small sugar farm. The raised plantation house, built in 1840 by Jean Armant, is abandoned and deteriorating.

27.7 Lutcher–Vacherie ferry landing. A skiff was operated in 1910 as the ferry to Lutcher; it was replaced by a small, motorized boat that took only pedestrians. In 1919 the first automobile ferry was a schooner that allowed two Model-Ts on board in the bow. The ferry was terminated when the Veterans Memorial Bridge from Gramercy to Wallace opened just downriver.

27.9 St. Philip Catholic Church was established in 1873; the present church and rectory buildings date from 1921. St Philip is a wood-frame country church built in what can be best called eclectic classical style.

28.3 St. James/St. John the Baptist Parish line.

The community of Wallace begins at the parish line, although no sign indicates this small enclave, originally called St. Philip because of its ecclesiastical parish. The area was settled by the first wave of Acadians, who arrived in the 1760s. Many of the refugees took part in the rebellion of 1768. In the 1860s Wallace boasted a rice mill and a cotton gin. Until 1885, residents received their mail

Hymel (Crescent) Plantation. Note the large cistern.
Courtesy St. James Historical Society

elsewhere; after they petitioned for a local post office and were successful through the efforts of Congressman Nathaniel Wallace, they renamed the settlement in his honor.

28.5 Numerous Creole-style cottages line the River Road in Wallace. Many of the facades have been modified, but the underlying structures are not difficult to discern.

29.3 The Schexnaydre House, a Creole cottage *circa* 1840, features an unusual dogtrot connection with the kitchen.

29.6 Veterans Memorial Bridge, connecting Wallace with Gramercy on the east bank. On both the upriver and downriver sides of the bridge are various Creole cottages and one of the few remaining rice barns in the area.

The Woodville Cemetery, a block or so behind River Road, dates to the last quarter of the nineteenth century. The cemetery was associated with the Woodville Benevolent Association, a black social service and burial organization founded in 1892.

30.3 The lowland area by the road is an old borrow pit.

30.7 The Wallace water tower is in the area of the settlement of Willow Grove, located at the nose of the broad Fifty Mile Point and thought to be named for a copse removed when settlers cleared the land. The old Willow Grove Store, dating from the late nineteenth century, was the first community post office but is no longer open. (Fifty Mile Point is at mile 145 AHP.)

Just downriver from the water tower is the site of Mialaret Plantation. Documents trace ownership of this property to 1785, when it was owned by a family named Roussel. A descendant, married to a Becnel, acquired title in 1846, after which the property was known as Becnel Plantation, a sugar producer. Antonin Mialaret purchased the property at sheriff's sale in 1867. The plantation house, described as "a magnificent mansion," as well as all other outbuildings save the sugarhouse were destroyed in 1884 by a tornado. In 1895 Alovon Granier purchased the property and renamed it Aurelia, for his wife, before selling out in 1919 to owners of neighboring Whitney Plantation. An eclectic Creole cottage remains just downriver from the location of the Mialaret Plantation big house. Some researchers date its existence to *circa* 1840; others suggest that it may have been built after the fateful tornado using old materials—although, if so, its *briqueté entre poteaux* construction needs explaining. Two cabins and a barn, modified from its origins in the late nineteenth century, also remain.

31.1 Whitney Plantation's location on Fifty Mile Point offered a commanding view of the river. The raised Creole plantation house with Classical Revival influences was built by Jean Jacques (sometimes called Jacob) Haydel *circa* 1790, although Haydel's ancestors had settled in the area during the 1750s. The house is solid brick on the first floor, bousillage on the second story, and was considered one of the best examples of painted wood architecture along the Mississippi River. Dominique Canova, an Italian immigrant artist in New Orleans, is thought to have painted the wall murals on the front and rear galleries of the house in 1850. The rear gallery, ceiling, and doors of the parlor are painted to resemble Dresden china, and the parlor ceiling is monogrammed M. H., for Marcelline Haydel, mistress of the house. In 1879 a fire destroyed Whitney's sugarhouse. Rice was also being raised commercially and became the primary crop. The quarters rows and milling complex originally paralleled the road, but river movement and subsequent development have reoriented the layout. Numerous outbuildings, including a kitchen, quarters, office, barn, shed, privy, pigeonnier, and turn-of-the-century store remain standing, although many of these outbuildings were heavily damaged in 1965 by Hurricane Betsy. Formosa Plastics, current owner of the property, wishes to sell the complex.

31.5 In this cane field is the approximate site of Ambrose Haydel's house, *circa* 1752—one of the oldest documented colonial dwellings along the River Road. Haydel (Heidel before gallicization) and family arrived on John Law's pest ships in 1721 and settled on the German Coast. Ambrose owned property on both sides of the river and was the progenitor of a large and successful family. Subsequent owners consolidated the property into Whitney Plantation.

The batture from Whitney past Evergreen is very wide because of movement of the river.

32.0 The extensive Evergreen Plantation property begins in this area. The plantation was in the Becnel family and known as Becnel Plantation until 1884, when a new owner called it Evergreen, supposedly because of the large number of evergreen trees on the property. The original house was probably constructed *circa* 1790 and remodeled in 1832 to the Classical Revival style. Evergreen was built by members of the same family that built Whitney, and the two houses were essentially identical. Now, only the solid brick walls (eighteen inches thick) and the Creole floor plan, minus two rooms, survive a remodeling that introduced Doric columns from ground to roof, a double curving stairway, fanlighted doorways, and a modified belvedere. The house was originally surrounded with formal Italianate gardens and gravel and brick walks, as well as avenues of trees.

The complex is the most complete plantation community extant along the River Road, with pigeonniers, garçonnières, kitchen, guesthouse, a Classical Revival privy, twenty-two slave cabins, office, and cemetery. The overseer's house, on the upriver side, is thought to predate the remodeling. Only the sugarhouse is missing. The beautiful oak allée leading to the site of the sugar factory was reputedly planted during the Civil War by a black woman, although her name is lost to history. In 1869 the property owners granted right-of-way to the railroad, although the river remained the significant transportation artery. Through the years the plantation had several owners, but after the 1927 flood and the 1929 stock market crash, the property fell into disrepair. In 1944 Matilda Gray of New Orleans purchased the house and began its restoration and renovation. It is said that 300,000 bricks were ferried across the Mississippi River from Uncle Sam Plantation (demolished for levee construction) to effect the restoration.

According to local lore, Evergreen has ghosts. At the end of the nineteenth century, four people in the same family died within less than two years at Evergreen. Some say that every night about six o'clock, the piano would play by itself—with no one in the room. The pianist is said to be the ghost of a young schoolteacher who often played the instrument at Evergreen before meeting an untimely death.

In front of Evergreen and along a portion of St. John River Road is a WPA sidewalk, a relic of the depression-era public works project that built continuous cement sidewalks along the River Road on both sides of the river. The sidewalk has survived only in places.

32.5 Junction La. 639. The Johnson Plantation slave cabins and overseer's house (renovated in the 1890s) were first owned by Bradish Johnson. The plantation was renamed Carroll by its new owners, Caire and Graugnard, in the latter part of the nineteenth century. The stretch of river here is called Willow Bend, for the channel's curve around the east bank's Forty-eight Mile Point.

32.9 The Bacas House is thought to have been built *circa* 1840–1850. It is a stylistic example of architecture in transition between Creole and Classical Revival, with bousillage walls, a steep hipped roof, and a full-length gallery with original columns. The house has been in the Bacas family since 1895. To the rear is the monumental Bacas live oak.

33.0 Nearby, this Creole cottage, fenced with traditional cypress picketing, is little altered except for a new roof added after Hurricane Betsy.

The fields represent the unofficial downriver boundary of the community of Wallace.

34.3 The Willow Bend School is an old community schoolhouse.

34.6 The Dugas House, *circa* 1814, is one of the earliest remaining one-story Creole cottages, close to its original appearance, although windows have been added on the front facade and an addition has been made to the rear of the house. It is situated on a long, narrow strip of property perhaps originally owned by a planter named Henderson (records are lacking) and has been in the Dugas family since 1906.

35.1 Several Creole and Acadian-style cottages.

35.8 A brick post in the fence along the road is all that now distinguishes the Dutreix House, built *circa* 1830. The unusual windows of this early Creole cottage cannot be seen through the overgrowth; only its rusting roof is visible. Between Dutreix and Columbia Plantation are several Creole cottages and a quarters cabin.

> "The road is still pleasant, but not as delightfully so as in St. Charles Parish. The planters hereabout do not seem to take quite as much pains in beautifying their homesteads and they are rather very fine, commodious farmhouses than splendidly ornamented villas. . . . There are, however, some very beautiful places in this parish. [Compared with St. Charles, there is] a much greater proportion of people of small means in this parish and more free colored. A good many people along the levee who appear to rely principally on the catfishery and woodchopping for the steamboats for a livelihood.
>
> "Edgard . . . [has] some ninety or a hundred buildings scattered along the levee road, two or three pretty nice stores, the parish buildings, well built of brick, a neat Catholic church, and a graveyard of considerable extent.
>
> "There are a large number of fine estates in St. John—Belle Point (A. Deslonde), Mount Airy (Joseph Lebourgeois), Esperance (Dr. Loughborough), and others. The planters, constituting the staple populations of the parish are, almost to a man, of the old Creole-gentleman type . . . the Anglo-Americans are few." J. W. Dorr, 1860.

36.3 Columbia Plantation house, built in the Creole style *circa* 1800, has been variously known as Marmillion, Matilda, and Columbia. The house was last moved in 1929, because of levee construction. Columbia once belonged to Valsin B. Marmillion, brother of Edmond Marmillion, who built San Francisco across the river. Valsin had a reputation for erratic behavior, including brutality toward his slaves. A two-room cottage, *circa* 1820, located behind the main house, was moved from St. Charles Parish. The Columbia Plantation overseer's house, *circa* 1835, also survives.

An oak allée, planted *circa* 1830, once extended from the house downriver to the St. John the Baptist Church in Edgard; some of the trees still remain. During the Civil War, gunboats fired at the plantation's large warehouse; half of it blew up.

36.7 Down the mill road, as the sign indicates, is the Caire-Graugnard Columbia sugar mill, visible across the cane field. The mill is thought to have been built in 1825, but the first mill on the site dated to 1810. Columbia was considered the oldest operating sugar mill in the United States when it closed in December 1994. The tiny Edgard depot, *circa* 1875, was moved by Mr. Graugnard to the grounds of the mill *circa* 1973. It is thought to be the only original depot building remaining in this area.

37.1 The community of Edgard was originally called St. John, after its church. It developed with the overflow populations from the German and Acadian settlements and in 1848 became the parish seat, replacing the community downriver now called Lucy. When the parish's first post office was established here in 1850, the town was renamed for postmaster Edgar Perret until it became known that another town already had the name Edgar. The community solved the problem by adding the *d*. The original jail and court-house were in use until 1900 and 1938, respectively; the current courthouse was built in 1967. The Texas and Pacific Railroad Depot was called St. John until 1909, when it was tardily renamed Edgard.

The Bon Secour Mutual Benevolent Association Hall is housed in a modest, modified shotgun. The black benevolent society developed after the Civil War to help freedmen help each other with financial expenses such as for burials. This and similar associations have continued as social clubs.

37.2 Graugnard House at Graugnard Court was built after the Civil War. Part of the Marmillions' oak allée is visible on the property.

37.4 The wood-frame Caire Store building dates to *circa* 1897; the brick structure—Caire Landing—was built *circa* 1860 and was moved back in 1881 because of a levee setback. Showboats stopped to entertain at the landing twice a year through the 1930s. The store was the largest for miles around, purveying general merchandise to west- and east-bank residents.

37.5 The Edgard–Reserve ferry landing was located across the street from the St. John the Baptist Church and cemetery. The original Catholic chapel, built in 1724 at Karlstein (downriver near Bonnet Carré Point), was replaced in 1770 by the Spanish colonial government with the St. Charles Borromeo Church, across the river at Destrehan. The change was made to punish settlers on the German Coast who had participated in the 1768 insurrection (residents on the east bank were friendlier to the Spanish). In 1772, however, it was agreed that a church would be restored on the west bank, although not in the old location. St. John the Baptist Church was constructed on four arpents of land expropriated from Jacques Dubroc, who was selected to "donate" the tract because he was a bachelor with no dependents. All the ecclesiastical accoutrements— bells, vestments, candles, and so on—at St. Charles Borromeo were divided and half given to the new church.

The first St. John the Baptist Church, a small, hand-hewn cypress structure, was destroyed in the hurricane and flood of 1821. It was immediately replaced with a second church, which burned in 1918 (however, three church bells—called Jeanne, Marie, and Josephine—were in a separate belfry and were saved). The current church, completed in the 1920s in the Roman Renaissance style, is on the same site as its predecessors. St. John the Baptist Church served both banks of St. John Parish until St. Peter's was built in Reserve in 1868.

Local lore says that Father Alexander Juille, who served as pastor from 1901 to 1904, put a curse on the church after he went to jail for slapping a young congregant; according to the story, his parishioners—with whom he was already having certain disagreements— refused to bail him out. When Catholics from nearby parishes finally rescued him, Father Juille stormed up the levee and pronounced a hundred-year curse. When the church burned in 1918, the fire was of course attributed to Father Juille's anger; for years afterward, whenever disaster struck the town, locals would affirm that "Père Juille vient encore"—Father Juille comes again.

The cemetery next door to the church was laid out in 1770. Levee work in 1881 cut through the old cemetery, and many gravesites washed into the river. Mrs. P. G. T. Beauregard, wife of the Confederate general, and members of John Slidell's family are buried here (Slidell was a pre–Civil War United States senator from Louisiana who became a Confederate diplomat). Until the early twentieth century, many of the tombstone inscriptions were written in French. The line of tombs located along the fence is called "Politicians' Row" and includes gravesites of extended families dating from the late eighteenth century through the 1920s.

37.8 The Caire-Jones House, *circa* 1835, is a raised two-story Creole-style home on tall piers. Alterations to the house include roof renovations after Hurricane Betsy and enclosing the downstairs floor. The staircase remains under the front gallery.

A small store, *circa* 1900, was Gendren's barbershop.

The Webre store, *circa* 1875, was located next to the original Webre cottage, *circa* 1815, which is no longer standing. The site is on a setback.

38.0 Kismet, built in 1840, is a Creole cottage, originally two stories, but the lower level was separated when the house was moved to escape the river. The addition of a screened porch is the only known major alteration since then.

This area of Edgard was called Tigerville and was part of a Mrs. Lorio's plantation. According to the local story, the area was called Paincourtville until a school superintendent visiting the local school was attacked by bulldogs, from which he fled in a panic. Thereafter, he referred to the place as Tigerville, and the name stuck.

38.8 A cluster of Creole cottages, two barns, a general store, a small store, and a quarters cabin are in this area upriver from the cane fields.

39.6 Goldmine Road recalls Goldmine Plantation. The house was built in the mid-nineteenth century. Confederate troops encamped in the Goldmine sugarhouse were fired upon by Federal gunboats in 1862. No original buildings remain. A narrow strip of trees in the middle of the cane field marks what is thought to be a relic pond from the Goldmine crevasse.

40.1 The Hempel House, *circa* 1835, is considered one of the best extant examples of a typical and unmodified small Creole cottage, with cabinets and porch on the back, a separate kitchen, and a cistern. Next door is an Acadian cottage built *circa* 1870.

40.2 The water tower heralds the community of Lucy, which, like other settlements in St. John Parish, is unincorporated and has no publicly posted town limits. The community was first settled in 1722, an upriver expansion of the German village of Hoffen. Some residents participated in the revolt of 1768. As parish seat from 1807 until 1838, the town became a significant steamboat landing, which promoted its onetime reputation as a center of gambling and fighting. Many residents were free men of color who owned property.

Before the Civil War, a tobacco factory operated in the community, but it did not reopen after the war. Much of the original settlement is in the river because of the continuous movement of the channel. In 1876 a post office was established, and the postmaster, one Charles Huget, named it for his true love. Then, according to custom, the village adopted the name of the post office. In 1896, when the gubernatorial election was "stolen" through voting fraud unprecedented even in Louisiana, a small riot broke out in Lucy between black and white residents as ballots were to be ferried to LaPlace across the river for counting. Numerous Creole-style cottages remain in Lucy.

40.3 Eastland is a late-Victorian cottage, built in the 1880s, with an L-shaped gallery.

40.4 In this area is a cluster of Creole-style cottages.

Downriver are several postbellum Creole cottages with cabinets along their rear galleries. The houses face sideways to the road, reoriented because a levee setback changed the direction of the road. When they were moved, they were placed in their original orientation, not rotated to face the new position of the road.

41.2 Because of levee setback, the Soraporu House, *circa* 1850, is parallel to the river as it currently flows, instead of facing it. A cluster of Creole-style cottages and quarters cabins can be seen just downriver.

41.6 Lucy is located on Bonnet Carré Point, a sharp elbow turn in the river and formerly an area highly vulnerable to river course changes. Until the later part of the nineteenth century, the east bank of the river was approximately where the west bank is now. The Bonnet Carré crevasse of 1874 took place directly opposite this point as the river scoured the outside of the bend. The riverbank at

Bonnet Carré continued to erode as late as the 1950s. The Lucy Setback (or Cutback) is the almost right angle turn in the road that follows the Corps of Engineers' revetment construction. The Darensbourg House, *circa* 1840, is on the left side of the road among several other Creole cottages.

42.5 Glendale Plantation house is a tidy, unimposing Creole raised plantation home begun *circa* 1802 by David Paine and renovated before the Civil War to include some early Classical Revival influences. The construction is brick and cypress with some bousillage; the timbers of the house are typically hand-hewn and pegged. The house is highly regarded for its impressive millwork, which has African motifs, imported octagonal tiles on the ground floor, and walls and wainscoting of brightly colored faux marbre. A stairway rises from the lower gallery to the second floor, and a pigeonnier remains on the grounds.

42.7 St. John the Baptist/St. Charles Parish line (whether there is a marker or not).

For the next several miles, the River Road passes through the area of the original German settlements. Attracted by the hyperbole of John Law in 1718, the Germans first settled near the Arkansas Post but found conditions there intolerable. They soon resettled here, at first about a mile and a half inland in an area that had been farmed by the Indians. After a devastating hurricane in 1722, the survivors moved to the river, seeking the highest ground—the natural levee. About the same time, more Germans arrived under the leadership of Karl Friedrich d'Arensbourg, who remained commandant of the German Coast for forty years. These Germans, unlike many of the initial wave, were not indentured and received small land grants. D'Arensbourg built a compound at river's edge; it was known as Karlstein, as was the settlement downriver from his property. On the upriver side, a settlement called Hoffen developed, a loose and tiny colony that extended from the upriver side of present-day Glendale to Killona. The first church of French colonial Louisiana, St. Jean des Allemands (St. John of the Germans), was established at Karlstein in 1724. Despite Indian attacks and flooding, the German settlement thrived.

T. Jeffreys, The Natural and Civil History of the French Dominions in North and South America *(1761): "[Ten*

*leagues above New Orleans] they have got extremely well cul-
tivated plantations and are purveyors of the capital, whither
they bring, weekly, cabbages, salads, fruits, greens and produce of all sorts, as well as vast quantities of wildfowl, salt
pork and many excellent sorts of fish. They load their vessels
on the Friday evening, towards sunset, and then placing themselves two together in a pirogue, to be carried down by the
current of the river without ever using their oars, arrive early
on Saturday evening at New Orleans where they hold their
market, whilst the morning lasts, along the bank of the river,
selling their commodities for ready money. After this . . . they
[row] their pirogues up the river against the stream and reach
their plantations in the evening."*

43.3 On the right is Hymelia Slough, a large pond gouged out by
the Hymelia crevasse of 1912. This body of water empties into a
bayou that leads to Lake des Allemands.

43.8 The Les Allemands historic marker recalls the original German settlement. In this area were residences on four-arpent properties.

> *From the 1724 census: "All these German families . . . raise
> large quantities of beans and mallows, and do much garden-
> ing. . . . They also work to build levees in front of their places.
> . . . Their small frontage on the river brings them so close to-
> gether that they look like villages."*

This is also the site of the Kennemore/Hymel Plantation, called
the property of O. Hymel by Persac, where the behemoth Hymelia
crevasse occurred in 1912. From the shell road atop the levee is
visible a body of water that is not the Mississippi River; it is a large
lake formed by the crevasse and now used for recreation. A crevasse
first occurred here in 1902, but the 1912 break was especially catastrophic. The river crashed through the levee—which was some
distance east of where it is now—and washed out so much of it that
it was impossible to repair. People panicked upon seeing the volume
of water that swept over the countryside, carrying away valuables,
cattle, and crops. Area plantations including Glendale, Hymelia,
Trinity, Rio Grande, and Waterford all suffered great damage.
Within five hours, the water had flowed all the way to Lucy—five

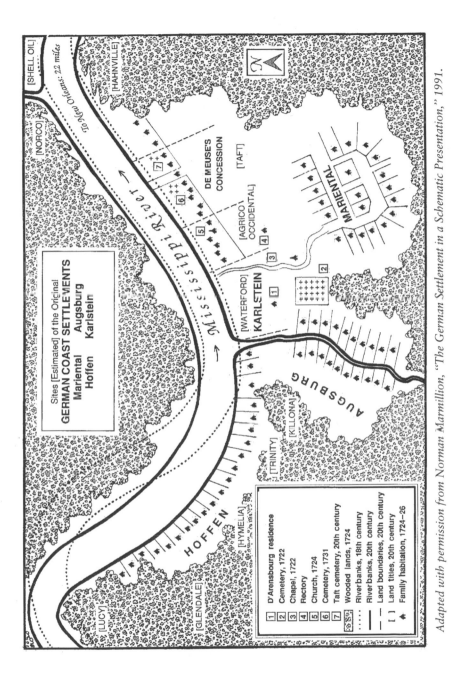

Sites [Estimated] of the Original
GERMAN COAST SETTLEMENTS
Mariental   Augsburg
Hoffen   Karlstein

MARIENTAL

DE MEUSE'S CONCESSION

[TAFT]

[AGRICO OCCIDENTAL]

[WATERFORD]
KARLSTEIN

AUGSBURG

HOFFEN

Mississippi River

To New Orleans: 22 miles

[SHELL OIL]
[NORCO]
[HAHNVILLE]
[LUCY]
[TRINITY]
[KILLONA]
[HYMELIA]
[GLENDALE]

1	D'Arensbourg residence
2	Cemetery, 1722
3	Chapel, 1722
4	Rectory
5	Church, 1724
6	Cemetery, 1731
7	Taft cemetery, 20th century
	Wooded lands, 1724
	Riverbanks, 18th century
	Riverbanks, 20th century
	Land boundaries, 20th century
[ ]	Land titles, 20th century
	Family habitation, 1724–26

Adapted with permission from Norman Marmillion, "The German Settlement in a Schematic Presentation," 1991.

miles above the break. It was the last major crevasse on this section of the river.

When the alarm was sounded, neighbors rushed to contain the leak by building a dike around the opening. But shortly, "water spurted all over the public road with waterspouts shooting seventy-five feet from the base of the levee. . . . In one half hour, the hole was fifty feet wide." Eyewitness account.

44.1   In these cane fields is thought to be the site of part of the German Coast settlements and, later, of Trinity Plantation, also known as LeSassier Plantation. Note the remnant WPA sidewalks here.

44.6   The sign indicates the approximate site of Mary Plantation, at the intersection of La. 3141, which connects to La. 3127.

Just downriver from La. 3141 is the settlement of Killona, site of Killona Plantation. Kentuckian Francis Webb lived at Killona during the Civil War. The tale is told that Union officers ransacked the plantation and auctioned portraits of Webb and his wife, among other properties. Friends bought the portraits and later returned them to Webb's family.

A post office was established here in 1887. The name Killona has been attributed both to an Indian word for "falling leaves" and to a corruption of the German for "Church of John" (perhaps in reference to the early St. Jean des Allemands Church). The Killona-Hahnville area was a focal point of the 1768 plot to overthrow Spanish governor Antonio de Ulloa. A strip of houses down La. 3141 dates from the lumbering era; Killona was an active mill town.

44.8   Freetown is a string of cabins formed into a community in 1866 by former slaves who settled or stayed here. (Freetown was a common name for such settlements.) The community no longer exists as an entity. It is thought that the village of Augsburg, one of the German settlements of 1722, was at this location.

In 1880 St. Charles Parish was the scene of the first labor strike in Louisiana when black workers on Whitehead (Waterford) and Dugan (Killona) Plantations struck for higher wages. The strike spread down the west bank, affecting eighteen plantations down to Ashton Plantation. The strikers were

The Locke Breaux Oak late in its centuries-long life.
Courtesy State Library of Louisiana

armed, and federal troops were sent out from New Orleans.
The leaders of the strike were arrested but later paroled.

45.2 The expansive Waterford I and II power plants and Waterford III nuclear power plant loom over the site of Waterford Plantation. Waterford III is thought to occupy the site of Karlstein. Waterford Plantation was owned by descendants of the d'Arensbourg (later spelled Darensbourg) family. Killona and Waterford Plantations were consolidated in the late nineteenth century by Richard Milliken. The next several miles are heavily industrialized and lack visual attractions.

46.4 IMC Agrico Chemical, formerly Hooker Chemical, is on the site of Providence Plantation. The first Catholic church in the colony—St. Jean des Allemands—was established in 1724 in this area at the village of Karlstein.

The famous Locke Breaux Live Oak was on the property. The tree was one of the most impressive of its species, with a trunk circumference of almost 36 feet, a height of 101 feet, and a limb span of 172 feet. It was called by various names—the Perret Oak

Delivering the mail in the now-vanished community of Taft.
Courtesy State Library of Louisiana

on Providence Plantation in 1791; the Davenport Oak in 1855; the Brou Oak in 1888, when the plantation was sold to Pierre and Joseph Brou. The tree's final name came from Samuel Locke Breaux. The property was bought by Colonial Dairy Products about 1935, and later sold to Hooker. The oak was estimated to be between three hundred and four hundred years old when it died in the late 1960s because of chemical pollution. Several massive stumps were removed in the early 1970s.

Just downriver, nothing remains of the community of Taft, where a post office was established in 1905. The town—a post office, a store, a few houses, and a single street—was named, according to local lore, for President William Howard Taft's brother Charles, who had lumber interests in the area.

47.6 Near the present intersection with La. 3142 was the site of Star Plantation. The Union Carbide plant owns the property of Holy Rosary Church, first constructed *circa* 1866. A replacement church built in the 1960s is downriver in Hahnville. The Holy Rosary Cemetery is still tucked near the road, dwarfed by its looming modern neighbors.

48.8 The Trosclair/Triche House, *circa* 1830, is a partially raised Creole cottage that has been altered. Part of Trosclair Plantation in the late nineteenth century, the house was renovated before the turn of the century and lost its roof and two chimneys during Hurricane Betsy. The modernized bricked sides and new roofline have significantly changed its appearance.

The nearby Zeringue House, an Acadian-style cottage thought to have been built *circa* 1805, was owned from 1815 to 1839 by Louis Edmond Fortier, who also owned Home Place in Hahnville. The original house is defined by the taller of the hipped roofs; on the upriver side of the house is a lower hipped roof covering an addition—the former Lucy schoolhouse, which was moved here.

49.4 Rosedon Street is the location of the Jacques Roussel House, now called Rosedon. This residence was built *circa* 1840 and belonged to Andre Dervin or Dorvin, who owned it until 1871. The house is symmetrical, with three pair of batten shutters, two chimneys, and two dormer windows. The floor plan consists of a central hall flanked on each side by two large rooms connected by a smaller room. When Shell Oil acquired the property on which the house sat (just next door upriver) in the 1970s, the Mollere family moved and remodeled the home. It is partially hidden from view by modern houses on the River Road but is still oriented to the river.

The Troxler House, *circa* 1840, is a hipped-roof Creole cottage. Several turn-of-the century cottages are located nearby.

50.3 A sign indicates the community of Hahnville. Records suggest that an Indian village called Quinnitassa was located here when the French explorers arrived. Hahnville is the historic and only parish seat; courthouses have been located on the same approximate site since the early eighteenth century, and records date from 1731. The settlement around the courthouse was simply called St. Charles Courthouse until 1872, when Otello J. Flagg, a carpetbagger judge, subdivided the area and created the town of Flaggville.

> *"I write . . . from St. Charles Court House. . . . This 'village'*
> *contains the courthouse building and jail [and a post office],*
> *which are of recent construction, and well and quite hand-*
> *somely built of brick, and some five or six houses, one of*
> *which is occupied as a store. The settlement is twenty-nine*
> *miles from New Orleans. The other post offices are Mc-*
> *Cutcheon's [McCutchon's] Landing on the left bank opposite*
> *this place, and Taylor's on the right bank, thirty six miles from*
> *New Orleans.*

"The value of real estate held by residents of the Parish of St. Charles is $1,646,900 and of non-residents is $56,366. . . . The few stores in the parish are nearly all scattered along the levee four or five miles apart and are small affairs. The largest and best stocked concern that I have yet seen is that of J. B. Gassen at Gassen's Landing and Ferry, 26 miles above the city. The total population of the parish is about 5,000, of whom about 900 are whites, 3,719 slaves, and 200 free colored." J. W. Dorr, 1860.

After the railroad was constructed in 1870, local luminary Michael Hahn bought land upriver from Home Place Plantation and subdivided it in 1873, calling his new village Hahnville. Hahn had opposed secession and had sworn his allegiance to the United States after New Orleans fell to Union forces in 1862. He served as (Union) governor of Louisiana in 1864. He also served briefly as a United States senator, and continued his political career as a state legislator, district judge, and congressman. He founded the St. Charles *Herald*, still in existence. Hahn died in Washington, D.C., in 1886, still regarded by some as a scalawag (a southern Union sympathizer) despite his many achievements.

Flaggville and Hahnville stood on opposite sides of the St. Charles Parish Courthouse, but after Flaggville lost its post office, the two settlements, with the courthouse, merged in 1880.

There is wide batture at Hahnville and a smattering of interesting cottages and vintage buildings.

51.1 Home Place Plantation, also known as the Keller House, was built on a Spanish land grant between 1787 and 1791 for Pierre Gaillard or his widow. The builder is thought to have been the mulatto Charles Pacquet, who designed the Destrehan Plantation house across the river. Architects note the remarkably sophisticated craftsmanship exhibited in the house. Home Place is considered a near-perfect example of a Creole raised plantation house with its wide gallery wrapped around all sides; there were no interior hallways. The original floor plan is two rooms deep. On the second floor the rooms are four across, two deep except for bathrooms built on the upstairs galleries. The ground floor is constructed of plantation-made bricks, and the rooms contain Italian marble; the second-story walls are cypress filled with bousillage. The white plaster on the walls is reportedly an inch thick. The enclosed first floor

German-born Michael Hahn served as governor of Union-occupied Louisiana in the last year of the Civil War—a fact for which some citizens of the state never forgave him.
Courtesy State Library of Louisiana

included a basement in which the wine room was surrounded by a decorative, protective grille. Louis Edmond Fortier, later a captain in the War of 1812, bought Home Place in 1806, and the plantation stayed in the Fortier family until 1856. P. A. Keller, an overseer on Terre Haute Plantation, bought the property in 1889. It is believed that the Keller family had arrived with the German settlement at Karlstein; local lore suggests the Kellers were related to d'Arensbourg and had possession of his gold sword. Keller renovated the house, moving the front stairway from under the gallery and relocating the attached kitchen to the rear of the house. The pecan tree allée was planted in 1900.

In 1893 the property was divided. The Kellers kept the upriver portion and in-laws received the downriver portion, which E. V. Haydel called Caneland Plantation. The Haydel house was built in 1895 but has been torn down.

51.4 Our Lady of the Most Holy Rosary Catholic Church is the replacement for the church at Taft.

In this area is thought to be the approximate site of Villeré Plantation, where in 1768 the plot was germinated to overthrow the Spanish colonial government. Joseph Villeré was a leader of the German Coast militia and an instigator of the insurrection. Villeré's sizable land grant extended from just above the courthouse downriver almost to Luling.

51.7 A historic marker designates Flaggville and the location of the courthouses. The first courthouse was replaced in 1826 with a handsome structure renovated in 1852. In August 1862, Federal troops camped on the courthouse lawn. In the 1870s the courthouse was the scene of violence between striking black laborers and local authorities. The present courthouse was built in 1973 to replace a 1926 building; the site is just to the rear of the previous courthouses—the parklike lawn in front of the new courthouse is where the earlier buildings stood. A St. Charles Parish law forbids the building of a courthouse anywhere else.

52.2 The Labry House was originally on Fashion Plantation property and bought by the Martin family in 1883. Fashion schoolhouse was across the street.

52.3 Fashion Plantation was the property of Confederate general Richard Taylor, son of president Zachary Taylor. The house was

Richard Taylor's Fashion Plantation in a Paret watercolor.
Courtesy Marcel Boyer from the watercolors of Father Joseph M. Paret

of raised West Indian design, on brick piers with a gallery and dormers. Taylor bought it in 1851 from G. W. Fullerton. Taylor's plantation was grand; he built an extensive library and became immersed in local politics. Taylor himself was a cooperationist and mild Unionist until secession in 1861. In September 1862, a skirmish took place at the plantation, and Union soldiers burned the house to the ground. After his property was confiscated by the U.S. government in 1865, Taylor suffered a reversal of fortune. After the Civil War, according to local lore, a group of his former slaves learned of his financial setbacks and offered him money, which he refused. The plantation was returned to his estate after his death and the property sold.

The Vial House, which is on the grounds of Fashion Plantation and sometimes thought to be Richard Taylor's house, was actually built about 1900 and was the home of Sheriff Leon Vial, who served from 1917 to 1939; his wife succeeded him as sheriff.

52.4 The Acadian-style Duhe Cottage was also part of Fashion Plantation and was owned in the 1850s through the Civil War by Richard Taylor. President Zachary Taylor's brother Thomas also lived here for a time. The exterior has been somewhat altered—the original columns and gallery railing have been replaced with iron filigree, and the house is on a concrete-block foundation, instead of piers.

From the St. Charles Herald, *March 1884: "The crevasses at Davis and Fashion have caused our back country to be submerged to a considerable extent. Surely the railroad companies will not allow these crevasses to remain open."*

53.4 A contemporary white rail fence marks Esperanza Plantation (*esperanza* is Spanish for "hope"). Here is the approximate site of the plantation of Jean Louis Labranche, located on the outside of a river bend. According to a newspaper account in 1858, cracks appeared in the levee and "before daybreak, the gap was sixty feet wide. The rushing waters created an eight foot high waterfall which could be heard from miles around. . . . The surge of water . . . was so strong that it tore off chunks of the riverbank creating floating islands, a mixture of land, wood and plants which made navigation hazardous." Ashton Plantation, just downriver, was incorporated in Esperanza after the turn of the century.

From the St. Charles Herald, *November 1884: "St. Charles Parish can point with pride to . . . Ashton Plantation where no . . . liquors or firearms [are] sold from the plantation store. This is certainly a step in the right direction."*

54.3 The Hale Boggs Bridge crosses the Mississippi River as I-310 and leads to Destrehan, U.S. 61 (the Airline Highway), and I-10, to both New Orleans and Baton Rouge. On this side of the river, the road connects with La. 3127.

Ranson Plantation, located in this area, belonged to antebellum planter Zenon Ranson, among the most prosperous and reputedly generous Creoles in this area. The raised Creole plantation house overlooked a broad lawn with allées along each side. The property was confiscated in 1864 from Louis, Zenon's son, who was a strong supporter of the Confederacy. It was returned to the family in 1867.

54.5 Ashton Road, on the downriver side of the bridge, denotes the site of Ashton Plantation, owned in the mid-nineteenth century by prosperous planter Ambrose Lanfear, according to Persac.

55.0 La. 52 is Paul Maillard Road, the main street of the community of Luling, first known as St. Denis. After the Civil War, Acadians settled here, and the town was sometimes called "Cajun

Town." In the 1870s an Englishman named F. A. Luling bought Ellington Plantation and various other properties downriver to Ama, and his name eventually was attached to the town. Downtown Luling includes some vintage commercial buildings. The Old Ferry Inn Lane up the levee once led to the Luling–Destrehan ferry landing and an old inn. Part of the Old Spanish Trail, which began as a horse path from New Orleans to the Spanish Southwest, followed River Road to Paul Maillard Road, where it turned west and became what is now U.S. 90. In 1938 a new levee forced the town front to retreat several blocks; some buildings were moved, others lost.

55.3 At Sugar House Road is Monsanto Park—the site of Ellington Manor Plantation, a Classical Revival home designed by the younger Charles Gallier in the 1840s. A beautiful garden with imported plants enhanced the grounds. The first floor of the house was rusticated stucco, the second floor clapboard. After ownership by F. A. Luling, the plantation was sold to John Barkley, once an adviser to President Herbert Hoover. Damaged by a tornado, the house was renovated in 1914, when Italianate influence was added. Later left uninhabited, it was bought in ruins by the Lion Oil Company and demolished in 1950. Part of the oak allée remains. The banisters from the porch were donated to a local church for altar railings.

55.5 The imposing and gnarled Lagarde Oak rises just to the right of the road; behind it is Lagarde House. The Lagarde Oak has local renown as a life-saver: when a local woman walking home during the hurricane of 1947 found that she could not fight the wind and rain, she took refuge in a niche in the tree's massive roots and safely rode out the storm. The discovery of a locket under the tree led to the story that gold and Spanish treasure were buried beneath it, but the tale proved completely false.

56.4 Lone Star Street indicates the site of Lone Star Plantation, owned by Pierre Sauve on Persac's map and in the 1880s and 1890s by the T. J. Sellers family, who had previously lived across the river at Diamond Plantation in Norco. Sellers lost his rice crop here to the 1884 Davis crevasse and augmented the new replacement levee by building a road parallel to the levee and high along its side; the traffic helped keep the earth on the inside of the levee well tamped.

56.7 Davis Road recalls Davis Plantation, first settled during the

A river baptism at Ama, 1939.
Courtesy State Library of Louisiana

Spanish colonial period. By the mid-eighteenth century, it was the property of Jacques Masicot, whose extended family owned the plantation until its purchase in 1852 by Ezra Davis. Davis Plantation had twenty-one arpents of frontage, perhaps the largest tract in the area. By the 1870s, Davis no longer owned the property and rice was the crop of choice, possibly grown by the St. Charles Homestead and Mutual Benevolent Aid Association, a farming co-op of freedmen.

56.9 Davis Pond is a relic slough and lowland area from the Davis crevasse. An inadequately closed rice flume, built in the levee to facilitate moving river water into the fields, was responsible for the devastating event in March 1884, when high water created a thousand-foot-wide breach in the levee. Parts of two parishes were flooded.

Davis Pond Freshwater Diversion Project, a large, long-term Corps of Engineers undertaking, is planned to help restore the coastal wetlands south of here by channeling Mississippi River water through a control structure and filters. The goal is to replenish freshwater loss in the coastal marsh and counteract saltwater intrusion from the Gulf of Mexico. This project is located on the upriver portion of Louisa Plantation and the downriver portion of Davis Plantation.

58.5 Archer Daniels Midland is located on the site of Louisa Plantation. Although land records indicate that settlement began here in 1773, the consolidation of smaller tracts into a plantation occurred during the mid-nineteenth century. The name was that of the daughter of Ambrose Lanfear, who bought the property at auction in 1850. Lanfear was an absentee owner and sold both Louisa and Ashton Plantations in 1866 after suffering devastating losses. The property changed hands several times and eventually supported a rice crop. Archer Daniels Midland bought it in 1985.

59.1 The community of Ama was named for the daughter of one of the early owners of Alice Plantation. The settlement was called Cooperville in the late nineteenth century. The Ama crevasse of 1891 caused destruction as far away as Lac des Allemands, south of Edgard.

60.4 St. Charles Aviation occupies the site of Alice Plantation, bought in 1893 by Thomas Sellers. The plantation grew rice and sugarcane. In the early 1900s, at the rear of their property, Sellers and his sons dug the Sellers Canal, extending from the Southern Pacific Railroad tracks to Bayou Verret. When the Hymelia crevasse occurred in 1912, Sellers and his family boarded a houseboat he had made and escaped out the canal and on to Grand Isle.

61.1 St. Charles/Jefferson Parish line.

SITES OPEN TO THE PUBLIC

Note: Admission may be charged. Unless otherwise noted, telephone numbers are area code 504. This list is not intended to be comprehensive, but merely to provide a handy thumbnail reference to important sites open to the public. Many churches and cemeteries can be found open as well.

Along the East Bank linear route:

LaBranche Dependency House, St. Rose. 468-8843.

Destrehan Plantation House. Destrehan. 764-9315.

Ormond Plantation House. Destrehan. 764-8544.

Bonnet Carré Spillway (exhibit diagram). Corps of Engineers office. 764-7484.

San Francisco Plantation House. Garyville. 535-2341.

Timbermill Museum. Garyville. 535-3202. Artifacts of the lumber industry and St. John the Baptist Parish history are on exhibit, as well as information about the Garyville National Historic District.

St. James Historical Society Museum. Lutcher. 869-9752. Artifacts, vintage photos, tools, etc. of St. James Parish history and culture.

Tezcuco Plantation House. Burnside. 562-3929.

Houmas House. Burnside. 473-7841.

Gillis W. Long Hansen's Disease Center. Carville. 642-4740.

In Baton Rouge:

Magnolia Mound Plantation. 343-4955.

The Old State Capitol Museum of Political and Governmental History. 342-0500. In the renovated neo-Gothic Old State Capitol building.

LSU Rural Life Museum. 765-2437. Collection of the everyday culture and heritage of the River Road from early settlement to the twentieth century, including an extensive array of artifacts, furnishings, tools, equipment, and outbuildings of plantation life.

USS Kidd *Nautical Museum.* 342-1942. Nautical displays, view of the Mississippi River.

Louisiana Arts and Science Center. 344-5272. View of the Mississippi River from the upstairs exhibit area.

Southern University. Red Stick sculpture overlooking the Mississippi River.

Along the West Bank linear route:

West Baton Rouge Museum. Port Allen. 336-2422. Exhibits on sugar culture, including a sugar mill model first exhibited at the 1904 Louisiana Purchase Exhibition.

Port Allen Lock. Port Allen. 343-3752.

Old Turnerville. Plaquemine. 687-5337. Two late-nineteenth-century houses furnished with antiques and memorabilia.

Plaquemine Lock Museum. Plaquemine. (800) 233-3560.

Nottoway Plantation House. White Castle. 545-2730.

Oak Alley Plantation House. Vacherie. 265-2151.

Laura Plantation House. Vacherie. 265-7690.

SELECTED BIBLIOGRAPHY

For more about the River Road, the following are just a few of the many sources available.

Books

Blume, Helmut. *The German Coast During the Colonial Era*. Translated by Ellen C. Merrill. Destrehan, La., 1990.

Bourgeois, Lillian C. *Cabanocey*. New Orleans, 1957.

Cable, George W. *The Creoles of Louisiana*. New York, 1884.

Cowdrey, Albert. *Land's End: A History of the New Orleans District U.S. Army Corps of Engineers and Its Lifelong Battle with the Lower Mississippi*. Baltimore, 1977.

Crété, Liliane. *Daily Life in Louisiana, 1815 to 1830*. Baton Rouge, 1978.

Davis, Edwin A. *Louisiana: A Narrative History*. 3d ed. Baton Rouge, 1971.

Fortier, Alcée. *Louisiana Studies: Literature, Customs, Dialects, History, and Education*. New Orleans, 1894.

Gaudet, Marcia G. *Tales from the Levee: The Folklore of St. John the Baptist Parish*. Lafayette, La., 1984.

Gleason, David King. *Plantation Homes of Louisiana and the Natchez Area*. Baton Rouge, 1982.

Kellough, Elizabeth, and Leona Mayeux. *Chronicles of West Baton Rouge*. Baton Rouge, 1979.

Laughlin, Clarence John. *Ghosts Along the Mississippi*. New York, 1961.

Riffel, Judy. *Iberville Parish History*. Dallas, 1985.

University of Southwestern Louisiana Center for Louisiana Studies. *Green Fields: 200 Years of Louisiana Sugar*. Lafayette, La., 1980.

Vlach, John Michael. *Back of the Big House: The Architecture of Plantation Slavery*. Chapel Hill, N.C., 1992.

Way, Frederick Jr. *Way's Packet Directory, 1848–1983.* Athens, Ohio, 1983.
Yoes, Henry E. *A History of St. Charles Parish to 1973.* Norco, La., 1973.

Map

Persac, Marie Adrien. "Plantations on the Mississippi from Natchez to New Orleans, 1858" (reproduction of original map). New Orleans, 1967.

INDEX